Studies in Development Economics and Policy

General Editor: **Anthony Shorrocks**

UNU WORLD INSTITUTE FOR DEVELOPMENT ECONOMICS RESEARCH (UNU-WIDER) was established by the United Nations University as its first research and training centre and started work in Helsinki, Finland, in 1985. The purpose of the institute is to undertake applied research and policy analysis on structural changes affecting developing and transitional economies, to provide a forum for the advocacy of policies leading to robust, equitable and environmentally sustainable growth, and to promote capacity strengthening and training in the field of economic and social policy-making. Its work is carried out by staff researchers and visiting scholars in Helsinki and through networks of collaborating scholars and institutions around the world.

UNU World Institute for Development Economics Research (UNU-WIDER)
Katajanokanlaituri 6B, FIN-00160 Helsinki, Finland

Titles include:

Tony Addison and Alan Roe (*editors*)
FISCAL POLICY FOR DEVELOPMENT
Poverty, Reconstruction and Growth

Tony Addison, Henrik Hansen and Finn Tarp (*editors*)
DEBT RELIEF FOR POOR COUNTRIES

George J. Borjas and Jeff Crisp (*editors*)
POVERTY, INTERNATIONAL MIGRATION AND ASYLUM

Ricardo Ffrench-Davis and Stephany Griffith-Jones (*editors*)
FROM CAPITAL SURGES TO DROUGHT
Seeking Stability for Emerging Economies

David Fielding (*editor*)
MACROECONOMIC POLICY IN THE FRANC ZONE

Basudeb Guha-Khasnobis (*editor*)
THE WTO, DEVELOPING COUNTRIES AND THE DOHA DEVELOPMENT AGENDA
Prospects and Challenges for Trade-led Growth

Aiguo Lu and Manuel F. Montes (*editors*)
POVERTY, INCOME DISTRIBUTION AND WELL-BEING IN ASIA DURING THE TRANSITION

Robert J. McIntyre and Bruno Dallago (*editors*)
SMALL AND MEDIUM ENTERPRISES IN TRANSITIONAL ECONOMIES

Vladimir Mikhalev (*editor*)
INEQUALITY AND SOCIAL STRUCTURE DURING THE TRANSITION

E. Wayne Nafziger and Raimo Väyrynen (*editors*)
THE PREVENTION OF HUMANITARIAN EMERGENCIES

Matthew Odedokun (*editor*)
EXTERNAL FINANCE FOR PRIVATE SECTOR DEVELOPMENT
Appraisals and Issues

Laixiang Sun (*editor*)
OWNERSHIP AND GOVERNANCE OF ENTERPRISES
Recent Innovative Developments

Studies in Development Economics and Policy
Series Standing Order ISBN 0–333–96424–1
(*outside North America only*)

You can receive future titles in this series as they are published by placing a standing order. Please contact your bookseller or, in case of difficulty, write to us at the address below with your name and address, the title of the series and the ISBN quoted above.

Customer Services Department, Macmillan Distribution Ltd, Houndmills, Basingstoke, Hampshire RG21 6XS, England

---

Macroeconomic Policy in the Franc Zone

Edited by

David Fielding

palgrave macmillan

in association with the United Nations University – World Institute for Development Economics Research

First published in 2005 by
PALGRAVE MACMILLAN
Houndmills, Basingstoke, Hampshire RG21 6XS and
175 Fifth Avenue, New York, N.Y. 10010
Companies and representatives throughout the world.

PALGRAVE MACMILLAN is the global academic imprint of the Palgrave Macmillan division of St. Martin's Press, LLC and of Palgrave Macmillan Ltd. Macmillan® is a registered trademark in the United States, United Kingdom and other countries. Palgrave is a registered trademark in the European Union and other countries.

ISBN-13: 978–1–4039–4952–3
ISBN-10: 1–4039–4952–2

This book is printed on paper suitable for recycling and made from fully managed and sustained forest sources.

A catalogue record for this book is available from the British Library.

Library of Congress Cataloging-in-Publication Data
Macroeconomic policy in the franc zone / edited by David Fielding.
p. cm.—(Studies in development economics and policy)
Includes bibliographical references and index.
ISBN 1–4039–4952–2 (cloth)
1. French franc area. 2. Monetary policy – Africa, French-speaking. 3. Monetary unions – Africa, French-speaking. 4. Franc, CFA – Africa, French-speaking. 5. Africa, French-speaking – Economic policy. I. Fielding, David, 1965– II. Series
HG3897.4.M28 2005
332.4′96′0917541—dc22 2005047557

10 9 8 7 6 5 4 3 2 1
14 13 12 11 10 09 08 07 06 05

Printed and bound in Great Britain by
Antony Rowe Ltd, Chippenham and Eastbourne

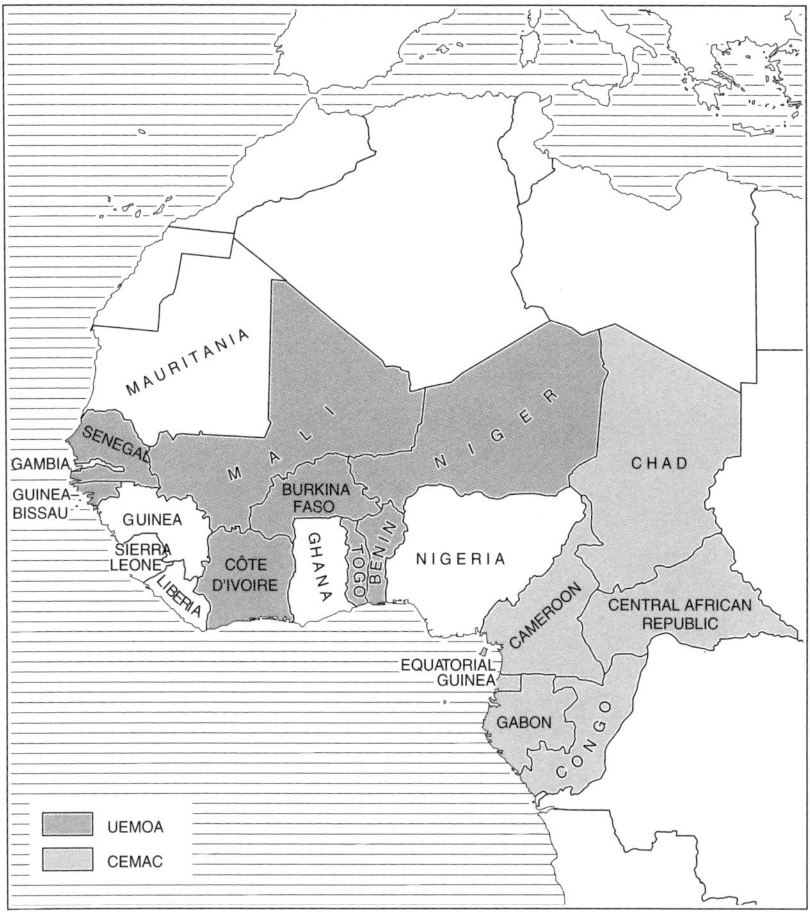

Monetary groupings in the Franc Zone, 2005

Contents

Part III The Franc Zone and Poverty

List of Figures

List of Tables

Foreword

The CFA Franc Zone is a unique financial institution that has rewarded its African members with an unprecedented degree of monetary and financial stability over the last forty years. In the past, this stability has been achieved at the cost of some macroeconomic inflexibility, leading to constitutional reforms in the 1990s designed to provide a foundation for sustained growth. This book deals with some of the issues arising from these reforms, using evidence relating to recent macroeconomic performance. It assesses the extent to which Franc Zone institutions face tensions resulting from heterogeneity among the member states, the degree of effectiveness with which they implement monetary policy and the impact that policy has on growth and poverty in the region. While the Franc Zone remains a haven of financial stability, it also faces serious challenges; this book provides an analytical framework with which to begin addressing such challenges.

Tony Shorrocks
Director, UNU-WIDER

Acknowledgements

This study has been prepared within the UNU-WIDER project on 'Long-Term Development in the CFA Zone Countries of sub-Saharan Africa', directed by David Fielding.

UNU-WIDER gratefully acknowledges the financial contribution to the project by the Finnish Ministry for Foreign Affairs. UNU-WIDER also acknowledges the financial contributions to the research programme by the governments of Denmark (Royal Ministry of Foreign Affairs), Norway (Royal Ministry of Foreign Affairs), Sweden (Swedish International Development Cooperation Agency – Sida) and the United Kingdom (Department for International Development).

Chapters 3, 6, 7 and 9 are reprinted from the *Journal of African Economies* 13(4) (2004), with the permission of Oxford University Press. The *Journal of African Economies* is produced by the Centre for the Study of African Economies (CSAE: http://www.csae.ox.ac.uk/) at Oxford University. CSAE applies modern research methods to Africa's economic problems, both microeconomic, with a focus on the problems facing individual producers (farms and firms) and macroeconomic, and is increasingly involved in policy debates assisting African governments and international organizations.

Notes on the Contributors

Jean-Paul Azam is Professor of Economics at the University of Toulouse and at the Institut Universitaire de France, and the Director of ARQADE (Centre for Research in Quantitative Applied Development Economics). He has served for some fifteen years as a resource-person with the AERC (African Economic Research Consortium), and as a consultant for, among others, the World Bank, the OECD Development Centre, and the Agence Française de Développement.

Lambert N'Galadjo Bamba is Professor of Economics at the UFRSEG and a researcher at the Ivorian Centre of Economic and Social Research (CIRES), Economic Policy Analysis Unit (CAPEC), at the University of Abidjan-Cocody. He is Technical Adviser to the ministers of tourism, education, and commerce. Outside his academic activities (which he continues to pursue), he is currently Permanent Secretary to the National Economic Policy Committee of Côte d'Ivoire (CNPE-CI), at the Economic Directorate of the Ministry of State, Economics and Finance.

Michael Bleaney is Professor of Economics at the University of Nottingham, where he has worked since 1978. He has published many papers in academic journals, and has been a Visiting Scholar in the IMF Research Department on several occasions.

Simeon Coleman is a research student and graduate teaching assistant at the Department of Economics, University of Leicester, UK, and worked as an intern at UNU-WIDER on the CFA Zones project. Previously he studied Agricultural Engineering, at the University of Science and Technology, Kumasi, Ghana.

David Fielding is Professor of Economics, University of Otago, New Zealand and director of the UNU-WIDER CFA Zones project. He is also a Research Fellow of the Centre for the Study of African Economies (CSAE), University of Oxford, and an External Fellow of the Centre for Research in Economic Development and International Trade, University of Nottingham, UK.

Kevin Lee is Professor of Economics at the University of Leicester, Dean of the University of Leicester Graduate School, an Honorary Research Associate at the University of Cambridge and Research Fellow at the University of Nottingham. Associate Editor of *Applied Economics*, Lee is a member of the UK's ESRC's Postdoctoral Fellowship and Research Studentships Panels, and member of the Executive Committee of the UK Council for Graduate Education. He has published widely on macroeconomics, labour and industrial organization.

Akira Nishiyama graduated from the School of Economics, University of Nottingham, UK and is currently Assistant Professor at Keio University, Japan.

Kalvinder Shields is Senior Lecturer in Economics at the University of Melbourne, Australia. Her research interests are broadly in the area of applied macroeconomics with a particular interest in growth and inflation dynamics and the role of survey-based information on expectations in macroeconomic models.

Anja Shortland is a Lecturer in Economics at the Department of Economics, University of Leicester, UK. She received her PhD in International Relations from the London School of Economics and her research interests are the political economy of finance and the macroeconomic effects of political instability.

David Stasavage is a Senior Lecturer in the Department of International Relations at the London School of Economics. He received his PhD from the Department of Government, Harvard University, and is a faculty associate of the Economic Organization of Public Policy Programme (STICERD). He serves on the editorial board of the journal *International Organization* and has recently been awarded a three-year ESRC Research Fellowship for a project entitled 'The Political Economy of Democratic Institutions: Transparency, Accountability, and Credibility'.

List of Abbreviations

AD	aggregate demand
ADF	Augmented Dickey–Fuller
AELE	Association Européenne de Libre–Échange
AERC	African Economic Research Consortium
ARQADE	Atelier de Recherche Quantitative Appliquée au Développement Economique (Centre for Applied Quantitative Research in Development Economics)
AS	aggregate supply
BCEAO	Banque Centrale des États de l'Afrique de l'Ouest (Central Bank of West African States)
BEAC	Banque des États de l'Afrique Centrale (Bank of Central African States)
CAPEC	Cellule d'Analyse des Politiques Économiques (Economic Policy Analysis Unit), University of Abidjan-Cocody
CAR	Central African Republic
CEMAC	Communauté Économique et Monétaire en Afrique Centrale (Central African Economic and Monetary Community)
CET	common external tariff
CFA	Colonies Françaises d'Afrique (French Colonies of Africa, original abbreviation)
CFA	Communauté Financière Africaine (African Financial Community, in the BCEAO area)
CFA	Co-operation Financière en Afrique Centrale (Financial Co-operation in Central Africa, in the BEAC area)
CFAF	CFA Franc
CFAFM	CFA Franc of Mali
CFP	Change Franc Pacifique (Pacific Franc Currency), originally Colonies Françaises Pacifiques (French Pacific Colonies)
CILSS	Côte d'Ivoire Living Standard Survey
CIRES	Centre Ivoirien de Recherche Économique et Sociale (Ivorian Centre for Economic and Social Research)
CNPE	Comité National de Politique Économique (National Committee for Economic Policy of Benin)
CNPE-CI	Comité National de Politique Économique (National Economic Policy Committee) of Côte d'Ivoire
CPI	consumer price index
CSAE	Centre for the Study of African Economies
DM	Deutsche Mark

DOTS	*Direction of Trade Statistics* IMF Yearbooks
EAC	East African Community
EACCU	East African Community Customs Union
EC	European Community
ECB	European Central Bank
ECOWAS	Economic Community of West African States
EEC	European Economic Community
EFTA	European Free Trade Association
EMU	European Monetary Union
ESRC	Economic and Social Research Council (UK)
FDI	foreign direct investment
FF	French Franc
FGT	Foster, Greer and Thorbeke
FIML	full information maximum likelihood
forex	foreign exchange
GDP	gross domestic product
GNP	gross national product
HICP	harmonized index of consumer prices
HP	Hodrick–Prescott
I3SLS	iterated 3-stage least squares estimation method
IDS	Institute for Development Studies
IFIs	international financial institutions
IFS	*International Financial Statistics*
ILO	International Labor Organization
IMF	International Monetary Fund
LDC	less developed country
MA	moving average
MD	monetary demand
MSM	Multilateral Surveillance Mechanism
NCFASSA	Non-Franc Zone SSA
OCA	Optimal Currency Area
OECD	Organisation for Economic Co-operation and Development
OLS	ordinary least squares
PPP	purchasing power parity
RPI	retail price index
SADC	South African Development Community
SAP	structural adjustment programme
SARB	South African Reserve Bank
SFI	Société Financière Internationale
Sida	Swedish International Development Co-operation Agency
SME	small and medium-sized enterprise
SMZ	Second Monetary Zone
SOE	state-owned enterprise
SPDS	Same Primary Data Source
SDR	special drawing rights

SSA	sub-Saharan Africa
STICERD	Suntory and Toyota International Centres for Economics and Related Disciplines
SVAR	structural vector autoregression
UEMOA	Union Économique et Monétaire Ouest-Africaine (Economic and Monetary Union of West African)
UN-ECA	United Nations Economic Commission for Africa
UNU	United Nations University
VAR	vector autoregression
VECM	Vector Error Correction Model
WAEMU	West African Economic and Monetary Union: see also UEMOA
WBDI	World Bank Development Indicators
WIDER	World Institute for Development Economics Research of the UNU
WIID	World Income Inequality Database

1
Introduction

David Fielding

There is an enormous variety in the currency arrangements and institutions across sub-Saharan Africa (SSA) in the early twenty-first century. This is a consequence of the different trajectories that African nations have taken since their independence from the former colonial powers (Belgium, Britain, France, Portugal and Spain) in the 1950s, 1960s and 1970s. The African nations' colonial experience has played a major role in shaping post-colonial institutions. However, there has been a great deal of divergence in the paths the different independent nations have taken. One of the most striking monetary institutions in the region is the CFA Franc Zone, a common currency area spanning most of the former French colonies of West and Central Africa. The first part of this chapter reviews the monetary history of SSA, highlighting the differences between the CFA Franc Zone and its neighbours. The second part reviews some of the more pressing policy questions facing the Franc Zone and its neighbours today, and explains how these questions are addressed in the rest of this book.

Post-colonial histories and institutions

The CFA Franc Zone

The CFA Franc Zone is a monetary system based on the institutions of the final phase of French colonialism, and encompasses most of France's former colonies. The African CFA Franc Zone is the major component of the world-wide Franc Zone, which also includes Monaco and some French overseas territories. The cornerstone of the Franc Zone is the use of currencies that the French Treasury guarantees to exchange for French Francs (now Euros) at a fixed rate.[1] In continental Africa member states are grouped into two regions, each of which has one central bank issuing a single currency – rather confusingly, both currencies are called the CFA Franc, CFAF – that is convertible with the French Franc/Euro at a fixed rate.

The Franc Zone evolved from the monetary institutions of the last phase of French colonial Africa. In 1955, five years before independence, the Metropolitan French authorities devolved the right to issue currency onto two newly created institutions: the Central Bank of Equatorial African States and Cameroon, later renamed the Bank of Central African States (*Banque des États de l'Afrique Centrale*, BEAC), and the Central Bank of West African States (*Banque Centrale des Etats de l'Afrique de l'Ouest*, BCEAO). These banks issued their own notes for use in French Equatorial Africa (including Cameroon) and French West Africa (including Togo). Their headquarters were originally in Paris, but later moved to Yaoundé in Cameroon and Dakar in Senegal.

(The history of acronym 'CFA' gives an interesting insight into attitudes towards political correctness in the francophone world. Its original meaning was *Colonies Françaises d'Afrique*. But after the African countries gained independence this interpretation was changed to *Communauté Financière Africaine* in the BCEAO area and *Coopération Financière en Afrique Centrale* in the BEAC area. Similarly, in New Caledonia and French Polynesia the 'CFP' mutated from *Colonies Françaises Pacifiques* into *Change Franc Pacifique*.)

After political independence (1960–62), the banks retained their function and their currencies, and the French Treasury continued to guarantee convertibility at 50 CFAF:1 FF. All of the newly independent Central African states – Cameroon, Chad, the Central African Republic (CAR), the Congo Republic and Gabon – adhered to this monetary union under the auspices of the BEAC. These were joined in 1985 by the former Spanish colony of Equatorial Guinea. In West Africa the new monetary area was smaller than the old colonial territory, because Guinea–Conakry had seceded from French control at the institution of the Fifth French Republic in 1955. Also, Togo seceded from the monetary union on gaining its independence, although it rejoined the union in 1963. The other states – Côte d'Ivoire, Dahomey (later Benin), Upper Volta (later Burkina Faso), Mali, Mauritania, Niger and Senegal – formed the Economic and Monetary Union of West Africa (*Union Économique et Monétaire Ouest-Africaine*, UEMOA) under the auspices of the BCEAO. Mali, however, was independent of UEMOA from 1962 to 1984, issuing its own CFA Franc, convertible at a rate of 100 CFAFM:1 FF. Mauritania completely seceded from the Franc Zone in 1973. The former Portuguese colony of Guinea–Bissau joined the union in 1997.[2]

The African CFA comprises two completely separate and independent monetary unions with two different currencies, although the two unions share many common features. The two unions constitute a complex array of contractual obligations on the part of the African states and France. Here we review those features of the Franc Zone constitutions that are likely to affect economic policy and economic performance.

The obligations fall into two categories. First, there are the constitutional principles designed to achieve the goal of complete financial integration between member states. Under this heading fall the guarantees of convertibility between CFA and French Francs (Euros), and the fixed exchange rate. Maintenance of the principles implies a heavy obligation on the part of France, with some obligations on the part of the Franc Zone. Second, there are the administrative structures to which member states bind themselves, and which prevent (or, at least, which are designed to prevent) African states free riding on French guarantees, and on each other. These entail considerable loss of economic sovereignty on the part of the African states.

The constitutions of the central banks of the Franc Zone describe the principles and institutional structures of the union. More details are to be found in Bathia (1986) and Vizy (1989). We will concentrate below on the details of the revised Franc Zone constitutions of 1972–73, which devolved policy-making authority from the French treasury to the central banks.[3] The members of the Franc Zone and France agree to act to ensure the following economic conditions:

(1) *Guaranteed convertibility*: Article 2 of the BEAC constitution states that the union is based on France's guarantee of unlimited convertibility of CFA Francs. Article 1 of the UEMOA convention stipulates that France will help member states to ensure the free convertibility of their currency. In practice, this means that the French Treasury will exchange CFA Francs for French Francs on demand. It also agrees to provide the Franc Zone central banks with as many French Francs as are needed to ensure the smooth running of the zone's financial system.

If this guarantee of convertibility were absolute, then there would be no black market for foreign exchange (forex): the official and parallel exchange rates would be the same. However, there have been exceptional short periods in which the rates have diverged somewhat. The main reason for this divergence is probably that although the French Treasury guarantees convertibility *now* at a certain exchange rate, there is a finite risk that the CFA Francs will be devalued, or that one or more countries will secede from the union. When rumours are rife, the implied risk of holding CFA Francs means that there is not full convertibility in practice. Nevertheless, the official and parallel market rates for CFA Francs have always been of the same order of magnitude, which is in itself a major achievement, compared with other African currencies.

(2) *A fixed exchange rate*: From 1948 to 1994 Article 9 of the BEAC constitution and Article 2 of the UEMOA convention stipulated a fixed rate of 50:1. The rate has been changed only once, to 100:1, in January 1994. The entry of France into the European Monetary Union (EMU) means that the rate is now defined in terms of Euros, but the current Euro rate is equivalent to 100:1 against the French Franc. The devaluation of the French Franc in August 1969 prompted the members of the Franc Zone to negotiate a system of compensation for French devaluations. Each year, the French

Treasury compensates for any loss of exchange by the two CFA central banks caused by falls in the value of the Euro–SDR rate, crediting the central banks accordingly. If the Euro appreciates the accounts are not debited, but the calculated gain by the CFA central banks is deducted from any future credits. The fixed exchange rate has meant that average inflation rates within the Franc Zone have not been significantly higher than those in France.

(3) *Free transferability*: Article 10 of the BEAC constitution states that 'transfers of funds between member states and France will be unrestricted'. Similarly, Article 6 of the UEMOA convention describes the 'freedom of financial relations between France and members of the Union'. This obligation on the part of the African states is not without qualification, and the practice of member states has not always been in harmony with the principle. International capital transfers are taxed, and occasionally (especially during the run-up to the devaluation in 1993) the transferability has been suspended. Nevertheless, there is usually a reasonable degree of capital mobility across the frontiers of each of the two monetary unions.

(4) *Harmonization of rules governing currency exchange*: Article 14 of the BEAC constitution stipulates that, 'with the exception of modifications necessitated by local conditions ... states will try to implement the exchange policy of the Franc Zone'. Article 6 of the UEMOA convention notes that the 'uniform regulation of the external financial relations of member states ... will be maintained in harmony with that of the French Republic'. These regulations cover such things as the remittance of salaries abroad (that is, outside the Franc Zone), foreign investment and borrowing from abroad.

The administrative structures of the Franc Zone are built around the BEAC and the BCEAO, which are the only institutions in the region granted the power to issue CFA currency. They also implement monetary policy, and finance and regulate government and private banking activity. The regulations the central banks are empowered to enact concern particular monetary aggregates. Overall control of monetary creation is sought through the close monitoring and regulation of the different components of the money stock.

In order to understand the way in which monetary policy is implemented, it is useful to consider the balance sheet of each central bank, which is of the form:

$$MON - CTE - NGD - NFA \equiv 0 \tag{1.1}$$

MON is the money base, *NFA* the net foreign assets of the central bank, *CTE* the net indebtedness of the private banking system to the central bank and *NGD* the net indebtedness of the governments of the Zone to the central bank. The balance sheet identity applies to individual countries as well as to the Zone as a whole, the central bank accounts being disaggregated by country.

The administration of the Franc Zone is based on accounts held by the central banks in Paris, the Operations Accounts. An Operations Account deficit constitutes a net foreign liability of the African central bank, so an increase in the deficit reduces *NFA*. It acts as a 'shock absorber' when there is an increase in domestic debt (*CTE* and *NGD*). So the local interest rates set by the BCEAO and BEAC do not have to be used to respond to external imbalances, at least in the short run.

The interest rate set on Operations Accounts overdrafts is punitively high. However, there is still an *a priori* worry that the overdraft facility will lead to excessive domestic credit creation in Africa. That is, *CTE* and *NGD* will tend to rise, and *NFA* will tend to fall, leading to persistent external deficits. However, in addition to the interest rate, the central banks have a number of ways of controlling the components of their balance sheets:

(1) Historically, a key tool for controlling CFA government debt was the '20 per cent rule'. Credits to government from the central banks (*NGD*) were limited to 20 per cent of the government's fiscal receipts for the previous year. If the government wanted to increase its expenditure, it had to increase its revenue. So there was always a link between credit creation and the budget deficit and, with government borrowing from abroad making up such a large fraction of total borrowing, between credit creation and the current account deficit. This imposed at least some fiscal discipline, and lower rates of money creation than in the rest of SSA. As part of the monetary reforms following the 1994 devaluation, net public borrowing from the BCEAO/BEAC has been further limited, so that now there is practically a '0 per cent rule'.

(2) With respect to the private sector, the central banks pursue an active policy of adjustment of the reserve assets ratio. An increase in the ratio will force up *MON*, offsetting any increase in *CTE* or *NGD* that might worsen the external balance. In fact, reserve assets ratios set by the BCEAO vary not only from month to month but also from country to country, according to the central bank's view on variations in excess liquidity over time and across countries. The central bank also operates *accords de classement*, vetting large loan applications by private sector institutions. In recent years these policy tools seem to have been effective. At the end of 2002, BCEAO loans to government were only 19.5 per cent of *MON*,[4] and loans to the private sector were only 1.1 per cent of *MON*. Most of the money base is covered by a positive net foreign asset position. In other words, the central bank was more or less operating a *de facto* currency board system, but with a built-in shock absorber. Similar observations are true of the BEAC.

In the past this was not always so, and in the 1980s lending to the public and private sector in Franc Zone countries – mostly to the larger ones, such as Côte d'Ivoire and Senegal, and disproportionately to their size – exceeded the size of the money base. Correspondingly, the net foreign asset position of both monetary unions was negative for long periods of time. There was considerable evidence to support the conjecture that the rules designed to limit credit creation were ineffective (Fielding 1996). But since the 1994 devaluation, which was designed to address the negative external balance of the CFA Franc Zone as a whole, the rules governing credit creation have been tightened and budgetary discipline – at the aggregate zone-wide level, at least – has been maintained.

Despite the problems faced by the CFA Franc Zone in the 1970s and 1980s, it has remained an area of relative monetary stability, with low inflation rates and moderate rates of monetary expansion. In this respect is has differed markedly from much of the rest of SSA, as we will see in the next section.

The rest of SSA

Political independence and the drive to monetary independence

Outside of the CFA Franc Zone, many of the newly independent African states chose to create their own national currencies and central banks. (The main exception was a number of former British colonies and front-line South African states.) These countries chose to distance themselves from their former political rulers in monetary terms as well as purely political terms. The group includes all the former Portuguese colonies that gained independence in the mid-1970s (Angola, the Cape Verde Islands, Mozambique, São Tomé and Príncipe, Guinea–Bissau prior to Franc Zone membership), the former Belgian colonies that gained independence in the early 1960s (Burundi, Congo DR, Rwanda), the former French colonies that opted out of the CFA (Guinea–Conakry, Madagascar) and some former British colonies (Mauritius, Nigeria, the Seychelles, Sudan). In addition, those countries that had long been independent (Ethiopia, Liberia) issued their own currency.[5]

The drive for monetary independence may have had a purely political motivation: an independent currency is a potent symbol of an independent nation. However, there was a more mundane fiscal rationale for currency devolution. The issue of base money is a source of revenue ('seigniorage'): in effect, printing new notes is – through the inflation it creates – a tax on those who already hold currency in circulation. This extra source of revenue could be extremely valuable for newly independent states with poorly developed tax collection systems.

In the late 1960s, the international context of this monetary autonomy was the Bretton Woods system. Most industrialized countries maintained a fixed exchange rate against the US Dollar, their central banks trading foreign exchange reserves in order to offset fluctuations in the demand for local currency. The newly independent African states participated in this system, pegging their new currencies against the US Dollar, or against some other industrialized country currency, or against a weighted basket of such currencies.

Two major factors led to the breakdown of these African currency pegs in the 1970s and 1980s. First of all, the Bretton Woods system collapsed in 1971–72, and most industrialized country currencies were floated against the Dollar. This made an individual African country's choice of currency for a peg more difficult. Pegging to the US Dollar (Franc, Escudo, Sterling) would lead to falling competitiveness in world markets when the Dollar (Franc, Escudo, Sterling) appreciated. Pegging to a weighted basket of currencies might alleviate this problem, if the weights reflected the relative importance of the different industrialized countries as trading partners. But changing trading patterns, especially after the 1973 oil price hike, complicated any such exercise.

Second, mounting budget deficits created an incentive to print more local currency than was warranted by national economic growth (and hence growth of demand for cash) under a fixed exchange rate system. Many governments squared the circle by imposing even more severe restrictions on people's ability to trade in foreign currency, while imposing a fixed exchange rate by fiat. That is, instead of maintaining a fixed peg by manipulating the local supply of foreign currency through the use of forex reserves, the authorities set a fixed rate by decree, and limited access to forex markets. Foreign currency was rationed. In any rationing system there is an incentive to trade on the black market. When foreign currency is scarce and its price is set artificially low, people will be willing to trade at a higher price on unofficial markets. The magnitude of the discrepancy is illustrated in Table 1.1, which shows the difference between official and black market exchange rates in Africa in 1985. Each number in the first column shows the percentage premium on the price of US Dollars on the black market. In many cases the official and black market rates were of completely different orders of magnitude.

The magnitude of the discrepancy reflects the magnitude of the economic inefficiency brought about by the rationing regime. Dollars trade at an exorbitantly high price on the black market when they are especially scarce, when it is almost impossible for consumers to find any currency to import what they cannot find locally, and for firms to find any currency to import essential raw material and component parts. So in the 1980s an end to foreign exchange rationing was usually top of the list of conditions attached to World Bank loans. The 1980s and 1990s saw an abandonment of fixed exchange rates across most of SSA, as shown in the remaining columns of Table 1.1. The exchange rate peg was replaced either by a free float (in which the local price of Dollars was driven entirely by the market, with no official intervention), or by an intermediate system. Intermediate systems include floating exchange

Table 1.1 Exchange rate regimes in sub-Saharan Africa, 1970–2000

	Black market premium 1985 (%)	Exchange rate regime			
		1970	1980	1990	2000
Southern Africa					
Angola	5415	[colony]	intermediate	intermediate	free float
Botswana	22	peg	peg	peg	peg
Congo DR	25	peg	peg	free float	free float
Lesotho	0	peg	peg	peg	peg
Madagascar	9	peg	peg	intermediate	free float
Malawi	30	peg	peg	peg	intermediate
Mauritius	0	peg	peg	peg	free float
Mozambique	4108	[colony]	intermediate	intermediate	free float
Namibia	[colony]	[colony]	[colony]	peg	peg
Seychelles	0	peg	peg	peg	peg
South Africa	0	peg	intermediate	intermediate	intermediate
Swaziland	0	peg	peg	peg	peg
Zambia	38	peg	peg	intermediate	free float
Zimbabwe	42	peg	peg	peg	intermediate
East Africa					
Burundi	25	peg	peg	peg	peg
Eritrea	[colony]	[colony]	[colony]	[colony]	peg
Ethiopia	122	peg	peg	peg	intermediate
Kenya	0	peg	peg	peg	intermediate
Rwanda	48	peg	peg	peg	free float
Somalia	147	peg	peg	peg	n/a
Sudan	29	peg	peg	peg	intermediate
Tanzania	259	peg	peg	intermediate	free float
Uganda	25	peg	peg	peg	free float
West Africa					
CFA Franc Zone[a]	0	peg	peg	peg	peg
Cape Verde	64	[colony]	peg	peg	peg
Gambia	7	peg	peg	free float	free float
Ghana	142	peg	peg	intermediate	free float
Guinea–Conakry	1414	peg	peg	intermediate	free float
Liberia	0	peg	peg	peg	peg
Mauritania	117	peg	peg	peg	intermediate
Nigeria	270	peg	intermediate	free float	intermediate
São Tomé	238	[colony]	peg	peg	free float
Sierra Leone	48	peg	peg	free float	free float
Per cent pegged		*100*	*87*	*63*	*32*

Notes: [a] The BEAC and BCEAO monetary areas. The data apply also to the Comorian Franc and the Djibouti Franc.
n/a = not available.
Sources: Schuler (2004); *World Currency Yearbook*.

rate regimes in which the authorities occasionally intervene to stabilize the value of the local currency, and pegs that are frequently adjusted in line with variations in the local demand for forex. The outstanding exception to the move towards floating exchange rates was the CFA Franc Zone. A few other countries have maintained a peg, but in terms of population and GDP they are small compared with the CFA area.

Attempts at monetary union in former British colonies

In the first years of independence in the mid-1960s, many former British colonies appeared to be following the same route as the Franc Zone countries. There were three separate monetary unions issuing currency tied to the Pound Sterling: the West African Currency Board (Gambia and Sierra Leone), the East African Currency Board (Kenya, Tanzania and Uganda) and the Central African Pound area (Malawi, Zambia and the remaining colony of Southern Rhodesia[6]). A single currency circulated in each of these areas, and currency issue was backed one-for-one by the Sterling reserves of each central bank. In some respects, the monetary links between these countries and the former colonial power were less extensive than in the case of the Franc Zone. The constitutions of the Anglophone monetary areas did not specify a large proactive role for British Treasury, and there was no direct equivalent of the Operations Account. Nevertheless, it was still possible in the mid-1960s that the monetary evolution of the former British colonies would closely resemble that of the former French colonies.

However, between 1964 and 1971 all three of these currency arrangements gradually dissolved. The British government was forced to devalue the Pound against the US Dollar in 1967, and with relatively little British interest in the Sterling Zone there was not much incentive for the newly independent states to pursue a link with the Pound Sterling. Moreover, political tensions between the different African states created pressure to set up national central banks issuing a national currency. Over 1964–66, Gambia and Sierra Leone abandoned the West African Pound. The countries then issued their own national currency using a currency board arrangement based on Sterling, but this was abandoned with the collapse of the Bretton Woods system in 1971. Kenya, Tanzania and Uganda retained the East African Shilling until 1966, but then moved through a short transitional phase with national currency boards to fully independent currencies by 1968. The Central African Pound was even more short-lived, surviving only to 1964. Thereafter, the management of the national currencies of these countries differed little from that in states that had instituted national currencies at independence.

Monetary integration in Southern Africa

The one other part of Africa in which monetary integration has been sustained for any length of time is the far south. Many of the front-line states bordering South Africa retained close economic links with the country, even when independence from Britain led to greater political divergence from the Apartheid government. Substantial labour flows across the South African border made economic independence impossible. The Rand circulated freely in Botswana, Lesotho and Swaziland, and also in Namibia, which remained under South African control until the 1990s. Over time these countries created their own central banks, which issued their own notes. But these new currencies circulated alongside the Rand, precluding any substantial degree of monetary independence. The national currencies have remained pegged against the Rand under a currency board system. There is a substantial amount of co-operation with the South African Reserve Bank, which makes payments to national governments in lieu of the seigniorage revenue earned through the issue of Rand notes that circulate outside South Africa.

With the end of Apartheid an expansion of regional economic co-operation has become politically feasible. The Southern African Development Community now incorporates the Rand Area discussed in the previous paragraph plus Angola, Congo DR, Malawi, Mauritius, Mozambique, the Seychelles, Tanzania, Zambia and Zimbabwe. However, these countries now have independent flexible exchange rate regimes,[7] and wider monetary co-operation is as yet entirely hypothetical.

Current policy issues

The costs and benefits of monetary union membership

The financial instability that resulted from monetary independence has prompted many countries to consider a greater degree of regional monetary co-operation. As documented by Bawumia (2002), the Lomé meeting of ECOWAS heads of state in 1999 set out detailed plans for regional monetary integration among both francophone and anglophone states in West Africa. The ultimate aim envisaged in these plans was a merging of the UEMOA with a yet-to-be-created anglophone monetary union, by as early as 2004. The Gambia, Ghana, Guinea–Conakry, Nigeria and Sierra Leone agreed to create a Second Monetary Zone (SMZ) by 2003. These deadlines have slipped somewhat, and it is envisaged that the single currency will be instituted in the near future. Nevertheless, there is a stated commitment to full monetary union in the near future. The institutional characteristics of the SMZ reflect some of the existing features of the UEMOA: an independent common central bank, no monetary financing for the public sector, pooled forex reserves and a stabilization fund to cushion temporary balance of payments shocks.

There is also some movement towards monetary union in East Africa, although plans are not yet as developed as in the ECOWAS area. In March 2004 Kenya, Tanzania and Uganda ratified the treaty creating the East African Community Customs Union (EACCU). The treaty established a common external tariff (CET) as a first step towards wider economic integration. The East African Community (EAC) treaty states that the customs union will be followed at some future date by a common market, and then by a monetary union; but the plan for a single currency is as yet less detailed than in West Africa.

In Southern Africa, the expansion of the Rand Zone to cover some or all of the other members of the South African Development Community (SADC) has also been discussed, although there is unlikely to be any formal move towards monetary integration in the near future.

Given the push towards monetary union in other parts of Africa, it is timely to review the evidence on the costs and benefits that monetary union has brought to CFA member states, and on whether monetary union elsewhere would entail similar benefits – and similar costs. In this section we will summarize existing evidence, and indicate how Part I of the book sheds new light on questions surrounding costs and benefits of monetary union.

Optimum currency area theory in Africa

The theory of optimum currency areas dates back to Mundell (1961). A monetary union is likely to bring substantial benefits to partner states in terms of lower transactions costs in international trade, and less risk for those engaged in trade. (A pegged exchange rate still entails some risk for those dealing with multiple currencies, if the peg can be adjusted.) This might promote economic growth.

Moreover, a consequence of monetary integration is that decisions about monetary policy are taken by a trans-national monetary authority. Each individual government has some influence over the policy of the central bank to which it adheres, with guaranteed seats on the board of governors of the central bank. But the power of any one government to influence central bank policy is limited. Moreover, the constitutions of each currency union put explicit bounds on the financial services that the central bank can provide to an individual government. As a consequence, the CFA central banks, for example, are credibly endowed with a degree of independence from government that would never be politically feasible within a single African state. So, potentially, the Franc Zone countries stand to gain from the benefits (in particular, low inflation) commonly associated with independent central banks that can credibly commit to low rates of monetary expansion. A credible commitment to a unilateral exchange rate peg without frequent devaluations might achieve the same results here as monetary union membership; but one might wonder how many African countries could credibly make such a commitment.

However, there are costs associated with monetary union membership. Within the Franc Zone, for example, monetary policy cannot be used to offset idiosyncratic shocks to an individual country that result in reduced economic growth, or unemployment, or external deficits. These losses may however be mitigated by the fact that the independence of the monetary policy-maker ensures that there are no large policy reversals attending a change in government, as has been the case elsewhere in Africa, particularly in the period after the collapse of the Bretton Woods system.

In assessing the actual or potential costs, it is important to remember that what matters most (in addition to the size of the shocks) is the degree of correlation across the members of the monetary union. If two countries sharing a single currency (and a single central bank setting a single interest rate) face shocks at different times that create movements in output and employment at different times, and if factors of production cannot move costlessly across international borders, then the lack of a country-specific monetary policy instrument will entail higher short-run volatility in output and employment in at least one of the countries than there need be with monetary autonomy. If the shocks are large enough and asymmetric enough, then the costs of monetary union will outweigh the benefits. The same comments can be made about shocks to prices and the real exchange rate.

Moreover, the smooth running of a monetary union requires that rules be in place to prevent one country's government generating more debt than another's. With a single currency, a higher level of debt in one country entails a monetary expansion across the whole monetary union, the costs of which are spread across all its members. So in a monetary union the costs for any one country of expanding its own debt are unusually low. In the absence of precommitment to low budget deficits there may well be a 'race to the bottom', with all countries facing a temptation to create excessive debt. So the smooth running of a monetary union is likely to require that all member states have a similar budgetary position prior to the formation of the union. If the status quo embodies asymmetric budgetary positions, then there are likely to be problems. In the cases of East Africa, Southern Africa and West Africa, some attention has already been given to the likely size of these costs for individual countries (potential costs for countries outside the Franc Zone, but actual costs for those inside), and to the question of what country groupings are likely to minimize the costs.[8]

Assessing the (potential) costs of monetary union

As shown in Table 1.2, the Franc Zone encompasses a wide range of African developing economies. All of the CEMAC countries except the Central African Republic (CAR) are now petroleum exporters, although petroleum exports from Chad and Equatorial Guinea are a recent phenomenon. *Per capita* income in the three established petroleum exporters (Cameroon, Congo and Gabon) is relatively high, over the US$2 a day mark, but in the other CEMAC countries it is less than US$1 a day. There is a corresponding discrepancy in other social development indicators, such as infant mortality. Population sizes range from over 16 million (Cameroon) to half a million (Equatorial Guinea). In the UEMOA, there is a similar discrepancy between

Table 1.2 Franc Zone: descriptive statistics, 2002 and 2003

UEMOA countries	Benin	Burkina Faso	Côte d'Ivoire	Guinea Bissau	Mali	Niger	Senegal	Togo
Agriculture value added (% of GDP), 2003	36	31	28	69	36	40	17	41
Industry value added (% of GDP), 2003	14	19	21	13	27	17	21	22
Services value added (% of GDP), 2003	50	50	52	18	37	43	62	37
Imports (% of GDP), 2003	26	23	30	88	38	26	40	47
Exports (% of GDP), 2003	14	9	46	51	27	16	30	34
GNI *per capita* (current US$), 2003	440	300	660	140	290	200	550	310
Life expectancy at birth, 2002	53	43	45	45	41	46	52	50
Infant mortality rate per thousand, 2002	93	107	116	130	122	155	79	87
Population (million), 2003	6.7	12.1	16.8	1.5	11.7	11.8	10.1	4.9

CEMAC countries	Cameroon	CAR	Chad	Congo	Equatorial Guinea	Gabon
Agriculture value added (% of GDP), 2003	45	61	38	6	7	9
Industry value added (% of GDP), 2003	19	25	17	61	89	67
Services value added (% of GDP), 2003	37	14	46	33	4	24
Imports (% of GDP), 2003	25	31	54	54	n/a	44
Exports (% of GDP), 2003	25	24	21	78	n/a	67
GNI *per capita* (current US$), 2003	640	260	250	640	n/a	3,580
Life expectancy at birth, 2002	48	42	48	52	52	53
Infant mortality rate per thousand, 2002	95	115	117	81	101	63
Population (million), 2003	16.1	3.9	8.6	3.8	0.5	1.3

the two relatively developed countries with *per capita* income over US$2 a day (Côte d'Ivoire and Senegal), and the five smaller countries with much smaller average income levels. One might wonder whether such a heterogeneous group of countries could possibly benefit from sharing a single currency. There is therefore a literature that tries to quantify the extent of macroeconomic heterogeneity among Franc Zone members, and the consequent cost of monetary union membership.

Several papers focus on the extent to which macroeconomic shocks differ between the Franc Zone economies and their neighbours, and among the Franc Zone countries themselves. These come up with several striking results, but one should note as an opening caveat that these results do depend on the prior assumptions about the structure of each economy that are necessary before information about shocks can be extracted from the available macroeconomic data. These papers are based on a formal econometric time-series analysis of macroeconomic data. Many employ the statistical framework of Blanchard and Quah (1989), but with differing assumptions about the underlying economic structure of the countries in question.

Hoffmaister, Roldós and Wickham (1998) compare the nature and sources of shocks in the Franc Zone countries – considered as a single whole – and fifteen neighbouring countries. They conclude that the Franc Zone countries are relatively less susceptible to shocks that originate within the domestic economy (for example, changes in local demand conditions), and relatively more susceptible to external shocks impacting on the price of imports and exports. If these asymmetries persisted with the creation of a wider ECOWAS monetary union, then there would be a cause for concern. The optimal monetary policy response to the domestic shocks is unlikely to be the same as the optimum monetary policy response to the external shocks, so the creation of a single central bank across the region would entail some welfare loss.

The Hoffmaister, Roldós and Wickham paper does not look explicitly at the potential differences between countries within the Franc Zone, or compare individual Franc Zone countries with their neighbours. Another paper that applies a similar, but not identical, methodology to Hoffmaister, Roldós and Wickham to individual Franc Zone countries is Fielding and Shields (2001). To a certain extent this paper's findings are consistent with those of Hoffmaister, Roldós and Wickham: for example, in terms of the relative importance of domestic shocks in countries outside the Franc Zone. In terms of the degree of homogeneity within the Franc Zone, however, the results are mixed and sensitive to the assumptions used to derive information about the size, timing and nature of the shocks. There do appear to be clusters of Franc Zone countries among which there is some homogeneity, but also some heterogeneity across the zone as a whole.[9]

Another way of assessing the size of the problem is to examine whether the degree of output volatility has actually been higher on average among the members of the Franc Zone. To our knowledge, Bleaney and Fielding (2002) is the only paper that addresses the issue of real output volatility directly. They find that the standard deviation of real GDP growth is significantly higher in Franc Zone countries than elsewhere. On average, the standard deviation is 1.4 percentage points higher.

One paper that looks at West African macroeconomic convergence from a more general perspective (with less reliance on time-series econometrics) and that includes a view of indicators of fiscal convergence, Bénassy-Quéré and Coupet (2003). Again the results are mixed, with differing degrees of homogeneity within and beyond the Franc Zone. Bénassy-Quéré and Coupet suggest that there is an economic rationale for an alternative partitioning of the Franc Zone on economic grounds. The current partition into the BEAC and BCEAO regions has an historical basis, and does not necessarily correspond to degrees of economic similarity. On the basis of current economic structure, the suggested grouping of the countries they study is (Benin, Burkina Faso, Mali, Togo), (Côte d'Ivoire, Senegal; plus Gambia), (Cameroon, CAR, Chad), (Congo, Gabon; plus Nigeria) and (Guinea–Bissau, Niger; plus Ghana, Sierra Leone).

There is a similar group of papers reviewing the degree of macroeconomic homogeneity within the SADC region. Agbeyegbe (2002), Grandes (2003) and Khamfula and Huizinga (2004) all look at the degree of asymmetry of macroeconomic shocks in Southern Africa. The Grandes paper focuses just on countries in which the Rand already circulates widely (South Africa plus Botswana, Lesotho, Namibia and Swaziland), but the other two look at data from across the SADC. Their attention is given principally to shocks to prices and/or the real exchange rate. There is a broad consensus that the Rand Zone countries face very similar shocks, which is not surprising given the degree of labour mobility between them. There is also some evidence that the macroeconomic shocks of a further group of countries (Malawi, Mauritius and Zimbabwe) are quite similar to the Rand Zone core. However, across the whole of the SADC there is a great deal of heterogeneity, which suggests that a monetary union encompassing the whole area would lead to substantial costs.

Papers that take a broader approach to the question of whether the SADC is an optimum currency area (looking at more than the degree of asymmetry of shocks) include Jenkins and Thomas (1998) and Sparks (2002). These papers also cover indicators of fiscal convergence, such as the debt–GDP ratio, and indicators of economic structure, such as the share of exports in GDP. The broader and less formal approach produces similar results. If one looks across the whole of the SADC region today, one sees a great deal of macroeconomic heterogeneity. The immediate creation of a monetary union across the whole area is likely to impose large costs on at least some countries.

Less has been written about the potential for monetary union in East Africa, but there is a paper by Mkanda (2001) that looks at a comprehensive range of macroeconomic indicators for Kenya, Tanzania and Uganda. The evidence of this paper is very mixed. There does appear to be a broad tendency towards alignment of real exchange rates in the three countries in the long run, with an increasing speed of convergence over the 1990s. (That is, the length of time and magnitude of real exchange rate divergences are becoming smaller.) There is also a high degree of correlation in movements of the terms of trade of the three countries. However, shocks to real GDP are not highly correlated. Also, the countries all share a similar production structure, which suggests that as yet there is limited scope for trade in the region.[10] With these mixed results, the immediate formation of a monetary union would be a gamble.

Assessing the benefits of monetary union[11]

A number of early studies sought to determine whether it is true that Africa's existing monetary unions in the Franc Zone promote economic growth. Studies comparing income growth rates include Devarajan and de Melo (1987) and Plane (1988a). The main obstacle to obtaining significant statistical results is the great diversity of economies both inside and outside the CFA. Devarajan and de Melo's solution is to fit an equation for the log of gross national product of seventy-four LDCs for the period, 1960–82. The equation is of the form:

$$y_{it} = b_0 + b_1 D_i + b_2 t + b_3 D_i t \qquad (1.2)$$

where y_{it} is log GNP of the *i*th country in year t and D_i is a dummy variable for membership of the CFA. The model is estimated for eleven categories, grouping together oil importers and oil exporters, and countries with *ex ante* low and high *per capita* GNP, for SSA as well as for the whole sample. In general, aggregate growth of CFA members is significantly lower than the aggregate for the rest of the sample, but this does not take account of the possibility of more adverse climatic and geographical conditions in Africa than elsewhere. When CFA members are compared with just the rest of SSA, statistically significantly better performance by CFA members appears for the high-income countries and for the high- and low-income countries pooled, whilst there is no statistically significant difference for low-income countries alone. Comparing two sub-samples, 1960–73 and 1973–82 (before and after the move to floating exchange rates in the international economic system) reveals more information. In the first period, the one significant result for SSA is that low-income CFA members grew more slowly, whilst in the second period the one (highly) significant result is the faster growth of high-income CFA members.

This approach is open to the criticism that its treatment of the factors determining economic growth is rather crude, allowing for no quantification of the effects of natural resources and geography on growth. Plane (1988a) tries to avoid this criticism by beginning with a general model of economic growth for sixty-one LDCs for the period, 1962–81, and for two sub-periods. (The partition is between 1970 and 1971.) The dependent variable in the cross-country regression is the average rate of growth of GNP over the period. Significant explanatory variables include *ex ante* population and population growth rate, a dummy for aridity of climate, variation in terms of trade, *ex ante per capita* GNP, the proportion of mineral extraction output in GDP, infant mortality rate and the proportion of the population with primary education. Plane then tests whether the cross-country residual is dependent on Franc Zone membership. Although the weighted average of residuals for the Franc Zone is positive, and the residual for Africa outside the Franc Zone negative, the difference is not significant.[12]

The evidence for a link between long-term growth and Franc Zone membership is therefore rather weak. However, another aspect of monetary union in Africa is the degree of central bank independence that it entails. Here, there is much stronger evidence. A number of papers using slightly different methodologies have consistently found Franc Zone membership to be associated with lower average rates of inflation, *ceteris paribus*. These papers include Plane (1988b), Elbadawi and Majd (1996) and Bleaney and Fielding (2002). The last of these makes a comparison between flexible exchange rate countries, countries with unilateral pegs and the Franc Zone. Controlling for other economic characteristics, it turns out that a unilateral peg does work as a nominal anchor, at least to some extent. Countries with unilateral pegs have experienced significantly lower average inflation rates. However, the effect is not as large as for the Franc Zone countries: average inflation rates in the Franc Zone are around 9 percentage points lower than for other pegged exchange rate countries. A natural interpretation of these results is that the central bank independence delivered by monetary integration lowers inflationary expectations more than a simple unilateral peg, which can always be revoked in the future.

One potential benefit of monetary union that has not received much attention in studies of Africa is the stimulus it might provide to wider economic integration – for example, by reducing the barriers to trade between member states. We will return to this question later.

What this book contributes to the optimum currency area analysis of the CFA Franc Zone

We have seen that papers dealing with the degree of macroeconomic heterogeneity among a group of African countries either took a relatively formal approach, focusing mainly on the characteristics of macroeconomic shocks in individual countries, or a less formal but broader approach. We have also seen that attempts to measure the potential benefits of Franc Zone membership have taken a variety of forms, with some robust conclusions with respect to inflation, but otherwise no conclusive results.

The chapters in Part I of this book advance this literature in several directions. Chapter 2 takes a broad approach to assessing the degree of macroeconomic heterogeneity among the UEMOA countries, and looks at the extent of their divergence in terms of many different nominal convergence criteria (that is, criteria relating to stated policy objectives, such as budget deficits and external debt, rather than measures of underlying structural heterogeneity). These criteria are the ones explicitly mentioned in the UEMOA 'convergence pact' instituted after the 1994 devaluation: the BCEAO now monitors these criteria. But this chapter takes a more formal approach to assessing nominal convergence than previous papers focusing on these criteria. In each case, the degree of convergence is measured within a consistent econometric framework. A striking result of the analysis is that there is markedly less convergence in those factors (such as budget deficits) relating to the policies of individual governments. Although we noted above that aggregate borrowing does not now lead to excessive monetary expansion, it appears that the aggregate measure masks considerable divergence in the situation of individual countries.

Chapter 3 relates to the existing literature on optimum currency area theory and macroeconomic shocks. One worry with existing work is that the econometric methodology relies on some strong, assumptions about the structure of African economies. Many papers rely on the econometric identification structure of Blanchard and Quah (1989), but they make different assumptions about the structure of the economy in the long run. For example, some papers are based on the assumption that output is independent of prices in the long run, but not vice versa (a vertical long run aggregate supply curve); and others are based on the assumption that prices are independent of output in the long run, but not vice versa (fixed exchange rates in small open economies with purchasing power parity, PPP). This is a consequence of the dearth of reliable high-frequency macroeconomic data in many CFA countries. Chapter 3 represents a new way of tackling the data problem. It analyses the data in as wide a range of CFA countries as possible, but employing measures of macroeconomic heterogeneity that do not rely on any theoretical identifying restrictions. The results relate to simple measures of macroeconomic heterogeneity, and the chapter uncovers groups of countries exhibiting some macroeconomic homogeneity. These groups are not completely orthogonal to the existing UEMOA–CEMAC grouping, but neither is the existing grouping necessarily a first-best outcome.

The first two chapters in Part I focus exclusively on CFA countries. Chapter 4 widens the geographical horizon by making a comparison of the macroeconomic characteristics of the CFA countries with those of their neighbours. It looks at the similarity between macroeconomic shocks on the Franc Zone and shocks on neighbouring countries. The approach to modelling shocks is formal (using time-series analysis), and the comparison between Franc Zone and non-Franc Zone countries is qualitative. The aim of the chapter is to see whether anything can be said about the sources of shocks to output and prices in different African countries. Does the 'hard' fixed peg of the Franc Zone mean that macroeconomic shocks there have a different explanation from shocks in countries with more flexible exchange rate regimes?

Wider policy questions

The conduct of monetary and exchange rate policy

Since the interesting times surrounding the 1994 devaluation, the CFA Franc Zone has enjoyed a period of relative monetary tranquillity. The external balances of the most indebted CFA members have improved somewhat, and there has been no discussion of any second devaluation, or of a de-linking of the CFA currencies from the Euro. The two central banks have re-oriented monetary policy, motivated by a desire to emulate what is seen as best practice in the Organization for Economic Co-operation and Development (OECD). The interest rate (alongside the reserve assets ratio and some credit controls) is considered as the prime monetary policy instrument. Central bank communiqués inform the public about monthly decisions on the value of the policy instruments, providing some rationale for the decisions. In this context, it is timely to assess the conduct of monetary and exchange rate policy in the Franc Zone.

If the BCEAO and BEAC are indeed operating in the fashion of an OECD central bank, then it ought to be possible to analyse their policies in the way that OECD central bank policies are analysed. With the exception of South Africa (Aron and Muellbauer 2002), Africa has received very little attention in the literature on monetary policy rules. So the first two chapters of Part II of the book analyse the use of BCEAO monetary policy instruments over the last decade. Chapter 5 focuses on the reserve assets ratio and chapter 6 on the interest rate. These chapters ask questions about the degree of consistency and transparency in the conduct of monetary policy. For example, can interest rate-setting in the UEMOA be described in terms of a Taylor Rule? Do changes in reserve asset requirements (which vary across member states) systematically reflect country-specific macroeconomic fluctuations, and do they promote or hinder nominal convergence?

Monetary policy, exchange rates and poverty

The final Part III of this book is designed to fill a gap in the existing literature by analysing the impact of monetary policy and institutions on the incidence of poverty in the CFA. The analysis of the relevant macro–micro linkages has received very little attention to date. Chapter 7 provides a broad view of the link between exchange rate institutions and poverty by performing a cross-country analysis in the style of the papers reviewed (pp. 16–17), but with an emphasis on changes in income distribution as well as changes in average income levels.

Chapters 8 and 9 focus on CFA countries, examining the transmission mechanisms that link changes in exchange rate or monetary policy to changes in the incidence of poverty. Chapter 8 analyses the channels through which the 1994 devaluation affected poverty in Côte d'Ivoire and Niger. Existing wisdom suggested that the devaluation would alleviate poverty, because it would generate a real exchange rate depreciation (an increase in the relative price of internationally traded goods), and most of the poor were small farmers engaged in the production of traded goods. However, it turns out that the picture is much more complex than this. Many of the urban middle classes in service sector employment, who lost most from the devaluation, used their income to finance informal sector activities employing workers from very poor households. The devaluation was associated with a contraction of this sector, which hurt the poor. Finally, chapter 9 analyses the monetary transmission mechanism in the UEMOA from a pro-poor perspective. In the short term, changes in monetary policy instruments can have an asymmetric impact on the prices of different commodities, not all of which adjust at the same rate. Within a monetary union, it can also have a geographically asymmetric impact on prices. So, in general, the brunt of monetary policy changes could be borne by the rich or by the poor, depending on whose consumption basket experienced the most price volatility in the wake of a monetary policy intervention. It turns out that the groups most likely to bear the brunt of such changes are the poor in a sub-set of the UEMOA countries.

Notes

1. Because convertibility has always been the responsibility of the French Treasury, and not the Banque de France, France's membership of EMU had very minimal institutional consequences for the Franc Zone.
2. In a parallel organization in Southern Africa, the island states of Madagascar and Comoros shared a central bank issuing yet another CFA Franc, although Madagascar seceded from the Franc Zone in 1973. So Comoros is now a semi-detached member of the African CFA Franc Zone, issuing a unique currency (the Comorian Franc) that is linked to the French Franc/Euro in the same way as the CFA currencies of continental Africa. The former French colony of Djibouti in the Horn of Africa also maintains a currency board linked to the Euro.
3. See de la Fournière (1973) for an account of the Franc Zone before the 1973 reforms.
4. These figures are net of IMF loans, which are channelled to individual governments via the central bank.
5. In Liberia, the monetary authority issues only coins, and the US Dollar circulates freely.
6. Now Zimbabwe.
7. Except the Seychelles, which maintains a basket peg.
8. There is a mainstream theoretical literature on the impact of central bank independence/fixed exchange rates focusing on the trade-off between higher output volatility and lower average inflation rates. See for example Rogoff (1985) and Cukierman, Leiderman and Spiegel (2003).

9. An earlier but more conceptually restrictive study by Horváth and Grabowski (1997) finds limited scope for integration among African countries, which – according to the methodology applied in this paper – typically face similar demand shocks but dissimilar supply shocks.
10. That is, there is little scope for inter-industry trade and the issue is not directly addressed.
11. This section focuses on the impact of Franc Zone membership on economic performance. We do not consider the impact of Rand Zone membership. Monetary policy in the Rand Zone is driven by a central bank (the South African Reserve Bank, SARB) that is certainly not independent of political influence, and does not have a particularly good track record with respect to the control of inflation.
12. Other studies of the impact of the Franc Zone on long-run growth include Devarajan and de Melo (1991) and Elbadawi and Majd (1996). The conclusions of these papers are similarly mixed.

References

Agbeyegbe, T. (2002) 'On the Feasibility of Monetary Union in the Southern African Development Community', Department of Economics Working Paper, City University of New York.

Aron, J. and J. Muellbauer (2002) 'Estimating Monetary Policy Rules for South Africa', in N. Loayza and K. Schmidt-Hebbel (eds), *Monetary Policy: Rules and Transmission Mechanisms*, Series on Central Banking, Analysis and Economic Policies, Volume 4, Central Bank of Chile.

Bathia, R. (1986) 'The West African Monetary Union: An Analytical Survey', IMF Occasional Paper 35, Washington, DC: IMF.

Bawumia, M. (2002) 'The Feasibility of Monetary Union in West Africa', Addis Ababa, Ethiopia: UNECA, mimeo.

Bénassy-Quéré, A. and M. Coupet (2003) 'On the Adequacy of Monetary Arrangements in Sub-Saharan Africa', THEMA, Working Paper, Université de Paris X Nanterre/Université de Cergy-Pontoise.

Blanchard, O. and D. Quah (1989) 'Dynamic Effects of Aggregate Demand and Supply Disturbances', *American Economic Review*, 79: 655–73.

Bleaney, M. and D. Fielding (2002) 'Exchange Rate Regimes, Inflation and Output Volatility in Developing Countries', *Journal of Development Economics*, 68: 233–45.

Cukierman, A., L. Leiderman and Y. Spiegel (2003) 'The Choice of Exchange Rate Bands: Balancing Credibility and Flexibility', *Journal of International Economics*, 622: 379–408.

de la Fournière, X. (1973) *La Zone Franc*, Paris: Presses Universités de France.

Devarajan, S. and J. de Melo (1987) 'Evaluating Participation in African Monetary Unions', *World Development*, 15: 483–96.

Devarajan, S. and J. de Melo (1991) 'Membership in the CFA Zone: Odyssean Journey or Trojan Horse?', in A. Chhibber and S. Fischer (eds), *Economic Reform in Sub-Saharan Africa*, Washington, DC: World Bank.

Elbadawi, I. and N. Majd (1996) 'Adjustment and Economic Performance under a Fixed Exchange Rate: A Comparative Analysis of the CFA Zone', *World Development*, 24: 939–51.

Fielding, D. (1996) 'Asymmetries in the Behaviour of Members of a Monetary Union: A Game-Theoretic Model with an Application to West Africa', *Journal of African Economies*, 5: 343–65.

Fielding, D. and K. Shields (2001) 'Modeling Macroeconomic Shocks in the CFA Franc Zone', *Journal of Development Economics*, 66: 199–223.
Grandes, M. (2003) 'South Africa's Monetary Area: An Optimum Currency Area: What Costs, Which Benefits?', DELTA Working Paper, Paris: Ecole des Hautes Etudes en Sciences Sociales/Ecole Normale Superieure.
Hoffmaister, A., J. Roldós and P. Wickham (1998) 'Macroeconomic Fluctuations in Sub-Saharan Africa', *IMF Staff Papers*, 45: 132–60.
Horváth, J. and R. Grabowski (1997) 'Prospects of African Integration in the Light of the Theory of Optimum Currency Areas', *Journal of Economic Integration*, 12: 1–25.
Jenkins, C. and L. Thomas (1998) 'Is South Africa Ready for Regional Monetary Integration?', in L. Peterson (ed.), *Post-Apartheid South Africa: Economic Challenges and Policies for the Future*, London: Routledge.
Khamfula, Y. and H. Huizinga (2004) 'The Southern African Development Community: Suitable for a Monetary Union?', *Journal of Development Economics*, 73: 699–714.
Mkanda, B. (2001) 'Is East Africa an Optimum Currency Area?', Department of Economics Working Paper 41, Gothenburg University.
Mundell, R. (1961) 'A Theory of Optimum Currency Areas', *American Economic Review*, 51: 509–17.
Plane, P. (1988a) 'Performances comparées en matiere de croissance économique', in P. Guillaumont and S. Guillaumont, *Strategies de Développement Comparées*, Paris: Economica.
Plane, P. (1988b) 'Performances comparées en matière de stabilité des prix', in P. Guillaumont and S. Guillaumont, *Strategies de Développement Comparées*, Paris: Economica.
Rogoff, K. (1985) 'The Optimal Degree of Commitment to an Intermediate Monetary Target', *Quarterly Journal of Economics*, 100: 1169–89.
Schuler, K. (2004) 'Currency Boards and Dollarization', http://users.erols.com/kurrency/.
Sparks, D. (2002) 'The Future of Monetary Integration in Southern Africa', Paper presented to the Conference *Exchange Rates, Economic Integration and the International Economy*, Ryerson University, Toronto, 17–18 May.
Vizy, M. (1989) *La Zone Franc*, Paris: CHEAM.

Part I

Convergence in the Franc Zone and Optimum Currency Area Theory

2

Analysis of the Convergence Process in the UEMOA Zone

Lambert N'Galadjo Bamba

Introduction

Economic integration between the members of the UEMOA is now undertaken under the auspices of a Multilateral Surveillance Mechanism (MSM), the aim of which is to ensure economic convergence. Although advocates of Optimal Currency Area (OCA) theory emphasize real convergence, and Loufir and Reichlin (1993) show that nominal convergence is expensive for 'poor' countries in the EEC and EFTA, the UEMOA has chosen to monitor nominal convergence. So this chapter investigates the speed of nominal convergence between the UEMOA countries.

We are limiting the time-span of this study to the period 1980–2001. This choice is motivated by two major factors. On the one hand, the 1980s was a decade of structural adjustment, which was designed to bring about convergence in economic policies through fiscal and sector reform. On the other, the UEMOA convergence pact dates from 21 December 1999.[1]

Existing empirical studies indicate that many single currency areas incorporate a degree of economic heterogeneity,[2] and recent theory[3] reveals the complexity of the conditions necessary for a region to be an OCA. In practice, the constitution of a monetary area usually results from a political and historical process, rather than an explicitly economic rationale. Nevertheless, the MSM indicates a genuine commitment towards convergence in the UEMOA.

The definition of convergence

The tests most frequently used in recent empirical economic research fall into four categories: dispersion indicators (Barro and Sala-í-Martin 1996: 424), tests based on the parameters of econometric models (Artis and Omerod 1991), regression-to-the-mean tests (Baumol 1986; DeLong 1988; Barro and Sala-í-Martin 1990) and cointegration tests. If convergence is a gradual and continuous process, the last three of these are not relevant because they test only for whether there has already been convergence. The UEMOA convergence pact incorporates a two-step convergence framework: from 1 January 2000 to 31 December 2005 the convergence of economic policies, and on 1 January 2006 the beginning of a period of stability. Convergence within the UEMOA is a dynamic process. So we use a methodology based on that of Haldane and Hall (1991) which takes convergence dynamics into account, as in Loufir and Reichlin (1993) and Bamba and Diomandé (2000).[4]

Consider a macroeconomic variable X_t for country *i* and for two reference countries, A and B. We want to know if country *i* converges towards country A or B, and at what rate. So we proceed with the following model:

$$X_{At} - X_{it} = a_{it} + b_{it} \cdot [X_{At} - X_{Bt}] + u_{it} \tag{2.1}$$

where a_{it} and b_{it} are time-varying parameters and u_{it} is white noise.

Country *i* converges towards country A when $E[\lim(b_{it})] = E[\lim(a_{it})] = 0$. Conversely, country *i* converges towards country B when $E[\lim(b_{it})] = 1$ and $E[\lim(a_{it})] = 0$. Equation (2.1) can be estimated using a Kalman filter. If a_{it} tends towards zero then we can test whether $E[\lim(b_{it})] = 0$, in which case X_{it} converges on X_{At}, or $E[\lim(b_{it})] = 1$, in which case X_{it} converges on X_{Bt}. If neither of these two conditions holds, then we have the following possibilities:

When $X_{At} < X_{Bt}$ asymptotically

$0 < E[\lim(b_{it})] < 1$	in which case $X_{At} < X_{it} < X_{Bt}$
$E[\lim(b_{it})] > 1$	in which case $X_{At} < X_{Bt} < X_{it}$
$E[\lim(b_{it})] < 0$	in which case $X_{it} < X_{At} < X_{Bt}$

When $X_{At} > X_{Bt}$ asymptotically

$0 < E[\lim(b_{it})] < 1$	in which case $X_{Bt} < X_{it} < X_{At}$
$E[\lim(b_{it})] > 1$	in which case $X_{it} < X_{Bt} < X_{At}$
$E[\lim(b_{it})] < 0$	in which case $X_{Bt} < X_{At} < X_{it}$

It is important to point out that if the variance of a_{it} is not finite, the convergence model cannot apply.

The ambiguity of this method lies in the choice of a reference country. Unlike Bamba and Diomandé (2000) we will use not only the leader country (Côte d'Ivoire) as a reference point, but also the norm defined by the UEMOA in its convergence pact. In our regressions, we will choose this norm as reference B, and Côte d'Ivoire as reference A. Choosing the norm as a reference point is intuitive: it is the UEMOA's chosen path. In choosing Côte d'Ivoire as the other reference point we wish to test whether there is convergence towards the largest and richest economy in the UEMOA.

The UEMOA convergence criteria

According to Additional Act No. 04/99 of 8 December 1999 modified by the Additional Act No. 03/2003 of 29 January 2003, there are two types of convergence criteria: first-order and second-order criteria. First-order criteria are those calling for corrective measures and at times even for sanctions if they are not adhered to. Second-order criteria are seen as structural indicators. Failure to attain these second-order criteria does not call for corrective measures.

There are four first-order criteria, to be met by 2005:

- The ratio of the budget surplus to nominal GDP should be greater than or equal to zero
- The average yearly inflation rate should be below three 3 per cent per annum
- The ratio of outstanding internal and external debt to nominal GDP should not exceed 70 per cent
- Payments in arrears: all internal and external arrears should be eliminated.

There are also four second-order criteria:

- The ratio of the public sector wage bill to tax revenue should not exceed 35 per cent
- The ratio of internally financed public sector investment to tax revenue should be at least 20 per cent
- The ratio of the current external deficit (excluding transfers) to nominal GDP should not exceed 5 per cent
- The average tax rate should be greater than or equal to 17 per cent.

These definitions correspond to specific objectives. The 1980s were marked by a continuous degradation of budget deficits and an over-valuation of the real exchange rate in almost all the countries of the Franc Zone. In this context, a balanced budget is a requirement of a sustainable level of public expenditure. The elimination of internal and external arrears lends credibility to monetary policy in an area where, because of the lack of a developed financial market, governments are forced to finance their budget deficit through money creation. It also aims to give a jump-start to the private sector. Using the inflation rate as a convergence criterion has two main objectives: to correct the misalignment of the real exchange rate and to create a favourable inflation differential between UEMOA and the world economy, particularly with the Euro area. The second-order criteria reinforce the budget adjustment effort, which is considered to be the key variable in this convergence process.

Data description

Since Guinea–Bissau joined the UEMOA only in 1997, our study omits this country. Also, because of a lack of data for outstanding debt, we must limit our observations to the seven other convergence criteria. The data relating to our study were obtained from the UEMOA Commission in Ouagadougou, the BCEAO, the National Committee for Economic Policy (CNPE) of Benin, the Department for Economic Forecasts in Abidjan, the Société Financière Internationale (SFI) and diverse other sources, mainly articles and magazine reports.

Figure 2.1 (the external deficit) shows considerable cross-country heterogeneity between the mid-1980s and 1996. From this year on, all UEMOA countries started reducing their external deficits, and Figure 2.1 suggests that there may have been a slight trend towards the UEMOA norm.

We also observe differences in the development of the tax rate in the countries of the union (Figure 2.2). Nevertheless, for the post-devaluation period, there appears to be a slight trend towards the UEMOA norm. Côte d'Ivoire performs best over the whole period. Figure 2.3 suggests that over 1985–94 all countries diverged from the UEMOA norm with respect to the wage bill. However, from 1994 onwards there was some reversal of this trend.

As the development of arrears payments in Côte d'Ivoire cannot be compared with that elsewhere, we present data for the six other countries. Figure 2.4 reveals slight variations in all countries with respect to the UEMOA norm up to 1993. After the 1994 devaluation, some countries (Burkina Faso, Mali and Senegal) complied with the UEMOA directives while others continued to show instability.

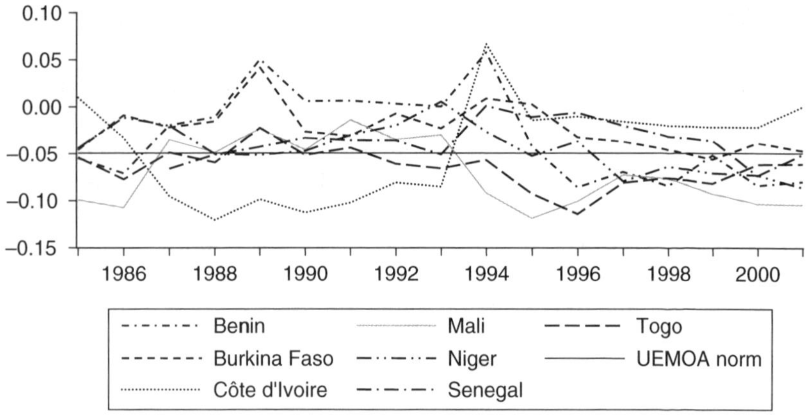

Figure 2.1 The external deficit as a fraction of GDP, 1986–2001

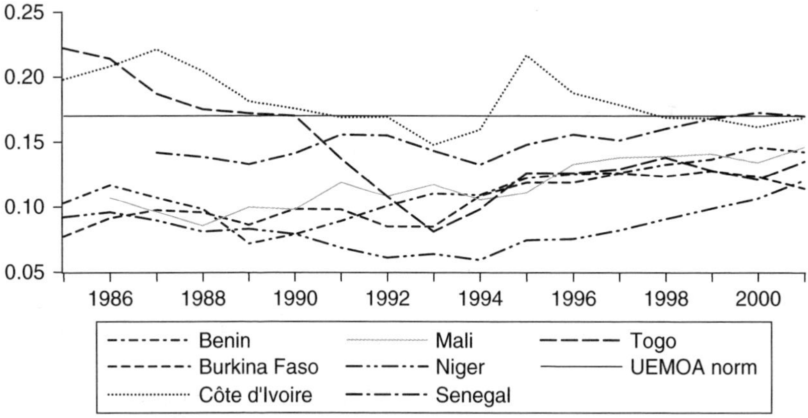

Figure 2.2 Tax revenue as a fraction of GDP, 1986–2001

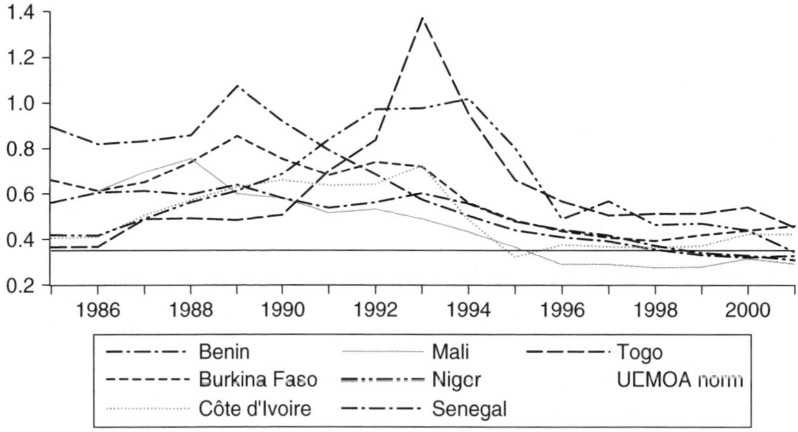

Figure 2.3 The public sector wage bill as a fraction of tax revenue, 1986–2001

Figure 2.5 indicates varying performance with respect to capital expenditure. Benin, Burkina Faso, Niger, Mali and Senegal show some convergence towards the UEMOA norm while the position of Togo worsened after the devaluation, as did that of Côte d'Ivoire following the coup of December 1999.

Up to 1993 there was substantial variation in inflation rates (Figure 2.6). Then the 1994 devaluation brought an inflationary trend to the entire region.

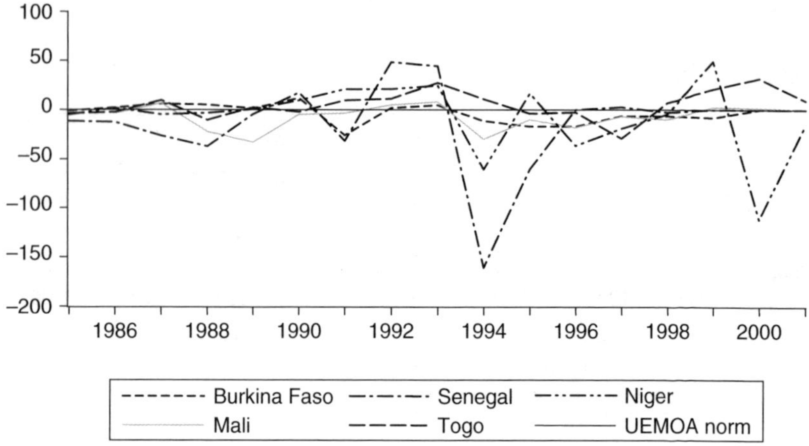

Figure 2.4 Payments in arrears, 1986–2001

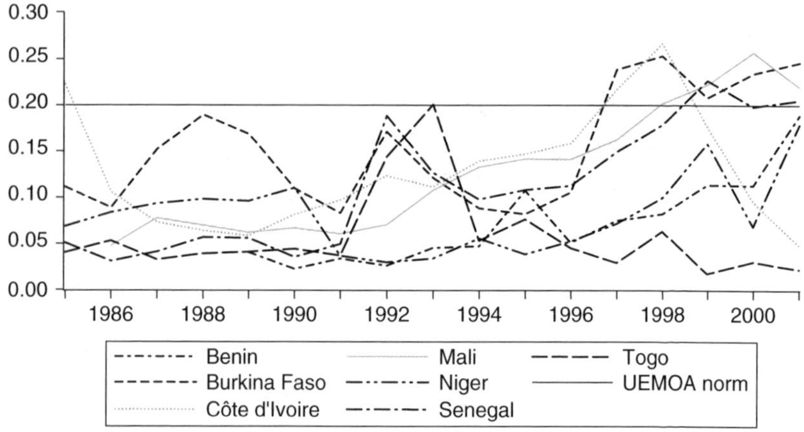

Figure 2.5 Public capital expenditure as a fraction of tax revenue, 1986–2001

The post-devaluation period was marked by inflation rates approaching those of Côte d'Ivoire, and smaller variations with respect to the UEMOA norm.

Data for the budget deficit (Figure 2.7) show that between 1980 and 1994 all UEMOA members tended towards a negative budget balance. From 1994 onwards they appear to show some convergence towards the UEMOA norm. The case of Togo is remarkable, the erosion of public finances reaching a

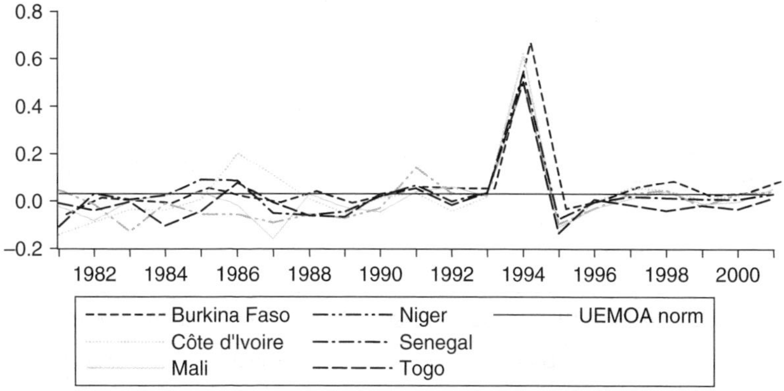

Figure 2.6 The annual inflation rate, 1982–2001

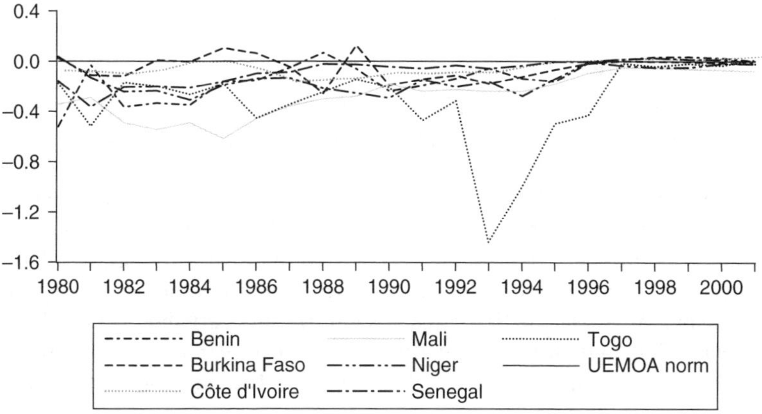

Figure 2.7 The budget balance as a fraction of GDP, 1980–2001

peak of 144 per cent in 1993 before converging at great speed towards the UEMOA norm.

Estimation and interpretation of results

The following section discusses the results of fitting (2.1) to the data for our convergence indicators using a Kalman filter technique.[5] This formal analysis is intended to complement the data description above.

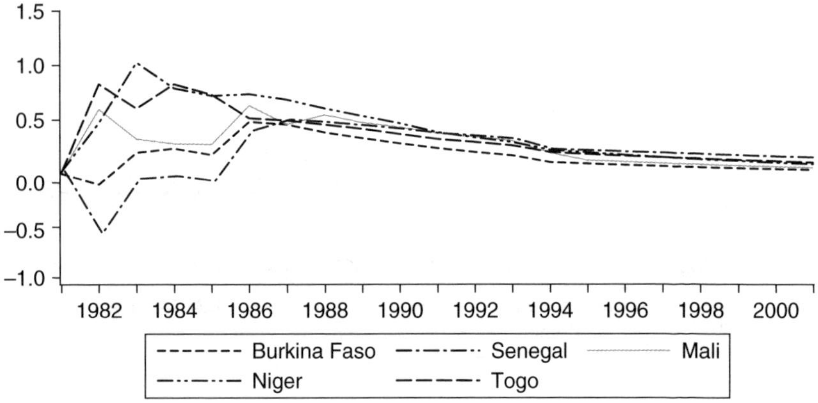

Figure 2.8 b coefficients for inflation, 1982–2001

The inflation rate

Figure 2.8 shows the slope coefficient b_{it} for the inflation rate. For this variable, we did not include Benin because insufficient data were available. The a coefficients are all stable, so we can analyse convergence by looking at the evolution of the b_{it}. The convergence of the slope coefficients shows that since the second half of the 1980s, UEMOA inflation rates have converged rapidly on a point between the 3 per cent UEMOA norm and Ivorian inflation. This result is explained by the policy adjustments carried out in co-operation with the BCEAO to deal with the real exchange rate overvaluation in UEMOA members. The high inflation of the devaluation year was an exceptional event. At least as regards inflation, UEMOA countries are converging on the norm defined by the union.

The budget deficit, capital expenditure, the external deficit, the tax burden, the wage bill and payments in arrears

Figures 2.9–2.16 show the b coefficients for these convergence indicators. In a few cases the b coefficient is missing because of an explosive a coefficient. No overall pattern is discernible in these figures. In many cases, there is substantial divergence away from the UEMOA norm and from the position of Côte d'Ivoire. There is certainly no evidence of a general trend towards convergence. As suggested by the raw data in Figures 2.1–2.7 there is no evidence that any country is systematically approaching the UEMOA norm with respect to these indicators.

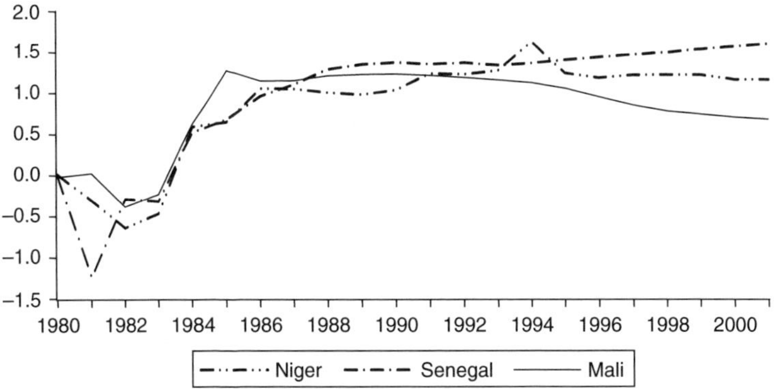

Figure 2.9 *b* coefficients for the budget deficit: Niger, Senegal, Mali, 1980–2001

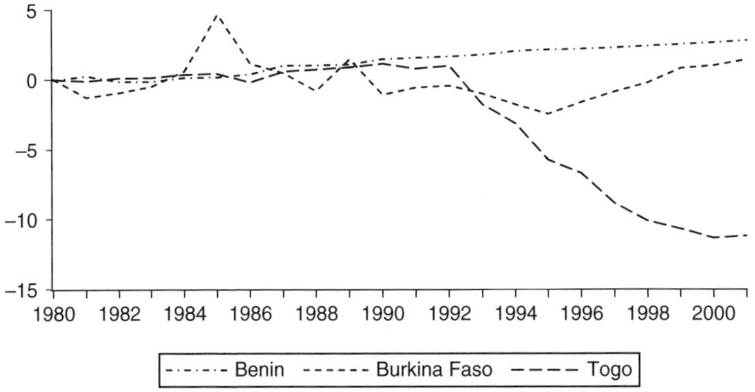

Figure 2.10 *b* coefficients for the budget deficit: Benin, Burkina Faso, Togo, 1980–2001

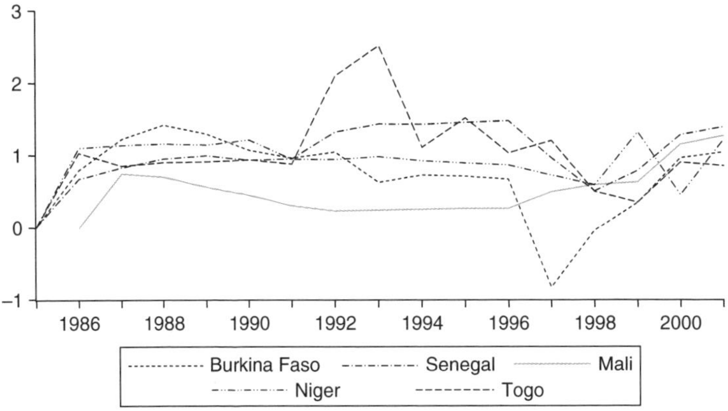

Figure 2.11 *b* coefficients for public capital expenditure, 1986–2001

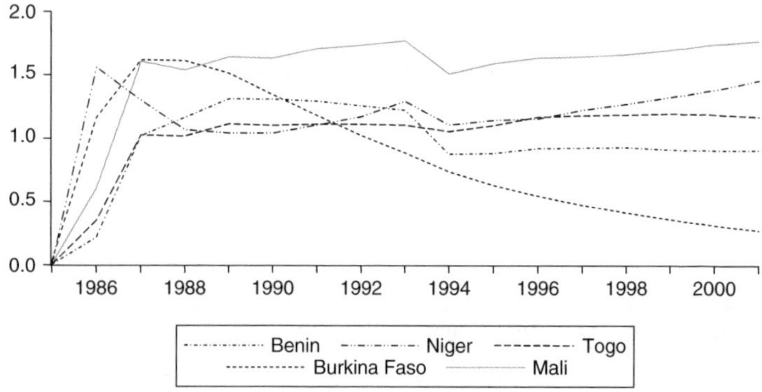

Figure 2.12 *b* coefficients for the external deficit, 1986–2001

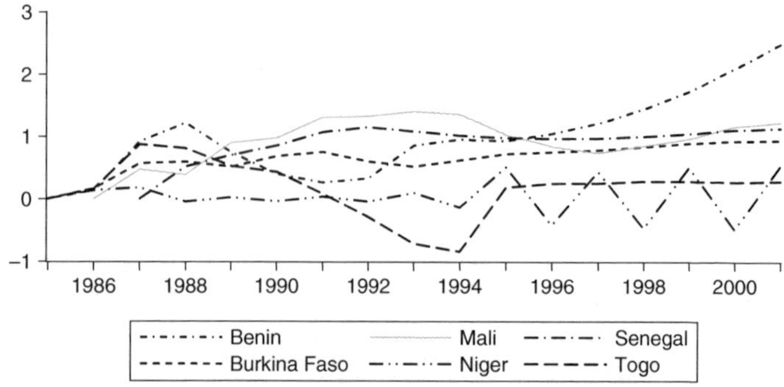

Figure 2.13 *b* coefficients for the tax rate, 1986–2001

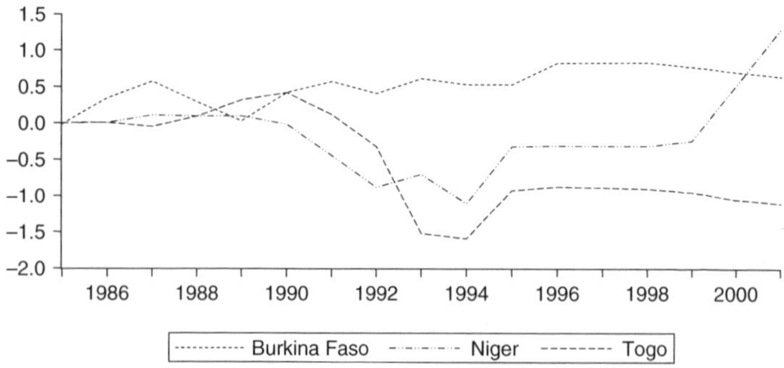

Figure 2.14 *b* coefficients for the public sector wage bill: Burkina Faso, Niger, Togo, 1986–2001

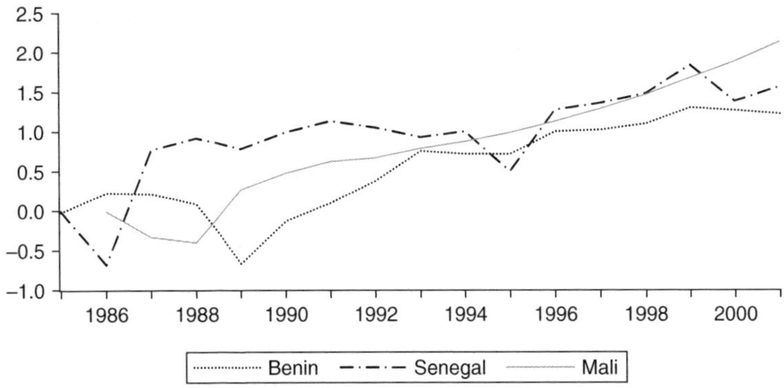

Figure 2.15 *b* coefficients for the public sector wage bill: Benin, Senegal, Mali, 1986–2001

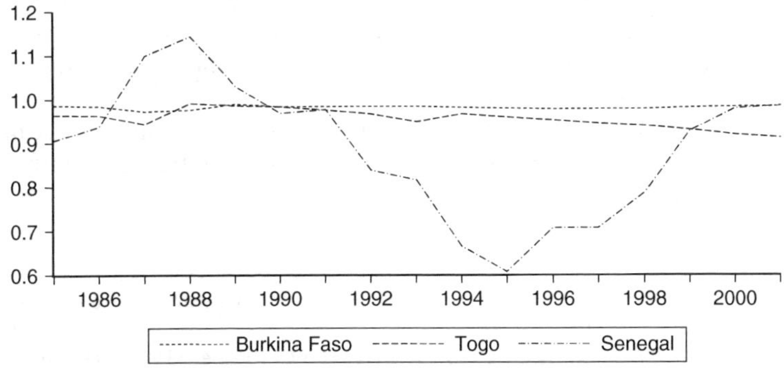

Figure 2.16 *b* coefficients for payments in arrears, 1986–2001

Conclusion

The purpose of our study has been to analyse convergence within the UEMOA from 1980 to 2001 by applying convergence criteria as defined by the UEMOA convergence pact. Convergence has been evaluated by using Côte d'Ivoire and the UEMOA norm as reference points. It appears that the convergence pact has not reduced the countries' instability *vis-à-vis* most of the UEMOA convergence criteria. The main exception to this is the inflation rate.

Our analysis calls for three important comments: First, with the exception of the inflation rate, all other UEMOA criteria are budget-related. Divergence was particularly manifest in these variables. This situation reflects only the difficulty in co-ordinating macroeconomic policies and fulfilling the convergence criteria in a union where the economies are continually exposed to external shocks. In this context, Ousmane and Masson (2002) have shown the influence of trade conditions and the business cycle on the performance of the countries faced with convergence criteria. The study reveals that, from 1994 to 1997, favourable business cycle and trade conditions permitted positive performance. But later unfavourable conditions undermined this trend.

The problem of co-ordinating fiscal policy in a monetary area must be addressed. Authors such as Cohen (1989) suggest that a credible monetary policy makes the co-ordination of budgetary policies superfluous, but this argument is not applicable to the UEMOA. Here, monetary policy credibility does not entail optimal budgetary policies. Co-ordination of fiscal policies may seem to be an impossible task compared with reinforcement of the monetary discipline that has brought about inflation convergence. But monetary discipline alone will not promote vigorous and sustainable economic growth.

Second, there is substantial cross-country heterogeneity with respect to convergence performance. This could be explained by the structural differences among the economies. The economies are subject to asymmetric shocks and react to shocks differently. Since fiscal policy is the only effective domestic instrument in the conduct of economic policy, variation in fiscal positions is only to be expected.

Third, our study shows that for most countries and most convergence measures, convergence episodes are short-lived. It remains to be seen whether the UEMOA will ever be able to attain stability.

Notes

1 Data for 2002 and 2003 are excluded because of the civil war in Côte d'Ivoire, the leading member of the UEMOA.
2 Mundell (1961), McKinnon (1963), Kenen (1969), Cooper (1977), Helpman and Razin (1982), Baumol (1986), Kindleberger (1986).
3 Bayoumi (1994), Ricci (1997), Beine and Docquier (1998), Neumeyer (1998).
4 The method used here is a variant of the test proposed by Haldane and Hall (1991), applied to some European Community (EC) nominal convergence indicators by Hall, Robertson and Wicksen (1992). The Kalman filter can be derived using classical statistical techniques, by applying Bayes' theorem (see Meinhold and Singpurwhalla 1983).
5 The model is fitted using E-views 3.1. See Bamba (2004) for more information on the Kalman filter and model estimation.

References

Artis, M. and P. Omerod (1991) 'Is there an "EMS" Effect in European Labour Markets?', CEPR Discussion Paper 598, London: CEPR.

Bamba, L. N. (2004) 'Analyse du processus de convergence dans la zone UEMOA', WIDER Research Paper 18, Helsinki: UNU-WIDER.

Bamba, L. N. and K. Diomandé (2000) 'Y a-t-il convergence des performances macroéconomiques au sein de l'UEMOA?' (Does Macroeconomic Performances' Convergence Exist within the WAEMU?), in *L'avenir de la zone franc* (*The Future of the Franc Area*), Paris: Editions Karthala et Codesria: 61–98.

Barro, R. and X. Sala-í-Martin (1990) 'Economic Growth and Convergence across the United States', NBR Working Paper 3419.

Barro, R. and X. Sala-í-Martin (1996) *Economic Growth*, Paris: Ediscience International.

Baumol, W. (1986) 'Productivity Growth, Convergence and Welfare: What the Long Run Data Show', *American Economic Review*, 76: 1072–85.

Bayoumi, T. (1994) 'A Formal Model of Optimum Currency Areas', CEPR Discussion Paper 968, London: CEPR.

Beine, M. and F. Docquier (1998) 'A Stochastic Simulation Model of an Optimum Currency Area', *Open Economies Review*, 9(3): 229–57.

Cohen, D. (1989) 'Monetary and Fiscal Policy in an Open Economy with or without Policy Coordination', *European Economic Review*, 33: 303–9.

Cooper, R. (1977). 'Worldwide versus Regional Integration: The Optimum Size of the Integrated Area', in F. Machulp (ed.), *Economic Integration, Worldwide, Regional, Sectoral*, London: Macmillan.

DeLong, J. B. (1988) 'Productivity Growth, Convergence and Growth: Comment', *American Economic Review*, 78: 1138–54.

Haldane, A. G. and S. G. Hall (1991) 'Sterling's Relationship with the Dollar and the Deutschemark: 1976–89', *Economic Journal*, 101(127): 436–43.

Hall, S. G., D. Robertson and M. R. Wicksen (1992) 'Measuring Convergence of the EC Economies', *The Manchester School*, 60, Supplement.

Helpman, E. A. and A. Razin (1982) 'A Comparison of Exchange Rate Regime in the Presence of Imperfect Capital Markets', *International Economic Review*, 23: 365–88.

Kenen, P. (1969) 'The Theory of Optimum Currency Areas: An Eclectic View', in R. A. Mundell and A. Swoboda, *Monetary Problems in International Economy*, Chicago: Chicago University Press.

Kindleberger, C. (1986) 'International Public Goods without International Government', *American Economic Review*, 76(1): 1–13.

Loufir, R. and L. Reichlin (1993) 'Convergence nominale et réelle parmi les pays de la CEE et de l'AELE' (Nominal and Real Convergence in EEC and EFTA Countries), *Revue de l'OFCE*, 43: 69–87.

McKinnon, R. (1963) 'Optimum Currency Areas', *American Economic Review*, 53: 717–25.

Meinhold, R. J. and N. D. Singpurwhalla (1983) 'Understanding the Kalman Filter', *American Statistician*, 37: 123–7.

Mundell, R. A. (1961) 'A Theory of Optimum Currency Areas', *American Economic Review*, 51: 657–65.

Neumeyer, P. A. (1998) 'Currencies and the Allocations of Risk: The Welfare Effects of a Monetary Union', *American Economic Review*, 88: 246–9.

Ousmane, D. and P. R. Masson (2002) 'Experience with Budgetary Convergence in the WAEMU', IMF Working Paper 02/108, Washington, DC: IMF.

Ricci, L. A. (1997). 'A Model of an Optimum Currency Area', IMF Working Paper 97/76, Washington, DC: IMF.

3

The Characteristics of Macroeconomic Shocks in the Franc Zone

David Fielding, Kevin Lee and Kalvinder Shields

Introduction

The main limitation to be faced when modelling the macroeconomics of the Franc Zone is that macroeconomic data for the poorest countries in the region are very limited, so it is infeasible to construct a structural macroeconometric model that encompasses the whole of the Franc Zone. In this chapter we navigate a way round this difficulty by fitting a Vector Error Correction Model (VECM) of annual output growth and inflation in Franc Zone member states that does not embody any restrictions to identify structural parameters. Instead, we draw out the information implicit in the fitted model by constructing persistence profiles for innovations in output and prices in each of the countries. These profiles permit us to investigate the degree of heterogeneity in the way each of the economies responds to macroeconomic shocks, and to see if there are identifiable sub-groups of countries across which there is a reasonable degree of homogeneity. Among such a group of countries the costs of a single currency would be relatively low, and the case for a monetary union much stronger. Our application of this methodology to the Franc Zone illustrates a way in which empirical macroeconomic analysis can be used to address questions about the costs and benefits of a single currency, even when data are relatively scarce.

The modelling framework

Overview

There are two established approaches to the estimation of regional shocks across a monetary global area and their consequences. The first (exemplified by Funke and Hall 1998) has focused on the identification of aggregate supply and demand shocks in each region, using long-run restrictions in the style of Blanchard and Quah (1989). Because the interpretation of these structural innovations is the subject of some controversy (Levtchenkova, Pagan and Robertson 1998), other authors (for example Giacometti and

Pinelli 1999) have chosen not to impose a particular set of theoretical long-run restrictions on their model. Instead they explore the dynamics of prices and output in each region through impulse response analysis. However, the application of impulse response analysis is not theoretically innocuous. The impulses to which the system's response is measured are orthogonalizations of the estimated reduced form innovations. These orthogonalizations (for example, Choleski decomposition) are not invariant to the ordering of the variables in the system. Implicit in the ordering is a theory about how the variables interact: in effect, a set of short-run restrictions.

We wish to avoid such restrictions, since our intention is to provide insights into national differences and similarities in the evolution of observed variables rather than in the structural model underlying them. Our analysis of the dynamics is conducted by constructing measures of persistence and persistence profiles, as described below.

The overall modelling approach is based on a vector autoregression (VAR) framework in national output growth and inflation. This framework provides a flexible method for characterizing the evolution over time of national output growth and inflation, as well as readily accommodating relatively complicated forms of international interactions and feedback.

Our model will include measures of output growth and inflation for the different nations of the Franc Zone. We begin by considering a general model of output growth and inflation for $i = 1, 2, \ldots, m$ nations. Assuming that output growth and inflation are stationary with deterministic means, then it is always possible to obtain an moving average (MA) representation of national output growth and inflation in the following form (see Wold 1983):

$$\Delta \mathbf{z}_t = \mu + \mathbf{A}(L)\varepsilon_t \tag{3.1}$$

In this expression $\Delta \mathbf{z}_t = (\Delta \mathbf{y}_t, \Delta \mathbf{p}_t)'$ represents a stacked $(2m \times 1)$ vector where $\Delta \mathbf{y}_t = (\Delta y_{1t}, \Delta y_{2t}, \ldots, \Delta y_{mt})'$ is a $(m \times 1)$ vector containing values on output growth in each of the m nations in time t, $\Delta \mathbf{p}_t = (\Delta p_{1t}, \Delta p_{2t}, \ldots, \Delta p_{mt})'$ is a $(m \times 1)$ vector containing values on inflation in each of the m nations in time t and Δ is the difference operator. $\mu = (\mu^y, \mu^p)'$ is a $(2m \times 1)$ vector, where $\mu^y = (\mu_1^y, \mu_2^y \ldots \mu_m^y)'$ and $\mu^p = (\mu_1^p, \mu_2^p \ldots \mu_m^p)'$ are both $(m \times 1)$ vectors and contain the mean values of output growth and inflation, respectively, in nations $i = 1, \ldots, m$. Similarly, $\varepsilon_t = (\varepsilon_{it}^y, \varepsilon_{it}^p)'$ for $i = 1, \ldots, m$ is a $(2m \times 1)$ vector of mean zero, serially uncorrelated innovations experienced by output growth (ε_{it}^y) and inflation (ε_{it}^p) in nation i at time t, with a covariance matrix Ω. In this multivariate model, $\mathbf{A}(L)$ is a matrix polynomial given by

$$\mathbf{A}(L) = \sum_{k=0}^{\infty} \mathbf{A}_k L^k, \quad \mathbf{A}_0 = \mathbf{I}_{2m} \tag{3.2}$$

and the (i,j)th element of $\mathbf{A}(L)$ is the lag polynomial $a_{ij}(L)$. Hence, for instance, in addition to the effects of current and past values of innovations on $\Delta \mathbf{z}_t$ in nation i itself, output growth (inflation) in nation i may also be affected by past values of shocks to nation j to output growth or inflation. Moreover, there may be a systematic association between the occurrence of shocks in nation i and those taking place elsewhere (captured by the non-zero off-diagonal elements of Ω).

Expression (3.1) has a fundamental moving average representation, and, in general, this can be approximated by a finite order VAR model of the form:

$$\mathbf{B}(\mathbf{L})\Delta \mathbf{z}_t = \Delta \mathbf{z}_t + \mathbf{B}_1 \Delta \mathbf{z}_{t-1} + \mathbf{B}_2 \Delta \mathbf{z}_{t-2} + \cdots + \mathbf{B}_q \Delta \mathbf{z}_{t-q} = \mu^* + \varepsilon_t \tag{3.3}$$

where $\mathbf{B}_s$ $(s = 1, 2, \ldots, q)$ are $(2m \times 2m)$ matrices of coefficients, and the (i,j)th element of $\mathbf{B}_s$, denoted b_{yipjs}, relates to the coefficient on inflation (denoted by p) in nation j, lagged by s periods, in the equation explaining output growth (denoted by y) in nation i. In this finite-order VAR model, output growth in nation i is explained by q lagged values of output growth in nation i, q lagged values of inflation in nation i, plus q lagged values of output growth and inflation in all other nations, and a random innovation, ε^y_{it}; that is:

$$\begin{aligned} \Delta y_{it} = \mu_i^{y^*} &+ \sum_{s=1}^{q} b_{yiyis} \Delta y_{i,t-s} + \sum_{s=1}^{q} b_{yipis} \Delta p_{i,t-s} \\ &+ \sum_{s=1}^{q} \sum_{j \neq i} b_{yiyjs} \Delta y_{j,t-s} + \sum_{s=1}^{q} \sum_{j \neq i} b_{yipjs} \Delta p_{j,t-s} + \varepsilon^y_{it} \end{aligned} \tag{3.4}$$

This type of model has a very large number of parameters. For example, if $q = 2$ and $m = 10$, the number of terms the right hand side of (3.4) equals 40, excluding the intercept and error terms. Such a model is likely to be over-parameterized, and its application to small macroeconomic time-series is unlikely to produce robust results. However, one plausible simplification of the model is to restrict the international feedback effects so that all foreign price or income changes have the same impact on country *i*s income (or prices). In this chapter, we fit a model that includes an aggregate income effect for the whole Franc Zone. For the aggregate price effects, we use a slightly more flexible specification, distinguishing between a price aggregate for country *i*s monetary union partners and a price aggregate for the countries of the other monetary union. (A similar disaggregation of the aggregate income expression turns out not to improve the fit of the model.) For any one country, the model can be represented as:

$$\Delta y_{it} = \mu_i^{y*} + \sum_{s=1}^{q} b_{yiyis} \Delta y_{i,t-s} + \sum_{s=1}^{q} c_{yis} \Delta \bar{y}_{-i,t-s} + \sum_{s=1}^{q} d_{yis} \Delta \bar{p}_{t-s}^{A} + \sum_{s=1}^{q} f_{yis} \Delta \bar{p}_{t-s}^{B} + \varepsilon_{it}^{y} \quad (3.5)$$

for the output growth equations and

$$\Delta p_{it} = \mu_i^{p*} + \sum_{s=1}^{q} b_{pipis} \Delta p_{i,t-s} + \sum_{s=1}^{q} c_{pis} \Delta \bar{p}_{-i,t-s}^{A} + \sum_{s=1}^{q} d_{pis} \Delta \bar{p}_{-i,t-s}^{B} + \sum_{s=1}^{q} f_{pis} \Delta \bar{y}_{-i,t-s} + \varepsilon_{it}^{p} \quad (3.6)$$

for the inflation equations. In (3.5) and (3.6),

$$\Delta \bar{y}_{-i,t} = \frac{1}{m-1} \sum_{h \neq i} \Delta y_{ht} \quad \text{and} \quad \Delta p_{-i,t-s}^{-A} = \frac{1}{m_0 - 1} \sum_{k \neq i} \Delta p_{kt} \quad (3.7)$$

where the first $k = 1, \ldots, m_0$ countries are members of monetary union A, the union to which country i adheres, and

$$\Delta \bar{y}_t = \frac{1}{m} \sum_i \Delta y_{it} \quad \text{and} \quad \Delta \bar{p}_t^{A} = \frac{1}{m_0} \sum_k \Delta p_{kt} \quad \text{and}$$
$$\Delta \bar{p}_t^{B} = \frac{1}{m - m_0} \sum_l \Delta p_{lt} \quad (3.8)$$

where the $l = m_0 + 1, \ldots, m$ countries are members of union B, the other monetary union.

The model represented by (3.5)–(3.6) imposes the following restrictions:

(1) Lagged output growth in countries other than i has a uniform effect on growth in i.
(2) Lagged inflation in countries other than i (but belonging to the same monetary union) has a uniform effect on inflation in i; the effect of inflation in countries of the other monetary union is also uniform.

(3) Lagged output growth in countries other than i has a uniform effect on inflation in i.
(4) Lagged inflation in countries other than i but belonging to the same monetary union has a uniform effect on output growth in i; the effect of inflation in countries of the other monetary union is also uniform.

Although such a model restricts the possible interactions that exist between different nations, it will be a good approximation of the true data generating process as long as there is not a great deal of heterogeneity in international feedback effects. Note also that there is no restriction on the structure of the correlation of contemporaneous shocks to different nations, so there is still scope for substantial international heterogeneity within the estimated model.

If important interactions exist between the levels of $\mathbf{z}_t$, the existing modelling framework can be readily adapted to allow for the presence of cointegrating relationships in the form of restrictions on the MA representation in (3.1). The error-correction form of (3.3) can be expressed as:

$$\Delta \mathbf{z}_t = \mu^* + \sum_{s=1}^{q} \Gamma_s \Delta \mathbf{z}_{t-s} - \Pi \mathbf{z}_{t-q-1} + \varepsilon_t \tag{3.9}$$

where Π is a $(2m \times 2m)$ reduced rank matrix determining the extent to which the system is cointegrated. Again, for empirical purposes, we restrict (3.9) and give the following form for output growth in nation i at time t:

$$\begin{aligned}\Delta y_{it} = {} & \mu_i^{y*} + \sum_{s=1}^{q} b_{yiyis} \Delta y_{i,t-s} + \sum_{s=1}^{q} c_{yis} \Delta \overline{y}_{-i,t-s} + \sum_{s=1}^{q} d_{yis} \Delta \overline{p}_{t-s}^{A} \\ & + \sum_{s=1}^{q} f_{yis} \Delta \overline{p}_{t-s}^{B} + \lambda_{yi} \left(y_{i,t-1} - \overline{y}_{-i,t-1} \right) + \lambda_{pi} \left(p_{it-1} - \overline{p}^{A}_{-i,t-1} \right) \\ & + \lambda_{zi} \left(\overline{p}^{A}_{i,t-1} - \overline{p}^{B}_{i,t-1} \right) + \lambda_i \left(y_{it-1} - p_{i,t-1} \right) + \varepsilon_{it}^{y}\end{aligned} \tag{3.10}$$

and an analogous expression can be written for the inflation. In (3.10) $\Delta \overline{y}_{-i,t}$ represents the (equal-weighted) aggregate of (log) output outside i and $\overline{p}^{A}_{-i,t}$ represents the (equal-weighted) aggregate of (log) prices outside i but in the same monetary union. $\overline{p}^{A}_{it}$ and $\overline{p}^{B}_{it}$ are similar aggregates for all of the countries in *i*s union (including i) and for all of the countries in the other union.[1] Hence, in its most general form, the model allows for the possibility for the same long-run relationship across all m nations between output levels, the same long-run relationship among price levels across all nations and for price and output series in nation i to be cointegrated.[2]

Measuring the persistence of shocks

The trans-national, multivariate VECM model presented above provides a flexible framework within which an analysis of output and price determination can be carried out. Of particular interest are the long-run responses of the variables in $\mathbf{z}_t$ to shocks, and the dynamics of adjustment to the long run. Lee and Pesaran (1993), Pesaran, Pierse and Lee (1993) and Lee and Shields (1998) provide the means for identifying the effects of specified types of shock, and for distinguishing between the effects of shocks common to all nations and those associated with individual nations. We can investigate the evolution of individual variables in response to shocks, without resorting to a *priori* restrictions, by using persistence profiles (see Lee, Pesaran and Pierse 1992, hereafter LPP). We will next provide a brief description of the measurement of the impact of shocks, showing how they may be used to construct measures of interest.

If a series is non-stationary, then the effects of a shock to the series is permanent and the size of the permanent effect of the shock is termed the 'persistence' of the shock. In LPP, a measure of persistence is suggested which can be applied to a trans-national model, and is based on the change in the conditional variance of $\mathbf{z}_t$ at the infinite horizon. If $\mathbf{z}_t$ is stationary, then eventually the series will return to its mean level with certainty, so the change in the conditional variance of predictions of $\mathbf{z}_t$ will tend to zero. Conversely, if $\mathbf{z}_t$ is $I(1)$, the conditional variance of predicted future $\mathbf{z}_t$ continues to grow as the forecast horizon extends. The extent of the permanent effect of a shock is thus reflected by the size of the growth in the conditional variance at the infinite horizon.

Specifically, referring to the multivariate, trans-national model described in (3.1)–(3.3), if $\mathbf{e}_t$ is a $(2m \times 1)$ selection vector with unity in its rth element, and zeros elsewhere, then the persistence of a shock to output $(1 \leq r \leq m)$ or prices $(m + 1 \leq r \leq 2m)$ in nation i is given by:

$$Q(z_i^1) = \left(\frac{e_r' \mathbf{A}(1) \Omega \mathbf{A}(1)' e_r}{e_r' \mathbf{A}_0 \Omega \mathbf{A}_0' e_r} \right)^{\frac{1}{2}} \tag{3.11}$$

where $\mathbf{z}_i^1 = (y_i^1, p_i^1)$, $\mathbf{A}_0 = \mathbf{I}_{2m}$. $Q(y_i^1)$ and $Q(p_i^1)$ are to be interpreted as measuring the permanent effect in nation i of the shock to output (or prices) that results from an innovation causing output (or prices) in that nation to rise by 1 per cent on impact. The persistence measures incorporate all of the interactions between variables in the system, insofar as they affect output (or prices) in nation i at the infinite horizon. Just as the asymptotic persistence measure given in (3.11) is of potential importance in understanding the response of the Franc Zone economies to shocks, so also is the path to the asymptote. This time profile of the response to shocks ('persistence profile') is calculated as in (3.10), but replacing **A**(1) (which represents the infinite horizon entity) with the corresponding *n*th horizon matrix, $\mathbf{A}(L) = \sum_{k=0}^{n} \mathbf{A}_k L^k$.[3] Both the asymptotic measure and persistence profiles will be discussed in the following section.

In a similar vein, we can calculate a measure of the permanent effect on nation *i*s output (or prices) of a unit shock to output (prices) in the whole monetary union by using the selection vector $\mathbf{w}_y$ (or $\mathbf{w}_p$). This is a $2m \times 1$ selection vector with ones in the first m (in the case of prices, the first $m+1$ to $2m$) elements, and zeros elsewhere. The persistent effect on nation *i*s output, when a shock causes economy-wide output to rise by 1 per cent on impact is given by:

$$Q(y_i^2) = \left(\frac{e_r' \mathbf{A}(1) \Omega\, \mathbf{A}(1)' e_r}{w_y' \mathbf{A}_0 \Omega \mathbf{A}_0' w_r} \right)^{\frac{1}{2}} \tag{3.12}$$

where the value of $r(1 \leq r \leq m)$ determines the selection of the output of a particular nation. An analogous expression can be given for the persistent effects of a unit shock to economy-wide inflation on national prices ($Q(p_i^2)$) by using $\mathbf{w}_p$ in place of $\mathbf{w}_y$ in (3.12) with

$$m + 1(\leq r \leq 2m)$$

It is possible to construct various decompositions of these persistence measures. Consider first decomposing the vector of shocks to each variable in each nation into three orthogonal components: a part due to a union-wide output shock, a part due to a union-wide price shock plus an idiosyncratic component. More formally,

$$\varepsilon_t = \overline{\varepsilon}_t^y \mathbf{w}_y + \overline{\varepsilon}_t^p \mathbf{w}_p + \varepsilon_t^d \tag{3.13}$$

where $\overline{\varepsilon}_t^y$ and $\overline{\varepsilon}_t^p$ represent the union-wide output and price shocks and ε_t^d is the $2m \times 1$ vector of idiosyncratic innovations. Now consider a typical ε_t – that is, one causing output in all nations to rise by 1 per cent on impact. For each nation *i*, it is possible to construct a persistence profile for output corresponding to the common-output shock component of this ε_t. This persistence measure will be denoted $Q(y_i^3)$. $Q(y_i^3)$ can be thought of as one component of $Q(y_i^2)$, the other main components being the output persistence measure corresponding to common shocks to prices (which we will call $Q(y_i^{3p})$) and that corresponding to the idiosyncratic innovation ε_t^d (which we will call $Q(y_i^{3x})$).[4]

An analogous exercise can be performed with price persistence profiles. Consider a typical ε_t causing prices in all nations to rise by 1 per cent on impact. For each nation i, it is possible to construct a persistence profile for prices corresponding to the common-price shock component of this ε_t. This persistence measure will be denoted $Q(p_i^3)$. $Q(p_i^3)$ can be thought of as one component of $Q(p_i^2)$, the other main components being the price persistence measure corresponding to common shocks to output $(Q(p_i^{3y}))$, and that corresponding to the idiosyncratic innovation $\varepsilon_t^d (Q(p_i^{3x}))$.

Formally, if

$$\Omega^y = E\left(\bar{\varepsilon}_t^{y^2}\right)\mathbf{w}_y\mathbf{w}_y', \quad \Omega^p = E\left(\bar{\varepsilon}_t^{p^2}\right)\mathbf{w}_p\mathbf{w}_p' \quad \text{and} \quad \Omega^d = E\left(\varepsilon_t^d \varepsilon_t^{d'}\right)$$

the two additional persistence measures are defined as:

$$Q(y_i^3) = \left(\frac{e_r'\mathbf{A}(1)\Omega^y\mathbf{A}(1)'e_r}{w_y'\mathbf{A}_0\Omega\mathbf{A}_0'w_y}\right)^{\frac{1}{2}} \quad \text{and} \quad Q(p_i^3) = \left(\frac{e_r'\mathbf{A}(1)\Omega^p\mathbf{A}(1)'e_r}{w_p'\mathbf{A}_0\Omega\mathbf{A}_0'w_p}\right)^{\frac{1}{2}} \tag{3.14}$$

where $1 \leq r \leq m$ and $m+1 \leq r \leq 2m$ for $Q(y_i^3)$ and $Q(p_i^3)$, respectively. In a similar way, we can construct persistence measures for output and prices corresponding to the idiosyncratic component of $\varepsilon_t, \varepsilon_t^d$.

In summary, we have three types of persistence measure for output growth (and inflation). Estimates of these three measures will be presented in the following section:

(1) $Q(y_i^1)$ (or $Q(p_i^1)$): a measure of how output (or prices) in each nation evolves in response to a typical shock to output (or prices) in that nation.
(2) $Q(y_i^2)$ (or $Q(p_i^2)$): a measure of how output (or prices) in each nation evolves in response to a typical union-wide shock to output (or prices).
(3) $Q(y_i^3)$ (or $Q(p_i^3)$): a measure of how output (or prices) in each nation evolves in response to the common-output shock component (or common-prices shock component) of a typical union-wide shock to output (or prices). Corresponding to this measure is a measure of persistence in response to the nationally idiosyncratic component.

All three measures are of potential importance in understanding how the Franc Zone economies respond to economic shocks. The first measure provides a basic indication of how similar or dissimilar the dynamics of output and prices are across Franc Zone nations. Similar values for persistence measures indicate a degree of homogeneity in the dynamics of each nation, although they do not indicate how similar shocks are across nations. For this reason the second two measures are also of potential interest.

The second persistence measure is of potential use in assessing the relative sizes of typical shocks to each country, and the consequences of differences in these sizes. If in some countries shocks are larger on average, then their $Q(y_i^2)$ measure will be relatively large at short horizons. If these relatively large shocks are attenuated by cross-country convergence over the longer term, then the $Q(y_i^2)$ measures at longer horizons will exhibit less heterogeneity. Even if prices are co-integrated across nations, so that there is no heterogeneity at the infinite horizon, there might nevertheless be heterogeneity in the paths to the asymptote. The larger the magnitude of such heterogeneity, the greater will be the degree of international price distortions resulting from the shock.

The usefulness of the second measure of persistence is predicated on knowledge about the degree of correlation of innovations on impact. The third measure of persistence complements the second, since it is based on that component of innovations in output (or prices) that is common to all nations. If persistence measures corresponding to the common innovations are large relative to the persistence measures corresponding to the idiosyncratic innovations then we can expect a larger degree of homogeneity in the movement of output and prices across nations, *ceteris paribus*. If the persistence measures corresponding to the idiosyncratic innovations are relatively large, then we can expect a greater degree of heterogeneity. The potential costs of sharing a single currency are likely to depend on how large this heterogeneity is.

Implicit in the construction of the $Q(y_i^2)$ and $Q(y_i^3)$ figures is a normalization: they are based on a shock that creates a unit change in Franc Zone-wide output on impact. On this basis, we can make observations about the relative costs for different countries of sharing a single currency, and whether these costs might be lower or higher in a world where the monetary unions had a different membership. We do not make any comments about the absolute costs of sharing a single currency: in the absence of any knowledge about the relevant policy-makers' utility functions, it is not possible to create a sensible metric for such an assessment.

Estimating measures of persistence

In this section we present our estimates of the three persistence measures discussed in the previous section, using the national real GDP and GDP deflator data from the World Bank Development Indicators (WBDI). These measures are based on a VECM model of annual price inflation and GDP growth in ten Franc Zone countries for the period 1967–2000. These are, in the UEMOA: Burkina Faso, Côte d'Ivoire, Mali, Senegal and Togo; and in the CEMAC: Cameroon, Central African Republic, Chad, Congo Republic and Gabon. The relevant data for the other four Franc Zone countries (Benin, Equatorial Guinea, Guinea–Bissau and Niger) were either not reported at all, or else were unreliable, for some of the sample period.

Time-series properties of the data and estimation of the VECM model

The first stage of our empirical analysis is to test for the order of integration of our price and output series, using the standard panel unit root test of Im, Pesaran and Shin (2003). We stack the regional output series and the regional price series and perform just two unit root tests, and under the assumption that all the output series and all the price series will be of the same order of integration, the test statistics have a standard normal distribution. (We think that the panel unit root tests are more appropriate here than univariate tests: we do not believe that the Franc Zone countries are so heterogeneous as to manifest different orders of integration of prices and output. But in any case, the application of a battery of univariate unit root tests does not alter our conclusions about the order of integration of the series.) The panel unit root test statistics are reported in Table 3.1. Table 3.1 indicates that the logarithms of both prices and output are difference-stationary, so the modelling framework in difference form outlined in the previous section is appropriate for our data. Figures 3.1–3.4 illustrate the output growth and inflation series that we use.

We also test for the four types of cointegration implicit in (3.9): cointegration between prices and GDP within one country, cointegration between national prices and the price aggregate in the appropriate monetary union, inter-union price cointegration and cointegration between national GDP and the Franc Zone average. In testing for cointegration between price and output in country i, residuals from an Engle–Granger regression are taken and standard unit root tests applied to the residuals. With regard to testing for cointegration existing between the same variable across countries, we again make use of the panel unit root tests of Im, Pesaran and Shin (2003). In this case, residuals from regressions over all countries of the country i variable on a union-wide aggregate of the same variable excluding country i are stacked and the standard panel unit root test is applied. Details of the cointegration results are provided in the Appendix in Table 3A.2 (p. 62). Briefly, we find that:

1. For no country is GDP cointegrated with prices.
2. For no country is GDP cointegrated with average Franc Zone GDP.

Table 3.1 Panel unit root test results

variable	t-bar stat.	variable	t-bar stat.
y	−0.583	p	+3.10
Δy	**−12.80**	Δp	**−7.77**

Notes: Figures in bold indicate rejection of the null that the series are $I(1)$ against the alternative that they are $I(0)$ at the 5 per cent level. The test is based on Im, Pesaran and Shin (2003), with no deterministic trend in the Augmented Dickey–Fuller (ADF) regressions.

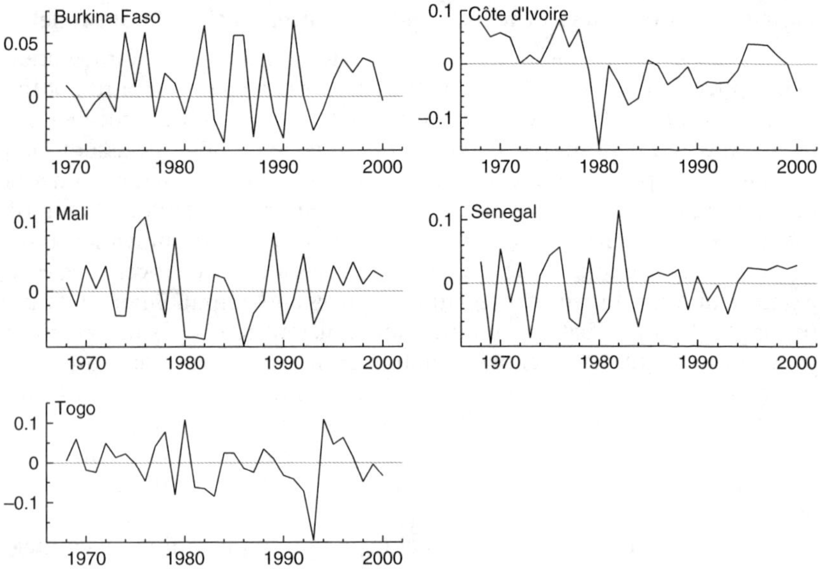

Figure 3.1 Annual GDP growth in five UEMOA countries, 1968–2000

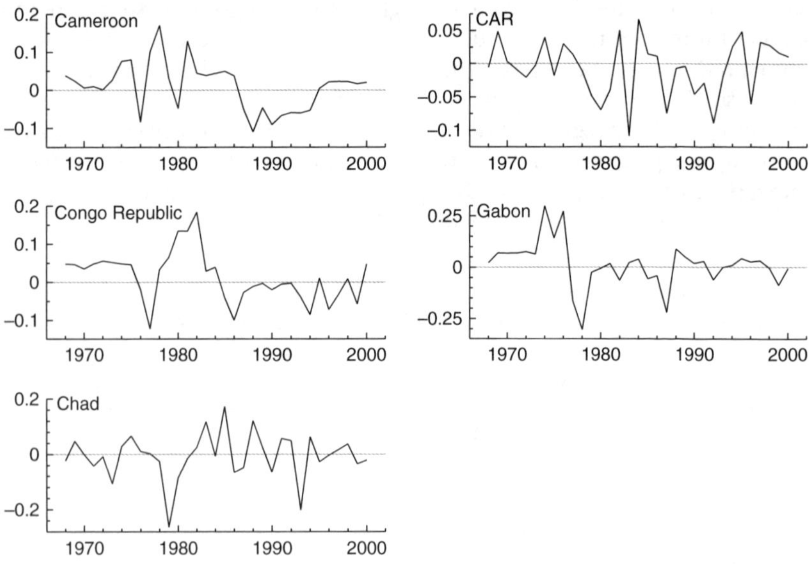

Figure 3.2 Annual GDP growth in five CEMAC countries, 1968–2000

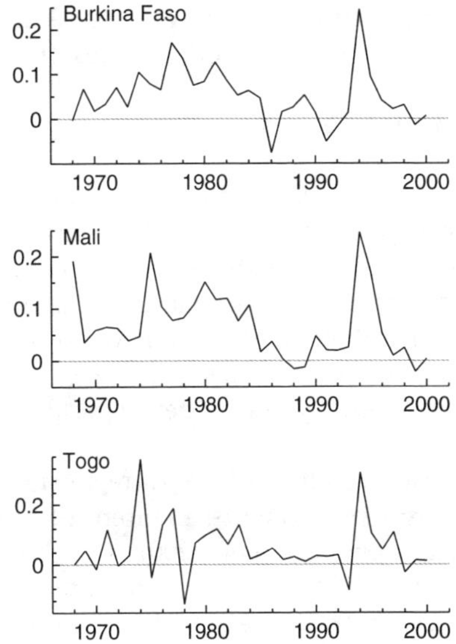

Figure 3.3 Annual inflation in five UEMOA countries, 1968–2000

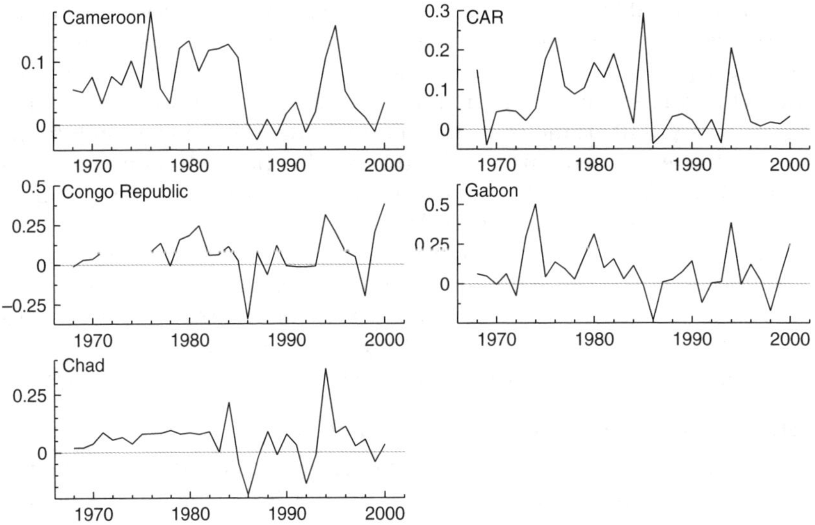

Figure 3.4 Annual inflation in five CEMAC countries, 1968–2000

3. For all countries prices are cointegrated with the union-wide aggregate, with a loading insignificantly different from [1, –1]. In other words, there is PPP in levels with a fixed wedge.
4. UEMOA prices are cointegrated with CEMAC prices.

So the estimated VECM is a restricted version of (3.9) in which λ_{yi} and λ_i are set to zero. The cointegration of national prices means that, by construction, persistence measures for Franc Zone-wide price shocks will converge asymptotically. However, the persistence profiles for national prices might still exhibit substantial heterogeneity, since the convergence is consistent with regional heterogeneity in short-run price dynamics. The absence of cointegration in regional GDP means that heterogeneity in persistence profiles is a possibility in both the short and the long term.

Table 3A.1 provides the detailed regression results. This set of regressions takes the form of (3.9), with two deterministic components: an intercept and a dummy variable for the post-devaluation period (1994–2000). The time-series for inflation in Figures 3.3–3.4 show that 1994 saw an atypically large shock to prices in many of the Franc Zone countries. The persistence profiles discussed below are based on estimated innovations other than the 1994 devaluation.

The unrestricted regressions contain many parameters that are individually statistically insignificant: with so many nuisance parameters, the power of diagnostic tests is very low and the standard errors on persistence measure very high. So Table 3A.1 reports a restricted version of the regression equations in which very small and statistically insignificant coefficients are set to zero.[5] The persistence profiles are based on this set of regressions.[6] Table 3A.1 shows many individual interactions between output and prices in the different members of the Franc Zone. In almost all cases inflation responds to the λ_{pi} error-correction term in (3.9). In other words, prices in a country respond to any divergence from PPP with the other members of its monetary union. In several of the CEMAC countries (but not in any of the UEMOA countries) the λ_{zi} error-correction term is significant. In other words, the long-run PPP that holds between the two monetary unions appears to be a consequence of CEMAC convergence on UEMOA prices. In this sense, the CEMAC area follows the UEMOA area. For all countries the devaluation dummy (*DUM94*) has a significant effect in the price equation.

Estimates of regional persistence in output

Figures 3.5–3.6 illustrate persistence profiles for output for each of the ten countries. Figure 3.5 shows the $Q(y_i^1)$ measures, which demonstrate, for each country, the consequences of a typical shock to the system causing output in that country to rise by one unit on impact. Figure 3.6 shows the $Q(y^2)$ measures, which demonstrate, for each country, the consequences of a typical shock causing output across all ten countries to rise by one unit on impact.

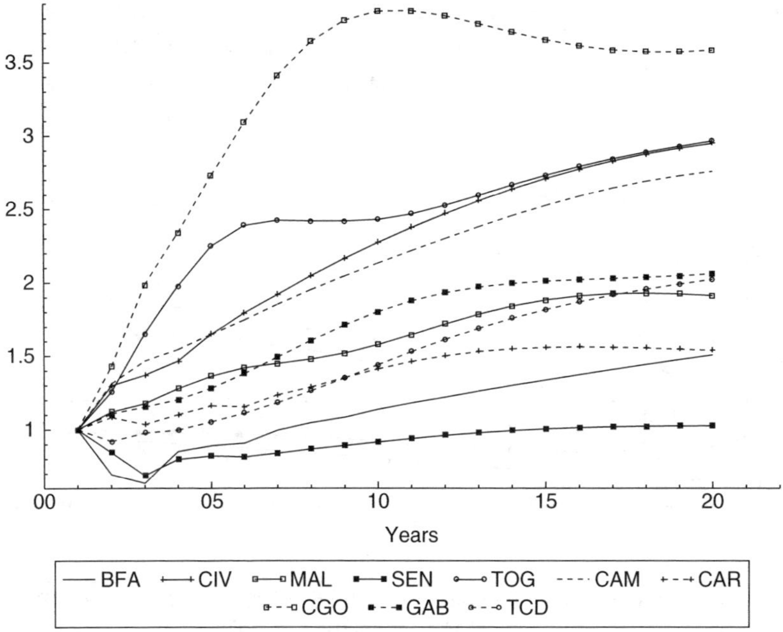

BFA	Burkina Faso	CIV	Côte d'Ivoire	MAL	Mali	SEN	Senegal
TOG	Togo	CAM	Cameroon	CAR	CAR	CGO	Congo Republic
GAB	Gabon	TCD	Chad				

Figure 3.5 Effect of a shock causing initial output to rise by one unit in country *i* ($Q(y^1)$)

The corresponding asymptotic persistence measures are listed in Table 3.2 with their respective standard errors.

Figure 3.5 shows a wide range of responses to a unit shock to output. In all cases, the initial shock is multiplied in the long run; this is partly due to the positive response of Δy_i to lagged $\Delta \bar{y}$ in many of the countries (Cameroon, CAR, Chad, Mali, Senegal, Togo). However, the range of estimated multiplier effects is very great, in both the short run and asymptotically: in Senegal, a unit shock leads to an eventual increase of 1.02; at the other extreme, a unit shock in Congo Republic leads to an eventual increase of 4.49.[7] There is no obvious pattern suggesting that a certain degree of persistence pertains to a certain type of economy.

This is not true when we move to Figure 3.6, which shows the persistence profiles for a typical shock leading to an aggregate increase in output of one unit across the Franc Zone. The four largest shocks on impact are in CEMAC countries (all the CEMAC countries except CAR); these are also four out of the five countries with the largest figures at the infinite horizon.[8] In other words,

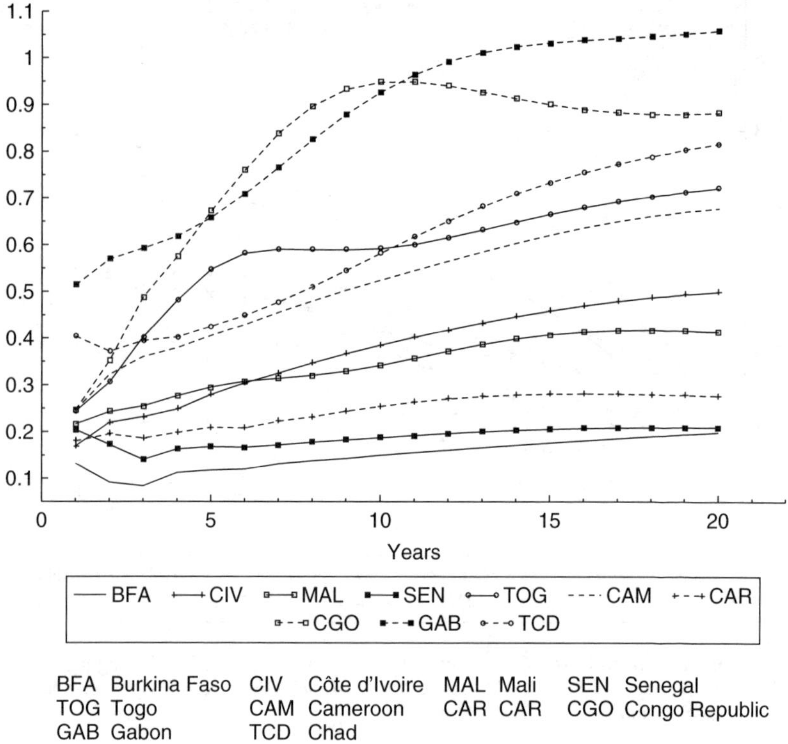

Figure 3.6 Effect of a shock causing an initial zone-wide rise in output of one unit ($Q(y^2)$)

the 'average' shock causing an aggregate increase in output across the Franc Zone is associated with relatively large initial output changes – on average – in the petroleum-exporting countries (Cameroon, Congo Republic, Gabon), plus one of their small CEMAC partners (Chad). Put another way, all of the CEMAC countries except CAR are typically subject to larger shocks than their UEMOA neighbours. Cross-country differences in levels of persistence are not great enough to change this picture substantially when we look at the impact of a typical shock in later years.

The $Q(y_i^2)$ measures indicate that output shocks in the petroleum exporters are typically larger on impact than in other countries, and have a larger long-run effect. The $Q(y_i^3)$ figures in Table 3.2 indicate that a very large part of these shocks is owing to country-specific effects. In other words, the idiosyncratic component of $Q(y_i^2)$, that is, $Q(y_i^{3x})$, is large relative to the components reflecting common shocks, that is, $Q(y_i^{3y})$ and $Q(y_i^{3p})$. This means that in the CEMAC area shocks to output (and the resulting output growth) are

Table 3.2 Asymptotic effects of different shocks to the system

	Effect of a shock causing initial output (prices) to rise by one unit in country *i*				Effect of a shock causing an initial zone-wide rise in output (prices) of one unit			
	$Q(y^1)$	s.e.	$Q(p^1)$	s.e.	$Q(y^2)$	s.e.	$Q(p^2)$	s.e.
Burkina Faso	2.2145	1.2664	2.6144	1.1697	0.2920	0.1670	0.2902	0.1298
Côte d'Ivoire	3.1904	1.4713	1.5507	0.6938	0.5403	0.2492	0.2902	0.1298
Mali	1.8072	1.7018	4.0043	1.7915	0.3914	0.3686	0.2902	0.1298
Senegal	1.0245	0.5308	3.3226	1.4865	0.2096	0.1291	0.2902	0.1298
Togo	3.9580	2.7251	1.5487	0.6929	0.9636	0.6634	0.2902	0.1298
Cameroon	2.9417	1.5606	2.8006	1.2530	0.7229	0.3835	0.2902	0.1298
CAR	1.4901	1.4392	2.0786	0.9300	0.2683	0.2591	0.2902	0.1298
Congo Republic	4.4883	5.5914	0.8255	0.3693	1.1049	1.3764	0.2902	0.1298
Gabon	3.0896	4.1652	0.8802	0.3938	1.5869	2.1393	0.2902	0.1298
Chad	3.0721	3.3620	1.8067	0.8083	1.2398	1.3568	0.2902	0.1298
	$Q(y^3)$ **share**	s.e.	$Q(y^{3p})$ **share**	s.e.	$Q(y^{3x})$ **share**	s.e.		
Burkina Faso	0.0654	0.0447	0.0275	0.0447	0.2766	0.1663		
Côte d'Ivoire	0.1583	0.0600	0.0074	0.0600	0.5156	0.2379		
Mali	0.1711	0.0646	0.0491	0.0646	0.3495	0.3958		
Senegal	0.0939	0.0329	0.0258	0.0329	0.1756	0.1384		
Togo	0.1356	0.1643	0.4778	0.1643	0.9135	0.6246		
Cameroon	0.2260	0.1051	0.2794	0.1051	0.6702	0.2677		
CAR	0.1239	0.0510	0.0261	0.0510	0.2348	0.2929		
Congo Republic	0.3139	0.2185	0.4587	0.2185	1.3002	1.5544		
Gabon	0.1689	0.2911	0.0961	0.2911	1.5540	2.0968		
Chad	0.0221	0.2215	0.1327	0.2215	1.2880	1.4371		
	$Q(p^3)$ **share**	s.e.	$Q(p^{3y})$ **share**	s.e.	$Q(p^{3x})$ **share**	s.e.		
All	0.2280	0.0395	0.0379	0.0395	0.2066	0.0792		

Notes: [a] The shares in each row do not sum exactly to the total effect $Q(z^2)$ because of non-zero covariance terms.

both relatively large and heterogeneous. If output stabilization is regarded as an important policy goal, and if monetary policy can be harnessed effectively to pursue this goal, then the CEMAC countries may face relatively large costs from sharing a single currency. Moreover the UEMOA countries, where shocks are much smaller (if no less heterogeneous), stand to gain from using a different currency from their petroleum-exporting neighbours. The one country for which there is a rationale for switching between monetary areas is the non-petroleum-exporting CAR, whose persistence profiles are closer to those of the UEMOA than of the CEMAC.[9]

Estimates of regional persistence in prices

Figures 3.7–3.8 illustrate persistence profiles for prices for each of the ten countries. Figure 3.7 shows the $Q(p_i^1)$ measures, which demonstrate, for each country, the consequences of a typical shock to the system causing prices in that country to rise by one unit on impact. Figure 3.8 shows the $Q(p_i^2)$ measures, which demonstrate, for each country, the consequences of a typical

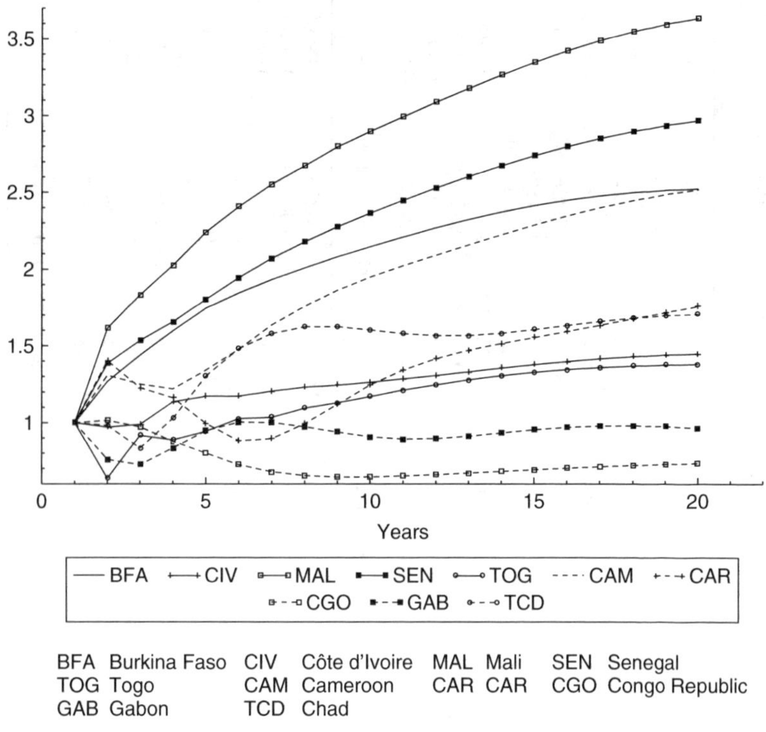

Figure 3.7 Effect of a shock causing initial prices to rise by one unit in country i ($Q(p^1)$)

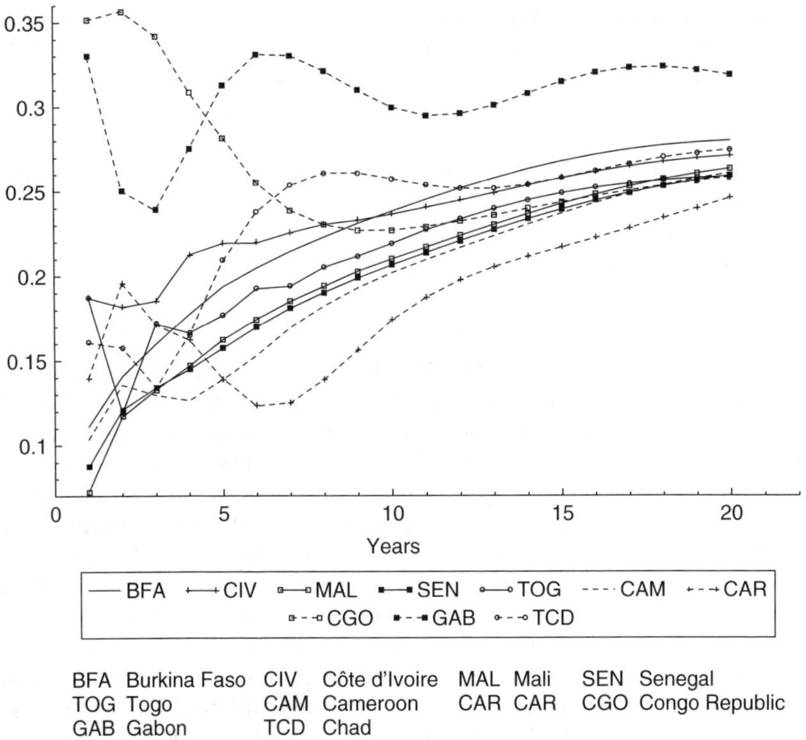

Figure 3.8 Effect of a shock causing an initial zone-wide rise in prices of one unit ($Q(p^2)$)

shock causing prices across all ten countries to rise by one unit on impact. The corresponding asymptotic persistence measures are listed in Table 3.2 with their respective standard errors.[10]

Figure 3.7 and Table 3.2 show that the $Q(p_i^1)$ price persistence measures are just as heterogeneous as the equivalent measures for output. In some cases (the two most oil-dependent countries, Congo Republic and Gabon) there is a very low level of persistence, and a unit shock to prices is somewhat attenuated in the long run. In the other countries there is a long-run multiplier effect ranging from a factor of 1.55 in Togo and Côte d'Ivoire to a factor of 4.00 in Mali.

As Figure 3.8 shows, this disparity does not lead to any heterogeneity in the $Q(p_i^2)$ measures in the very long run, because prices across all of the countries are cointegrated. However, the convergence is very slow, and the heterogeneity in the size of the shocks on impact is substantial. A typical shock leading to a unit increase in aggregate prices on impact is associated with a price increase of 0.35 in Congo Republic and of 0.33 in Gabon; in all the other countries, the figure is less than 0.2. Even at the four-year horizon, the persistence measures for Congo Republic and Gabon are 0.31 and 0.28, respectively, the next highest figure being 0.21 (Côte d'Ivoire). In other words, price shocks are typically very much larger in the two most oil-dependent countries, and long-run price convergence is not fast enough to eradicate this difference at any time horizon likely to be of interest to a policy-maker.

Table 3.2 includes information about the $Q(p_i^3)$ components of $Q(p_i^2)$. Price cointegration means that these figures are the same for all countries at the infinite horizon, though the stylized facts discussed here are also generally true of the $Q(p_i^3)$ measures for different countries at finite horizons. $Q(p_i^{3x})$ is roughly as large as $Q(p_i^{3p})$ at the infinite horizon, and $Q(p_i^{3y})$ is very much smaller. In other words, the fraction of $Q(p_i^2)$ (that is, the asymptotic effect of a typical shock causing aggregate prices to rise by one unit on impact across the Franc Zone) that is accounted for by the response to a common price shock is about as large as the fraction accounted for by the response to an idiosyncratic shock. Given the relative homogeneity of the $Q(p_i^2)$ persistence profiles for the eight Franc Zone countries excluding Congo Republic and Gabon (see Figure 3.8), this means that a policy-maker concerned primarily with price stabilization is much more likely to meet her objectives with a monetary area that excludes the two large petroleum exporters.

Overall, the picture for the price persistence profiles is very similar to that for output persistence profiles. The heterogeneity and persistence of shocks is generally lower for the UEMOA countries than for the CEMAC countries, and therefore presents fewer problems in reaching hypothetical stabilization objectives. The profile for some CEMAC countries (just CAR in the case of output shocks, but also Cameroon and Chad in the case of price shocks) is close to that for the typical UEMOA country. So the difficulty of meeting output/price stabilization objectives in the UEMOA would not be substantially greater if these countries shared the UEMOA currency. However, the two big CEMAC petroleum exporters, Congo Republic and Gabon, are always the exception. Price and output shocks in these two countries are typically larger than elsewhere, and these shocks have a high degree of persistence.

Summary and conclusion

We have fitted a VECM model of output and prices in ten Franc Zone countries, in order to explore the characteristics of inflation and output growth dynamics in the region. The dynamics are characterized in terms of persistence profiles, an approach that avoids the imposition of questionable identifying restrictions in a data set including some very low-income countries about which little is known from a macroeconomic perspective.

In this way we can make some observations about the relative degree of macroeconomic heterogeneity in the two monetary unions that make up the Franc Zone, about relative difficulty of achieving price and output stabilization objectives under the current configuration of countries and about the relative merits of alternative configurations.

A common pattern that emerges in our results is that there is less heterogeneity in the macroeconomic dynamics of the UEMOA countries than there is among the CEMAC members, and so the costs of adhering to a single currency are likely to be lower, *ceteris paribus*. To some extent, the heterogeneity to be found among the CEMAC countries has been a consequence of the presence of two economies – Congo Republic and Gabon – that have been heavily dependent on mineral exports, particularly petroleum. In some ways, the macroeconomic dynamics of some of the other CEMAC members have been closer to those of the UEMOA. This is even true to some extent of Cameroon, which is a petroleum exporter but has a more diversified export base.

If the Franc Zone adopted a single currency in place of the existing two, the presence of large petroleum exporters would probably make the achievement of stabilization objectives in the current members of the UEMOA more difficult. These results are likely to reinforce the reluctance of the UEMOA to respond positively to the stated aim of the non-Franc Zone members of ECOWAS – including Nigeria – to form a monetary union across the ECOWAS area.

Appendix

Table 3A.1 The fitted regression equations

Regressors	Burkina Faso	Côte d'Ivoire	Mali	Senegal	Togo	Cameroon	CAR	Congo Republic	Gabon	Chad
Dependent variable = Δy_{it}										
Intercept	0.0590	0.0136	−0.0052	0.0205	−0.0510	−0.0140	−0.0119	0.0574	−0.0237	0.0178
	(4.6275)	(1.0730)	(−0.3841)	(1.3044)	(−2.2173)	(−0.8005)	(−0.7443)	(2.9211)	(−0.8211)	(0.6975)
Δy_{i-1}	−0.4388		−0.2927	−0.2927	0.2011	0.2011	−0.3630		0.1123	−0.1697
	(−2.6180)		(−1.5498)	(−1.5498)	(1.1941)	(1.1941)	(−1.8442)		(0.6278)	(−0.8239)
Δy_{i-2}	−0.3777		−0.2376	−0.2376				0.1929		
	(−2.1923)		(−1.3867)	(−1.3867)				(1.0838)		
Δy_{-1}		0.8235	0.4448	0.4448			0.7384	−1.1894		0.7339
		(2.7794)	(1.4885)	(1.4885)			(1.8538)	(−2.9467)		(0.9126)
Δy_{-2}					0.5725	0.5725	0.3784	−0.8081		
					(1.6544)	(1.6544)	(1.2276)	(−2.1701)		
Δp_{-1}^{UEMOA}					0.3946					
					(2.4727)					
Δp_{-2}^{UEMOA}	0.1736									
	(2.0018)									
Δp_{-1}^{CEMAC}						0.4197	0.2454		0.3117	0.2481
						(3.3500)	(2.1265)		(1.2081)	(1.1585)
Δp_{-2}^{CEMAC}							−0.2456			
							(−1.8797)			
$p_i - p_{-1}^{UEMOA}$	−0.1483		0.0785	−0.0820	−0.3827			0.1882	−0.2287	−0.1683
	(−2.3497)		(0.7708)	(−0.7745)	(−2.2305)			(1.8308)	(−2.4713)	(−1.9964)
p_{-1}^{UEMOA}		−0.2289	0.2269		0.5499	−0.1493	−0.1890			
p_{-1}^{CEMAC}		(−3.0634)	(1.4863)		(2.4256)	(−1.2431)	(−1.2465)			
DUM94	−0.0306	−0.0052			0.1792		0.0885	−0.1615		
	(−1.0063)	(−0.3841)			(3.1509)		(1.8453)	(−2.6965)		

Continued

Table 3A.1 Continued

Regressors	Burkina Faso	Côte d'Ivoire	Mali	Senegal	Togo	Cameroon	CAR	Congo Republic	Gabon	Chad
R^2	0.3900	0.5078	0.2682	0.1892	0.4148	0.0521	0.3240	0.5074	0.2834	0.1650
σ	0.0286	0.0359	0.0451	0.0448	0.0527	0.94	0.0407	0.0533	0.1069	0.0856
LMAC p^a	0.01	0.14	0.06	0.14	0.28	0.32	0.94	0.70	0.45	0.58
FF p^b	0.68	0.38	0.79	0.91	0.05	0.80	0.14	0.75	0.25	0.73
Normality p^c	0.19	1.00	0.31	0.27	0.73	0.97	0.84	0.27	0.99	0.88
Heterosc. p^d	0.31	0.57	0.30	0.02	0.54	0.4616	0.76	0.41	0.07	0.08
Dependent variable = Δp_{it}										
Intercept	0.0001	0.0135	0.0201	0.0005	0.0090	0.0239	0.0283	0.0549	0.0010	−0.0154
	(0.0081)	(0.4676)	(1.9745)	(0.0340)	(0.2762)	(2.1716)	(1.3521)	(1.1666)	(0.0216)	(−0.5989)
Δp_{i-1}				0.4251	−0.8468		−0.3784			
				(3.3541)	(−3.3738)		(−2.0969)			
Δp_{i-2}		−0.3020			−0.4159					−0.2154
		(−1.0174)			(−2.2480)					(−1.1439)
Δy_{-1}					1.1705				−1.1800	−0.9376
					(1.6639)				(−1.0656)	(−1.5419)
Δy_{-2}	0.4026		−0.1767	0.2882	0.7743		−0.5993			0.6730
	(1.3565)		(−0.8632)	(1.1722)	(1.1843)		(−1.2230)			(1.3116)
Δp_{-1}^{UEMOA}	0.5229	0.4996	0.6148		1.1431					
	(4.2554)	(1.8589)	(7.6053)		(3.1312)					
Δp_{-2}^{UEMOA}		0.7726								
		(1.6080)								
Δp_{-1}^{CEMAC}						0.3789	0.5361	0.3774		0.3244
						(4.2672)	(3.2798)	(1.0870)		(1.8254)

Δp_{-2}^{CEMAC}									0.5842	0.4002
									(1.4055)	(1.7470)
$p_i - p_{-1}^{UEMOA}$		−0.2299	−0.2937	−0.1789	−0.2773	−0.2381	−0.2701	−0.0791	−0.1319	
		(−1.6734)	(−4.8003)	(−2.0442)	(−1.2180)	(−2.1200)	(−3.7880)	(−0.3909)	(−0.8768)	
p_{-1}^{UEMOA}						0.2252	−0.3073		1.1286	0.5742
p_{-1}^{CEMAC}						(1.2654)	(−1.4979)		(1.9392)	(2.3339)
DUM94	0.2522	0.3337	0.2507	0.2494	0.2837	0.0935	0.1996	0.2613	0.2921	0.2817
	(5.5564)	(4.1695)	(8.2783)	(6.6983)	(3.0719)	(2.2111)	(3.2833)	(1.8420)	(1.9522)	(3.5330)
R^2	0.6031	0.5059	0.8394	0.6696	0.5245	0.5483	0.6333	0.1470	0.4083	0.6365
σ	0.0425	0.0745	0.0283	0.0341	0.0779	0.0404	0.0568	0.1345	0.1313	0.0668
LMAC p	0.94	0.16	0.29	0.96	0.35	0.32	0.40	0.14	0.05	0.63
FF p	0.24	0.46	0.63	0.58	0.14	0.72	0.61	0.73	0.43	1.00
Normality *p*	0.23	0.97	0.10	0.97	1.00	0.63	0.90	1.00	0.19	1.00
Heterosc. *p*	0.43	0.20	0.12	0.30	0.12	0.18	0.69	0.45	0.74	0.46

Notes: [a] In each part of the table '*LMAC p*' is the *p*-value from an LM test for first-order residual autocorrelation, figures *greater* than 0.95 indicating rejection of the null of no autocorrelation at the 5 per cent level.

[b] '*FF p*' corresponds to a RESET test for the validity of the functional form.

[c] 'Normality *p*' corresponds to a Jacque–Bera test for residual normality.

[d] 'Heterosc. *p*' corresponds to a test for heteroscedasticity.

Table 3A.2 Cointegration test results[a]

Cointegration between output and price in country *i*	
Country	**ADF test statistic**
Burkina Faso	−0.87
Côte d'Ivoire	−3.08
Mali	−1.35
Senegal	−1.35
Togo	−3.65
Cameroon	−1.52
CAR	−2.33
Congo Republic	−1.06
Gabon	−2.21
Chad	−1.53
Panel tests for cointegration	
Cointegration between output in country *i* and average CFA	***t*-bar test statistic**
Output	−0.79
Prices	**−3.04**[b]

Notes
[a] The upper part of the table gives ADF test statistics based on a regression of the Engle–Granger residuals as described in the text, and contain a constant term. The lower part of the table gives the t-bar test statistic based on Im, Pesaran and Shin (2003) with no deterministic trend in the ADF regressions.
[b] Figures in bold indicate rejection of the null that the series are $I(1)$ against the alternative that they are $I(0)$ at the 5 per cent level.

Notes

1. A specification using average import weighted aggregrates yielded almost identical results and did not improve the fit of the model.
2. This would be the case, if, for instance, all the series were driven, equiproportionately, by the same (stochastic) trend, such that the series do not diverge in the long run.
3. See Lee and Pesaran (1993) and Lee and Shields (1998) for further details of how persistence profiles can be derived.
4. The three components do not sum exactly to $Q(y_i^2)$ because this expression also incorporates some covariance terms.
5. Formally, the specification search rule, while ensuring the stability of the system, excludes coefficients with t-ratios with absolute values less than one only if the F-test for the joint exclusion of restrictions is satisfied.
6. The variables omitted from the restricted regression are not jointly significant, and the restricted regression is to be preferred on the basis of the Akaike Information Criterion. The diagnostic statistics reported in Table 3A.1 suggest the absence of residual autocorrelation and heteroscedasticity in the regressions. In one or two

cases the null of residual normality might be rejected, but the omission of the offending residual outliers does not substantially alter our results.

7. At the infinite horizon standard errors are rather high, making it difficult to assess which asymptotic effects are significantly different from each other. However, the standard errors on the effects at a shorter horizon are somewhat smaller. For instance, in the cases of Chad, Congo Republic, Mali and Togo, the standard errors on impact are smaller by a factor of approximately twenty, while for CAR, Gabon, Bukina Faso, Côte d'Ivoire and Cameroon, they range roughly from respectively being a sixth to a twelfth of the infinite horizon standard errors – and, for Senegal, approximately three times smaller.
8. Togo from the UEMOA joins the group of high-persistence profile countries at longer horizons. Its typical initial shock is almost as large as for the CEMAC countries, and its multiplier effect is the second largest of the ten.
9. If Cameroon, Congo Republic and Gabon all export petroleum, why are their output shocks not very correlated? Gabon exports a wide range of minerals other than petroleum (for example, manganese) and, in Cameroon, the share of petroleum exports in GDP is rather smaller than in the other countries.
10. Again, as in the case of the output profiles, the persistence profiles are estimated relatively more precisely at the short horizon compared to the infinite horizon. For instance, for Burkina Faso, Chad, Mali and Senegal, the short-horizon standard errors are, respectively, in the range of roughly nine–sixteen times smaller relative to their long-run counterparts, while for Cameroon, CAR, the Congo Republic, Côte d'Ivoire, Gabon and Togo, the respective range is approximately between two and six times smaller.

References

Blanchard, O. and D. Quah (1989) 'Dynamic Effects of Aggregate Demand and Supply Disturbances', *American Economic Review*, 79: 655–73.

Funke, M. and S. Hall (1998) 'Aggregate Demand and Aggregate Supply in UK Regions', *Journal of Economic Studies*, 25: 260–76.

Giacometti, R. and D. Pinelli (1999) 'Asymmetric Shocks and Long-Run Economic Performances Across Italian Regions', Bergamo: University of Bergamo, unpublished manuscript.

Im, K., M. Pesaran and Y. Shin (2003) 'Testing for Unit Roots in Heterogenous Panels', *Journal of Econometrics*, 115: 53–74.

Lee, K. and M. Pesaran (1993) 'Persistence Profiles and Business Fluctuations in a Disaggregated Model of UK Output Growths', *Richerche Economiche*, 47: 293–322.

Lee, K., M. Pesaran and R. Pierse (1992) 'Persistence of Shocks and their Sources in a Multisectoral Model of UK Output Growth', *Economic Journal*, 102: 342–56.

Lee, K. and K. Shields (1998) 'Modelling Sectoral Output Growth in the EU Economies', Report for the European Commission, www.le.ac.uk/economics/kcl2.

Levtchenkova, S., A. Pagan and J. Robertson (1998) 'Shocking Stories', *Journal of Economic Surveys*, 12: 507–32.

Pesaran, M., R. Pierse and K. Lee (1993) 'Persistence, Cointegration and Aggregation: A Disaggregated Analysis of Output Fluctuations in the US Economy', *Journal of Econometrics*, 56: 57–88.

Wold, H. (1983) *A Study in the Analysis of Stationary Time Series*, Uppsala: Almqvist–Wiksell.

4

Variance Decomposition of Macroeconomic Shocks in the Franc Zone and other Sub-Saharan African Countries

Simeon Coleman

Introduction

Most countries in sub-Saharan Africa (SSA) are generally considered to be small economies, and are often the price-takers on the world market. However, since the 1980s, most African countries have increasingly been implementing policy reforms aimed at boosting economic growth and promoting their integration into the world economy. To the extent that they are open, the quest comes with the added burden of a greater sensitivity to the external environment, in addition to the domestic disturbances that may occur. Aside from the geographical and political heterogeneity that exist within African countries, marked differences in economic performance, especially over the 1980s, have led to the question of whether being in a monetary union in this part of the world has caused the Franc Zone countries to respond differently to macroeconomic shocks, relative to the non-Franc Zone countries. There is also a question whether such economies have fared better or worse than their neighbours who are not part of the monetary union (see Devarajan and de Melo 1991; Devarajan and Rodrik 1991; Clement 1994; Elbadawi and Majd 1996; Ghura and Hadjimichael 1996).

In relation to the generally poor growth in almost all of Africa, some studies have sought to investigate the factors affecting long-run growth in this part of the world (see, for example, World Bank 1994; Ghura and Hadjimichael 1995). In fact, some studies have suggested that such dismal performances are best explained by understanding the unstable macroeconomies (see Ramey and Ramey 1995; Sachs and Warner 1996; Collier and Gunning 1999). To do this, a thorough understanding of the sources (and responses) of macroeconomic shocks in these economies is important. Despite the generally poor growth, there were also some significant differences in economic performance between countries, and economic blocs in SSA. Notable among these differences are those observed between the countries within the Franc Zone, having a fixed exchange rate regime *vis-à-vis* the French Franc (and with the Euro since 1999) and countries outside the Franc Zone. Among the important comparative studies on the topic are, for example, Elbadawi and Majd (1996); Hoffmaister, Roldós and Wickham (1998); Fielding and Shields (2001); Kose and Reizman (2001).[1]

This chapter seeks to contribute to these studies by providing some information regarding the relative importance of macroeconomic shocks to the real exchange rate, real output and real money balances within a sample of twelve Franc Zone countries and four non-Franc Zone countries. Franc Zone countries considered are Benin, Burkina Faso, Cameroon, CAR, Chad, Côte d'Ivoire, the Congo Republic, Gabon, Mali, Niger, Senegal and Togo. Non-Franc Zone countries included in the study are Ghana, Kenya, Nigeria and Sierra Leone.[2] The Franc Zone and the non-Franc Zone countries of SSA provide a good test case of how the countries in SSA respond to macroeconomic shocks, both domestic and external. This chapter, however, focuses mainly on domestic disturbances.

With macroeconomic instability generally perceived as a main inhibitor to growth in developing countries, knowledge about the relative importance of macroeconomic shocks should be of value. To the extent that countries within the Franc Zone pursue a high degree of policy co-ordination, the ability of individual countries to pursue independent stabilization policies is limited. It is therefore of some interest to identify the relative importance of the macroeconomic shocks in each of these countries, and also in the non-Franc Zone countries. Second, on the basis that the oil-producing countries are more likely to face similar shocks, we decompose the macroeconomic shocks of aggregated groups of oil producing and non-oil-producing Franc Zone countries and determine the similarities or otherwise of the decompositions. Third, this chapter draws a comparison between the decompositions observed from the Nigeria data and the oil-producing Franc Zone group.

In relation to this chapter, although previous studies such as Fielding and Shields (2001) and Hoffmaister, Roldós and Wickham (1998) investigate macroeconomic shocks within SSA, we note that there are some important differences that we need to highlight. Fielding and Shields (2001) identify shocks to output and prices in the economies of twelve countries that make up the Franc Zone of SSA over the period 1962–97. Hoffmaister, Roldós and Wickham (1998) investigate the sources of macroeconomic fluctuations in SSA by comparing – as two sub-groups – eight Franc Zone countries and fifteen non-Franc Zone countries by measuring the relative importance of domestic versus external shocks for the period 1971–93. Fielding and Shields (2001) consider inflation, output growth and growth in nominal money stock and condition on foreign price inflation, our model considers real exchange rate appreciation, real output growth and the growth in real money balances for each region. Our focus on real exchange rate growth is in line with the questions this chapter seeks to address, which include the role of the exchange rate regime in influencing the other determinants associated with macroeconomic stability. Second, we condition our domestic variables on a wider scope of variables from the economy of the largest trading partner. Third, like Fielding and Shields but unlike Hoffmaister, Roldós and Wickham, our statistics for the Franc Zone are based on underlying regressions that are country-specific.

Focusing on the decomposition of macroeconomic shocks, our method extends the traditional atheoretic VAR analysis and uses economic theory and time-series analysis to determine the sources of disturbances to economic variables. A UNU-WIDER Research Paper (Coleman 2004) gives a broader analysis of shocks in SSA based on an (albeit contentious) assumption that countries within each of the Zones can be aggregated. In the next section we present the theoretical basis for our model and provide some insight into the empirical basis for our analysis. We then discuss the data sources before presenting our estimations and results.

Model estimation and identification

This section presents the theoretical issues considered in arriving at the model used in this chapter. It also summarizes the empirical methodology that is employed in our decomposition of macroeconomic shocks.

Theoretical considerations

In order to analyse the source of shocks, we need to impose some theoretical restrictions on our VAR. In this sense, we rely on more untested assumptions than chapter 3 in this volume. Nevertheless, we have taken some care to make these assumptions realistic and few in number.

Reform by SSA countries aimed at improving integration into the world market has been designed to increase growth through more efficient allocation of economic resources. In many ways, this has rendered the sub-region more susceptible to both domestic shocks and the after-effects of economic shocks of their trading partners. With economic growth and macroeconomic stability a prime policy objective in the developing world, the need to increase output and to attract foreign direct investment (FDI) is paramount. Any improvement in this regard will be highly influenced by the capability of the macroeconomy to withstand shocks.

In a small open-economy framework, domestic variables are likely to be affected by the world economy but not vice versa. For this reason, we examine the influence of growth in output and in interest rates in the economies of the most important trading partner and use these as conditioning variables.[3] We need some long-run theoretical restrictions to identify structural shocks in our VAR, and for this we make use of the aggregate demand (AD) equation, the aggregate supply (AS) equation, the money demand (MD) and a relative price equation, which makes use of the concept of relative purchasing power parity (PPP). In the rather complex economies of SSA, financial sectors are in various stages of development, political institutions are usually major players in the economy, prices and wages are sticky and there is considerable private sector activity with strong dependence on international institutions and trade. The concept of aggregate demand – which in theory is used to measure the ability and the willingness of individuals and institutions to purchase goods and services – may be influenced by more factors outside national control than the norm. In (4.1), we present an inverted version of an AD equation where the growth in aggregate demand (Δy) is a function of the interest rate growth (Δr) and the growth in real exchange rate (Δp):

$$\Delta r = a_0 + a_1 \Delta y + a_2 \Delta p; \quad \text{typically } a_1 \leq 0, \;\; a_2 \leq 0 \tag{4.1}$$

The willingness to invest and/or consume domestically will be influenced partly by changes in the real interest rates Δr, and partly by competitiveness, which is influenced by real exchange rate growth Δp.

Equation (4.2) presents a simplified AS equation, where the growth in AS is expressed as a function of the growth in the real interest rate Δr:

$$\Delta y = b_0 + b_1 \Delta r; \quad \text{typically } b_1 \leq 0 \tag{4.2}$$

Producers must consider the real effects of changes in interest rates on the capital stock.

Long-run money demand is presented as a function of growth in real income [Δy], the real interest rates [Δr], and the real exchange rate [Δp]. This represents a long-run money market equilibrium locus (LM curve) with currency substitution:

$$\Delta m = c_0 + c_1 \Delta y + c_2 \Delta r + c_3 \Delta p; \quad \text{typically } c_1 \geq 0 \geq c_2, \;\; c_3 \geq 0 \tag{4.3}$$

In (4.4) we present a form of relative PPP, which allows for a steady long-run growth in the real exchange rate, and also the possibility of an equilibrium long-run real exchange rate (when $f_0 = 0$). Real exchange rate fluctuations have important consequences for competitiveness, fiscal sustainability and monetary policy. A prolonged real appreciation may have an adverse effect on a country's competitiveness, as it induces a switch from home goods to foreign goods, which could possibly lead to a recession. The real exchange rate affects debt repayment, a very important factor for countries in SSA, as most are rather highly indebted.

$$\Delta p = f_0; \quad \text{typically } f_0 \geq 0 \tag{4.4}$$

The interest rate data available for the sample are inadequate.[4] We, therefore, adopt the method by Fielding and Shields (2001) to construct a reduced form for (4.1)–(4.3) by substituting (4.1) into (4.2) and (4.3). Any shock to the resulting equation will, therefore, not be branded as either a strict demand shock or a supply shock, but rather broadly as a real output shock.

In an open economy, individuals and firms may choose to hold their wealth (or assets) in either the domestic or foreign economy. The countries in question being relatively small participants in an increasingly interdependent world, we allow for external influence on the domestic economy. The variable often included in literature is the foreign real interest rate (see for example, Leventakis 1993; Khalid 1999) and there is some evidence to show that when trade and economic links exist among countries or regions, changes in national income (GDP) may influence the domestic income (see Desruelle, Khan and Nord 1998: Table 1.2). For completeness, we condition the equations above on some selected foreign variables – real output growth (Δy^*) and real interest rate (Δr^*) of the largest trading partner. Therefore, in an open-economy framework, our long-run economic model can be summarized as:[5]

$$\Delta p = q_0 + q_1 \Delta y^* + q_2 \Delta r^* \tag{4.5}$$

$$\Delta y = d_0 + d_1 \Delta p + d_2 \Delta y^* + d_3 \Delta r^* \tag{4.6}$$

$$\Delta m = g_0 + g_1 \Delta y + g_2 \Delta p + g_3 \Delta y^* + g_4 \Delta r^* \tag{4.7}$$

where q_n, d_n, g_n are derived from (4.1)–(4.4).

In (4.6), given the typical inter-relationships between the variables in the VAR, the sign of d_1 may be positive or negative, hence this possibility allows for the impact of a shock to the real exchange rate on Δy being ambiguous. Typically, the expected outcome of a real exchange rate appreciation is that the effect on output is negative. But in our model it may be either positive or negative depending on whether the product of b_1 (the elasticity of AS with respect to the real interest rate) and a_1 (the slope of the AD curve in (4.2)) is less or greater than 1. As predicted by economic theory, the elasticity of the real money demand growth with respect to the real exchange rate growth g_2 will be positive. Also from the initial equations, we would expect the slope of (4.7) with respect to the real output growth g_1 to be positive, which is also consistent with economic theory.

Equations (4.5), (4.6) and (4.7) represent the long-run solution to a restricted VAR, and thus we estimate the dynamics of the three variables: the real exchange rate growth (Δp), the growth in real income (Δy) and the growth in real money balances (Δm). The variables Δy^* and Δr^* (external variables) are considered to be purely exogenous to the domestic economy. This triangular structure of (4.5)–(4.7) applies only in the long run, but the variables are simultaneously determined in the short run. As an example, in the short run, when PPP does not have to hold, the model allows the real exchange rate to be influenced by all the other variables in the VAR. According to the model, the demand for real money balances, even in the long run, is influenced by real exchange rate (via domestic and foreign price inflation, for domestic purchases and for transaction purposes), interest rate changes (through both transaction requirements and portfolio allocation decisions, which could cause reallocation of money holdings), income (due to the increased level of activity and demand for liquid assets that accompany increases in income). Allowance is made for the influence of the external exogenous variables, Δr^* and Δy^*, which are likely to be more significant with stronger trade linkages.

In the short run, therefore, the model without any restrictions can be expressed in matrix form as:

$$\begin{bmatrix} \Delta p_t \\ \Delta y_t \\ \Delta m_t \end{bmatrix} = \alpha(L) \begin{bmatrix} \Delta r_t^* \\ \Delta y_t^* \end{bmatrix} + B(L) \begin{bmatrix} \varepsilon_{1t} \\ \varepsilon_{2t} \\ \varepsilon_{3t} \end{bmatrix} \tag{4.8}$$

Where $B(L)$ is the 3×3 matrix of lag polynomials that summarizes the dynamics of the model. $\alpha(L)$ represents the coefficients, which depict the contemporaneous effects of the exogenous variables on the endogenous variables. Finally, the vector containing the pure structural innovations ε_{it} are the pure structural shocks to the real exchange rate appreciation, the growth in real output (as defined earlier in this section), and the growth in real money demand.

Empirical methodology

Structural vector autoregression (SVAR) models use the long-run properties of the variables to identify and recover the economic shocks. In our SVAR model, we use the approach of Blanchard and Quah (1989) to achieve this where the long-run restrictions together with the independence of shocks (orthogonality conditions) are used to recover the structural shocks. The restrictions are used to distinguish and isolate the short-run effects of any shocks. The long-run restrictions, though based on the methodology used in the Blanchard and Quah (1989) framework, are imposed on a macroeconomic structure that is different in terms of both variables used and size. One advantage of this methodology is that it is based on long-run restrictions that are derived from economic theory. Although there is some criticism (see Sims 1980) of some 'incredible identifying restrictions' being used at times to identify SVARs, this methodology is widely used. Secondly, it is somewhat less controversial, at least in comparison to empirical evidence that imposes short-run or impact restrictions. We note that in using the Blanchard and Quah methodology, variations of this approach have been used by many researchers and in many different contexts, as in Bayoumi and Eichengreen (1994); Bergmann (1996); Funke and Hall (1998); Keating and Nye (1999) for OECD countries; Enders and Lee (1997), Bergmann, Cheung and Lai (2000) in investigating the dynamics of real exchange rates; Fielding and Shields (2001) in evaluating shocks within the Franc Zone.

In our model, the basic vector of three endogenous variables Z_t is given as:

$$Z_t = (\Delta p_t, \Delta y_t, \Delta m_t)^T \tag{4.9}$$

The vector of external conditioning variables is also given as $M_t = (\Delta y_t^*, \Delta r_t^*)^T$. The model can therefore be summarized as:

$$Z_t = \alpha(L)M_t + B(L)\varepsilon_{i,t} \tag{4.10}$$

The reduced form of (4.10) requires us to identify an invertible matrix (say, H) such that the reduced form innovations u_t may be expressed as $u_t = H\varepsilon_{it}$. Alternatively (4.10) may be expressed in a more compact form as:

$$Z_t = \mu + \varphi_1 M_t + \Xi_t u_t \tag{4.11}$$

Estimation of this reduced form VAR (4.11) will provide us with the information required to identify and recover the structural shocks using the Blanchard and Quah (1989) methodology. Since the reduced form residuals, u_t, are not uncorrelated across variables [$\text{cov}(u_t u_t') = \Omega$)], we cannot make any explicit inferences from these, hence the need for identification and isolation of the pure structural shocks.

In the model with n endogenous variables, we need n^2 restrictions to exactly identify the structural shocks. The identification of our three-variable system will therefore require nine restrictions: six $[n(n+1)/2]$ of which are achieved through the orthogonality condition of the variance of the structural shocks (that is, $\text{cov}(\varepsilon_t \varepsilon_t') = I_3$) and three being from the long-run restrictions. In line with the Blanchard and Quah (1989) methodology, the imposition of the long-run restrictions, resulting in the long-run structure of (4.5)–(4.7), provides the remaining three restrictions needed to identify the model exactly and allows us to recover the structural shocks. In relation to (4.8), the three long-run restrictions are imposed such that, given the ordering of Z_t, the 3×3 matrix $B(L)$ is lower triangular. Therefore $B_{12} = B_{13} = B_{23} = 0$.

Data sources

The sample as described earlier contains twelve Franc Zone countries and four non-Franc Zone countries. The variables of the reduced form VAR include both endogenous variables (the real exchange rate growth, real output growth and growth in the real money demand) and exogenous variables (growth in foreign real income and the foreign real interest rate).

Annual data is collected over the period 1961–99, and the real exchange rate sequence is calculated as the ratio of the change in the domestic price index to foreign price indices. The GDP deflator is used as a proxy for the domestic price mainly because of the lack of complete consumer price index (CPI) data for some countries within the study. In addition, this index is based on a broader class of goods in the economy and encompasses prices of investment goods, as well as consumer good prices. The source of this price index is the 2001 World Bank Development Indicators (WBDI) series and the 2002 World Bank Africa Database CD-ROM. The foreign price index is measured in terms of domestic currency by multiplying by the bilateral nominal exchange rate. Data for real income for all the countries, including that for the foreign economy, are taken from the same sources as the price indices above. Growth is therefore measured as the annual change in the logarithm of real GDP (in local currency units). Using a broad definition of money (M2), the money series is measured as the sum of currency outside banks, demand deposits other than those of the central government, time deposits, savings deposits and foreign currency deposits. The data is taken from the same sources as the price indices and corresponds to lines 34 and 35 in the IMF *IFS* database. The Δm series is taken as the annual change in the logarithm of the real money balances.

Estimation and results

This section presents some information on the VAR estimation and also reports and discusses the results. We use *E*-views to estimate the VAR coefficients and, through preliminary tests, select a lag order of two (supported by the Akaike Information Criteria) of the unrestricted VAR. The 1994 collective devaluation of the CFA Franc *vis-à-vis* the French Franc is a rare occurrence, which introduces some distortion into estimation. Also, initial time-series plots of the money variable used in the VAR for Kenya indicate a sizeable spike in 1966, which is consistent with an unusual shock to the money supply. These unusual but significant incidents distort the normality of the residuals for the Franc Zone countries and for Kenya. For this reason we introduce exogenous dummy variables *D94* and *D66*, respectively, to isolate these effects. Their inclusion is necessary to ensure the normality of the observed residuals.

Presented in Table 4.1 is a summary of some regression diagnostic statistics from the unrestricted VAR. As a brief summary, we present the R^2 values for each equation in the VAR, the standard error and the Jacque–Bera statistic for normality of the residuals.

In these tables, the R^2 values for all the countries considered show some significant variations, but are all above 0.2 and typically above 0.5. In each

Table 4.1 Summary of unrestricted VAR regression diagnostics

		R^2	s.e.	Normality of residuals[a]
(a) Δp equation	ben	0.72	0.061	4.200 (0.122)
	bfa	0.74	0.067	3.708 (0.147)
	cam	0.85	0.047	6.327 (0.042)
	car	0.68	0.083	4.558 (0.100)
	civ	0.68	0.073	5.186 (0.074)
	chd	0.55	0.078	5.522 (0.063)
	con	0.44	0.113	3.002 (0.222)
	gab	0.66	0.077	3.910 (0.141)
	mal	0.82	0.061	3.314 (0.190)
	niger	0.43	0.095	3.978 (0.013)
	sen	0.80	0.055	4.260 (0.118)
	tog	0.59	0.078	1.427 (0.489)
	gha	0.42	0.327	2.086 (0.352)
	ken	0.21	0.200	3.879 (0.143)
	nigeria	0.85	0.159	5.231 (0.073)
	sr-lone	0.31	0.378	3.135 (0.208)
(b) Δy equation	ben	0.64	0.052	3.387 (0.183)
	bfa	0.50	0.063	3.823 (0.147)
	cam	0.39	0.089	3.76 (0.151)
	car	0.54	0.067	3.313 (0.190)
	civ	0.74	0.066	4.595 (0.100)
	chd	0.25	0.120	2.746 (0.253)
	con	0.46	0.103	3.025 (0.220)
	gab	0.61	0.119	4.375 (0.112)
	mal	0.75	0.047	5.132 (0.076)
	niger	0.45	0.109	2.893 (0.235)
	sen	0.66	0.049	3.082 (0.214)
	tog	0.36	0.099	1.861 (0.394)
	gha	0.62	0.130	4.567 (0.109)
	ken	0.30	0.181	3.239 (0.197)
	nigeria	0.31	0.170	2.856 (0.239)
	sr-lone	0.40	0.058	3.639 (0.162)
(c) Δm equation	ben	0.68	0.095	4.606 (0.100)
	bfa	0.56	0.069	2.756 (0.252)
	cam	0.63	0.103	3.045 (0.218)
	car	0.51	0.113	3.031 (0.219)
	civ	0.54	0.106	3.082 (0.214)
	chd	0.37	0.148	3.515 (0.172)
	con	0.52	0.113	3.887 (0.143)
	gab	0.62	0.127	4.389 (0.111)
	mal	0.40	0.096	3.510 (0.172)
	niger	0.27	0.137	2.824 (0.243)
	sen	0.58	0.090	5.945 (0.051)
	tog	0.44	0.146	3.985 (0.136)
	gha	0.49	0.110	2.278 (0.320)
	ken	0.80	0.150	2.756 (0.252)
	nigeria	0.24	0.160	4.735 (0.093)
	sr-lone	0.50	0.186	1.350 (0.508)

Notes: [a] VAR residual normality test done by Jacque–Bera Normality tests with null hypothesis that all residuals are multivariate normal; figures in parenthesis represent the p-values from the $\chi^2(2)$ distribution.

of the equations, the R^2 column indicates good explanatory power, which is somewhat encouraging. This is more so in the Franc Zone countries.

To allow for identification and recovery of the structural shocks ε_t, the restrictions as outlined in the section on empirical methodology are imposed.

Stability and stationarity

Our variables are initially tested for the presence of unit roots. ADF unit root tests justify the use of first differences, which are $I(0)$ and stationary.[6] Diagnostic tests on the lag structure show that the VAR as a whole is stable (stationary). The inverse roots of the characteristic autoregressive (AR) polynomial (see Lütkepohl 1991) are all found to have a modulus less than one, and lie within the unit circle. Our results show that the VAR as used for each country is stable. The stability is necessary for the validity of the results, including standard errors and impulse responses.

Variance decomposition

In principle, VARs are very useful in determining how variables interact with each other in the economy. If, say, ε_{1t} shocks explain none of the forecast error variance of the real exchange rate, then the sequence evolves independently of its own shocks, and Δp will be a purely endogenous variable. If, at the other extreme, it explains all of its forecast error variance, then the change in the real exchange rate is said to evolve independently of other variables in the model. In this chapter, the analysis of the variance decompositions is meant to show the relative importance of each innovation and will form a basis for our short-run analyses. We present below a summary of the variance decomposition results for each of the structural shocks ($\varepsilon_{i,t}$) for each country considered. The structural innovations derived from (4.5), (4.6) and (4.7) are represented by ε_{it}^{p}, ε_{it}^{y} and ε_{it}^{m}, respectively.

In Tables 4.2(a) and 4.2(b), the extent to which output growth shocks and money shocks explain real exchange rate fluctuations varies somewhat across the countries. Output shocks explain an important part of the real exchange rate fluctuations in Benin, Chad, Congo and Togo. The effect is somewhat smaller in all the other Franc Zone countries, and close to zero in Gabon. Money shocks are important in all the countries within the CEMAC. This contrasts with the countries of the West African Monetary Union (except Mali).[7] In Niger, the real exchange rate seems to be largely self-driven, evolving almost independently of the structural shocks to other variables in the model. In the non-Franc Zone countries, the importance of output shocks seems to be generally higher than in any of the Franc Zone countries in explaining real exchange rate fluctuations. The role of money shocks is, however, less uniform. In Nigeria and Sierra Leone, money shocks do explain significant movements in real exchange rate fluctuations, but this is not so in Ghana and Kenya. These results imply that changes in monetary policy, in the countries

Table 4.2(a) Percentages of forecast error variance decomposition of the ε^p_{it} (periods 1–5) due to each shock: individual CFA countries

	Period	s.e.	ε^p_{it}	ε^y_{it}	ε^m_{it}
ben	1	0.061	93.827	6.136	0.035
	2	0.064	85.249	14.717	0.032
	3	0.065	85.340	14.602	0.056
	4	0.065	85.438	14.503	0.057
	5	0.065	85.334	14.607	0.057
bfa	1	0.067	99.291	0.672	0.035
	2	0.071	98.354	1.606	0.038
	3	0.073	98.368	1.587	0.043
	4	0.073	98.373	1.583	0.042
	5	0.074	98.360	1.596	0.042
cam	1	0.047	67.755	2.261	29.982
	2	0.055	51.714	1.924	46.360
	3	0.058	55.039	3.136	41.823
	4	0.059	54.537	4.106	41.356
	5	0.059	53.869	5.157	40.972
car	1	0.083	87.725	2.110	10.163
	2	0.089	75.772	2.598	21.629
	3	0.090	74.379	2.542	23.078
	4	0.091	73.291	2.770	23.937
	5	0.091	72.884	2.884	24.231
chd	1	0.078	89.270	8.413	2.580
	2	0.081	82.431	14.943	2.624
	3	0.082	80.850	14.632	4.516
	4	0.082	80.214	14.733	5.052
	5	0.082	80.073	14.883	5.043
civ	1	0.073	97.489	2.474	0.035
	2	0.075	92.629	7.211	0.159
	3	0.077	91.662	8.161	0.176
	4	0.077	91.291	8.533	0.175
	5	0.077	91.210	8.614	0.174
con	1	0.113	89.076	6.742	4.181
	2	0.121	83.367	10.712	5.920
	3	0.122	83.541	10.515	5.942
	4	0.123	83.668	10.438	5.892
	5	0.123	83.685	10.431	5.883
gab	1	0.077	73.733	0.099	26.166
	2	0.086	59.449	0.534	40.016
	3	0.087	60.264	0.605	39.130
	4	0.088	60.368	1.029	38.602
	5	0.089	60.313	1.028	38.657
mal	1	0.061	78.552	4.297	17.150
	2	0.072	75.083	4.941	19.974
	3	0.074	72.615	6.791	20.592
	4	0.074	72.099	7.312	20.587
	5	0.074	72.070	7.355	20.573

Continued

Table 4.2(a) Continued

	Period	s.e.	ε^p_{it}	ε^y_{it}	ε^m_{it}
niger	1	0.095	99.637	0.359	0.002
	2	0.097	98.706	1.290	0.002
	3	0.098	98.485	1.510	0.004
	4	0.098	98.475	1.519	0.004
	5	0.098	98.475	1.519	0.004
sen	1	0.055	96.624	3.357	0.018
	2	0.060	94.404	5.560	0.035
	3	0.061	94.579	5.386	0.034
	4	0.062	94.563	5.402	0.034
	5	0.062	94.58	5.396	0.034
tog	1	0.078	99.649	0.295	0.055
	2	0.086	93.874	6.072	0.052
	3	0.090	85.708	14.059	0.231
	4	0.091	84.049	15.709	0.241
	5	0.091	84.017	15.736	0.246

Table 4.2(b) Percentages of forecast error variance decomposition of ε^p_{it} (periods 1–5) due to each shock: non-CFA countries

	Period	s.e.	ε^p_{it}	ε^y_{it}	ε^m_{it}
gha	1	0.327	60.916	38.779	0.304
	2	0.344	63.409	36.062	0.528
	3	0.375	54.137	43.939	1.923
	4	0.379	53.655	44.174	2.170
	5	0.381	53.073	44.596	2.329
ken	1	0.203	70.748	28.848	0.402
	2	0.218	63.498	35.610	0.891
	3	0.223	64.721	34.420	0.857
	4	0.223	64.636	34.479	0.883
	5	0.224	64.234	34.885	0.881
nigeria	1	0.360	75.828	22.946	1.225
	2	0.378	69.863	23.423	6.712
	3	0.381	69.208	24.175	6.616
	4	0.384	68.130	25.059	6.809
	5	0.385	67.856	25.164	6.978
sr-lone	1	0.327	74.328	11.117	14.494
	2	0.344	75.590	9.410	14.999
	3	0.375	69.973	15.537	14.489
	4	0.379	70.065	15.704	14.230
	5	0.381	70.033	15.661	14.304

where the money shocks are significant, will be important determinants of the real exchange rate.

In terms of the variation in output (Tables 4.3(a) and 4.3(b)), the following points can be highlighted. First, real exchange rate shocks explain a significant proportion of output variations in all of the Franc Zone countries, with the exception of Niger and Togo. Money shocks account for a significant proportion in some Franc Zone countries, but the effect is marginal in Cameroon, Chad and Côte d'Ivoire, and insignificant in Benin, Burkina Faso, Niger, Senegal and Togo. With the exception of Kenya, the non-Franc Zone countries show that both real exchange rates and money shocks dominate in explaining output movements.

Tables 4.4(a) and 4.4(b) show that both output and real exchange rate shocks play a role in explaining variations in money, although the effects are marginal in Cameroon, Niger and Togo.

Because of administrative and institutional rules and the commitment to fixed exchange rate, the Franc Zone countries cannot individually use the nominal exchange rate as policy tool. Moreover, the degree that policy co-ordination is important for the Franc Zone countries, it is worth noting that similar responses to macroeconomic shocks will be preferred, to enable a joint policy response beneficial to all members. Tables 4.2(a–b)–4.4(a–b) indicate that the variance decompositions do not follow a clear pattern for the Franc Zone countries, which indicates some macroeconomic heterogeneity. These results imply that some joint policy responses to common macroeconomic shocks may not yield common outcomes for Franc Zone members. Nashashibi and Bazzoni (1994) discuss some of the costs of the Zone's fixed parity commitment in relation to adjustment to macroeconomic shocks. They find that the internal adjustment strategies followed by Franc Zone countries could not correct the imbalances caused by the macroeconomic shocks suffered by most of SSA even though relative stability in prices was still maintained.[8]

The importance of monetary shocks in explaining other shocks in the non-Franc Zone countries is in line with the observed failure by most of these countries to achieve price stability. One difference compared with the Franc Zone (except in Kenya), is that money shocks play a more significant role in explaining output and real exchange rate fluctuations. This suggests that in flexible exchange rate regime money shocks are more likely to have real effects.

In Tables 4.5(a)–4.5(c) we present results from an aggregated sample of oil-producing and non-oil-producing Franc Zone countries.[9] Under the assumption that oil-producing Franc Zone countries are more likely to face similar output shocks, the variance decomposition of output shocks will be of particular interest. Table 4.5(b) shows that money shocks explain a significant portion of output shocks for the oil-producing group. It can therefore be argued that there is a stronger relationship between money and output shocks

Table 4.3(a) Percentages of forecast error variance decomposition of the ε_{it}^{y} (periods 1–5) due to each shock: individual CFA countries

	Period	s.e.	ε_{it}^{p}	ε_{it}^{y}	ε_{it}^{m}
ben	1	0.052	55.494	44.381	0.124
	2	0.057	56.958	42.927	0.113
	3	0.057	57.033	42.809	0.157
	4	0.057	57.109	42.730	0.159
	5	0.058	57.130	42.709	0.159
bfa	1	0.063	13.418	86.411	0.170
	2	0.063	13.397	86.370	0.231
	3	0.064	13.260	86.474	0.265
	4	0.064	13.341	86.393	0.265
	5	0.064	13.349	86.384	0.265
cam	1	0.089	11.923	85.785	2.291
	2	0.096	10.398	87.605	1.995
	3	0.101	9.875	85.839	4.285
	4	0.103	9.865	85.981	4.153
	5	0.105	9.860	85.994	4.145
car	1	0.067	37.437	59.544	3.017
	2	0.072	33.108	58.077	8.814
	3	0.074	30.875	58.774	10.349
	4	0.076	29.816	58.835	11.348
	5	0.077	29.115	58.966	11.918
chd	1	0.120	65.552	33.813	1.084
	2	0.121	64.862	33.914	1.519
	3	0.124	62.326	33.504	2.863
	4	0.124	62.132	33.446	3.040
	5	0.124	62.112	33.464	3.045
civ	1	0.066	2.215	94.513	3.271
	2	0.069	7.862	88.122	4.015
	3	0.070	8.013	87.610	4.376
	4	0.070	8.017	87.607	4.374
	5	0.070	8.017	87.605	4.377
con	1	0.103	72.604	6.714	20.681
	2	0.121	56.927	12.075	30.997
	3	0.123	57.726	11.917	30.356
	4	0.124	58.183	11.698	30.118
	5	0.125	58.270	11.663	30.065
gab	1	0.119	3.866	96.129	0.003
	2	0.144	20.595	67.242	12.161
	3	0.154	26.274	61.421	12.304
	4	0.157	28.437	59.000	12.562
	5	0.159	28.039	57.704	14.256
mal	1	0.047	6.446	90.906	2.647
	2	0.054	10.259	76.826	12.914
	3	0.056	10.100	70.954	18.945
	4	0.057	10.312	68.991	20.696
	5	0.058	10.309	67.865	21.825

Continued

Table 4.3(a) Continued

	Period	s.e.	ε_{it}^{p}	ε_{it}^{y}	ε_{it}^{m}
niger	1	0.109	0.004	99.845	0.149
	2	0.110	0.019	99.719	0.260
	3	0.111	1.329	98.407	0.263
	4	0.112	1.463	98.272	0.263
	5	0.112	1.465	98.270	0.264
sen	1	0.049	6.819	93.177	0.003
	2	0.051	9.647	90.338	0.013
	3	0.051	9.881	90.101	0.017
	4	0.051	9.912	90.070	0.017
	5	0.051	9.923	90.058	0.017
tog	1	0.099	0.346	99.104	0.548
	2	0.104	1.927	97.403	0.669
	3	0.105	3.130	96.021	0.847
	4	0.105	3.291	95.825	0.882
	5	0.106	3.280	95.834	0.885

Table 4.3(b) Percentages of forecast error variance decomposition of ε_{it}^{y} (periods 1–5) due to each shock: non-CFA countries

	Period	s.e.	ε_{it}^{p}	ε_{it}^{y}	ε_{it}^{m}
gha	1	0.133	50.458	27.770	21.770
	2	0.137	47.147	30.852	22.000
	3	0.159	36.528	47.027	16.444
	4	0.163	38.965	45.023	16.011
	5	0.165	38.727	44.880	16.392
ken	1	0.185	96.762	3.209	0.028
	2	0.194	93.434	6.534	0.031
	3	0.207	81.891	18.027	0.080
	4	0.208	82.009	17.821	0.168
	5	0.210	81.392	18.439	0.168
nigeria	1	0.169	45.541	29.486	24.972
	2	0.207	35.961	47.216	16.821
	3	0.219	32.671	46.570	20.758
	4	0.221	32.499	46.312	21.187
	5	0.222	32.587	46.235	21.176
sr-lone	1	0.058	0.447	58.327	41.225
	2	0.064	16.335	48.714	34.949
	3	0.068	23.779	44.995	31.224
	4	0.070	23.306	45.993	30.700
	5	0.070	23.317	46.005	30.676

Table 4.4(a) Percentages of forecast error variance decomposition of ε_{it}^{m} (periods 1–5) due to each shock: individual CFA countries

	Period	**s.e.**	ε_{it}^{p}	ε_{it}^{y}	ε_{it}^{m}
ben	1	0.129	1.087	5.147	93.764
	2	0.130	5.575	5.492	88.932
	3	0.130	11.784	6.291	81.923
	4	0.130	11.871	6.612	81.515
	5	0.130	11.885	6.662	81.451
bfa	1	0.069	2.345	2.823	94.830
	2	0.071	8.800	2.659	88.539
	3	0.074	12.529	6.035	81.435
	4	0.074	12.523	6.113	81.363
	5	0.074	12.552	6.156	81.291
cam	1	0.103	10.413	0.026	89.560
	2	0.115	15.648	3.180	81.171
	3	0.125	23.444	3.948	72.606
	4	0.126	23.033	3.996	72.970
	5	0.127	24.143	3.984	71.871
car	1	0.113	43.895	9.189	49.915
	2	0.114	43.393	9.101	47.504
	3	0.116	42.239	8.868	48.892
	4	0.116	41.961	8.876	49.162
	5	0.116	41.757	8.949	49.292
chd	1	0.148	1.662	1.313	97.023
	2	0.158	3.098	1.642	95.258
	3	0.162	2.966	6.296	90.736
	4	0.163	2.956	6.265	90.777
	5	0.163	2.977	6.278	90.744
civ	1	0.106	2.552	5.845	91.601
	2	0.107	4.418	5.701	89.879
	3	0.110	7.179	7.117	85.702
	4	0.110	7.201	7.161	85.637
	5	0.111	7.346	7.149	85.504
con	1	0.113	3.626	22.100	74.272
	2	0.119	4.720	22.326	72.952
	3	0.119	4.992	22.500	72.507
	4	0.120	5.130	22.419	72.450
	5	0.120	5.162	22.402	72.435
gab	1	0.127	19.960	3.331	76.708
	2	0.154	32.829	2.282	64.887
	3	0.162	34.660	4.231	61.107
	4	0.165	36.106	4.324	59.568
	5	0.168	36.816	4.251	58.932
mal	1	0.096	6.533	27.401	66.065
	2	0.096	6.732	27.350	65.917
	3	0.097	6.586	28.978	64.434
	4	0.098	6.523	29.053	64.423
	5	0.098	6.520	28.984	64.495

Continued

Table 4.4(a) Continued

	Period	s.e.	ε^p_{it}	ε^y_{it}	ε^m_{it}
niger	1	0.137	6.473	0.084	93.441
	2	0.138	7.396	0.629	91.973
	3	0.138	7.401	0.655	91.942
	4	0.138	7.406	0.656	91.937
	5	0.138	7.406	0.657	91.935
sen	1	0.090	1.356	7.182	91.460
	2	0.095	6.140	10.968	82.891
	3	0.096	7.747	11.154	81.098
	4	0.096	8.082	11.122	80.795
	5	0.096	8.166	11.113	80.795
tog	1	0.146	1.231	0.000	98.768
	2	0.147	1.267	1.440	97.292
	3	0.149	1.246	3.356	95.397
	4	0.149	1.273	3.452	95.273
	5	0.149	1.296	3.451	95.252

Table 4.4(b) Percentages of forecast error variance decomposition of ε^m_{it} (periods 1–5) due to each shock: non-CFA countries

	Period	s.e.	ε^p_{it}	ε^y_{it}	ε^m_{it}
gha	1	0.115	5.250	3.226	91.523
	2	0.120	7.767	5.389	86.843
	3	0.132	7.971	18.93	73.092
	4	0.135	9.935	19.47	70.591
	5	0.135	10.182	19.38	70.431
ken	1	0.151	66.137	8.161	25.701
	2	0.158	61.649	14.887	23.462
	3	0.169	55.555	23.677	20.766
	4	0.169	55.717	23.540	20.741
	5	0.170	55.838	23.613	20.548
nigeria	1	0.152	9.887	0.170	89.941
	2	0.171	16.510	10.724	72.764
	3	0.176	15.716	10.384	73.899
	4	0.176	15.701	10.363	73.934
	5	0.176	15.697	10.373	73.928
sr-lone	1	0.186	0.168	82.845	16.985
	2	0.210	1.564	75.181	23.254
	3	0.230	1.306	72.057	26.635
	4	0.239	1.341	69.965	28.693
	5	0.246	1.311	68.670	30.017

Table 4.5(a) Percentages of forecast error variance decomposition of ε^p_{it} (periods 1–5) due to each shock: oil- and non-oil-producing CFA countries

	Period	s.e.	ε^p_{it}	ε^y_{it}	ε^m_{it}
Oil	1	0.079	92.230	0.029	7.739
	2	0.083	84.888	0.107	15.004
	3	0.084	84.698	0.169	15.131
	4	0.084	84.511	0.191	15.297
	5	0.084	84.503	0.193	15.303
Non-oil	1	0.072	98.738	1.261	0.000
	2	0.075	96.047	3.945	0.007
	3	0.076	95.416	4.566	0.017
	4	0.076	95.310	4.671	0.017
	5	0.076	95.291	4.691	0.017

Table 4.5(b) Percentages of forecast error variance decomposition of ε^y_{it} (periods 1–5) due to each shock: oil- and non-oil-producing CFA countries

	Period	s.e.	ε^p_{it}	ε^y_{it}	ε^m_{it}
Oil	1	0.113	14.965	81.137	3.896
	2	0.118	19.298	73.616	7.084
	3	0.119	19.820	73.142	7.037
	4	0.119	19.848	73.107	7.044
	5	0.119	19.851	73.104	7.043
Non-oil	1	0.082	19.963	79.931	0.104
	2	0.082	20.572	79.284	0.143
	3	0.082	20.569	79.270	0.160
	4	0.082	20.569	79.270	0.160
	5	0.082	20.569	79.270	0.160

in the oil-producing sample compared to the non-oil-producing group. In Table 4.5(a), money shocks are also important in explaining fluctuations in the real exchange rate for the oil-producing group. Output shocks are not important.

A comparison of output shocks between Nigeria and the oil-producing sample in response to an output shock shows some significant similarities. There is, however, an obvious difference in the proportion of the output shock explained by fluctuations in money – it is much higher in Nigeria than in the oil-producing Franc Zone group. This indicates that transmission of money shocks to the real sector is less marked within the oil-producing Franc Zone countries than in Nigeria, although they are likely to experience similar oil-price shocks.

Table 4.5(c) Percentages of forecast error variance decomposition of ε_{it}^{m} (periods 1–5) due to each shock: oil- and non-oil-producing CFA countries

	Period	s.e.	ε_{it}^{p}	ε_{it}^{y}	ε_{it}^{m}
Oil	1	0.120	24.337	17.351	58.310
	2	0.125	27.193	16.424	56.382
	3	0.126	26.824	16.385	56.790
	4	0.126	26.893	16.371	56.735
	5	0.126	26.885	16.370	56.743
Non-oil	1	0.114	2.602	0.496	96.901
	2	0.114	2.630	0.530	96.839
	3	0.115	2.787	0.644	96.568
	4	0.115	2.796	0.653	96.550
	5	0.115	2.799	0.655	96.545

The decomposition of output shocks in Kenya shows that – unlike in the other non-Franc Zone countries – a minimal proportion of the variance is explained by money shocks. By contrast, the real exchange rate plays the most significant role in explaining fluctuations in Kenyan output. With Kenya's economy highly dependent on the manufacturing sector, capital goods form a high share of imports, and fluctuations in the real exchange rate are correspondingly more important.

Conclusions

Using the Blanchard and Quah (1989) decomposition, this chapter identifies and decomposes structural shocks to three important variables (real exchange rate appreciation, real output growth and the growth in real money balances) in the macroeconomies of twelve Franc Zone countries and four non-Franc Zone countries over the period 1961–99. While there is no *a priori* reason to think that Franc Zone countries' response to macroeconomic fluctuations will be identical, the policy co-ordination and restrictions on individual adjustment strategies within a monetary union suggest that we might see some homogeneity.

However, our results of forecast error variance decomposition do not show a clear pattern of response in the countries within either part of the Franc Zone. The heterogeneity within the Franc Zone with respect to macroeconomic shocks implies that a common policy response to external imbalances and growth disturbances may be sub-optimal. The heterogeneity may be due to differences in national production factors, geography and natural resources, and also wage and price flexibility. Boughton (1991) and Elbadawi and Majd (1992) both provide some interesting discussion on the optimality and homogeneity of the CFA Franc Zone.

Nevertheless, common patterns do emerge in the data. In particular, money shocks generally feature more prominently in explaining macro-economic shocks in the CEMAC than in the West African monetary union, and even more prominently in most of the non-Franc Zone countries. They also appear to be more important in the oil-producing sub-group than in the non-oil-producing sub-group.

Notes

1. Kose and Reizman (2001) examine the role of external shocks in explaining macro-economic fluctuations in African countries by using a quantitative, stochastic, dynamic multi-sector equilibrium model calibrated for a 'typical' African country. The external shocks examined include trade shocks (fluctuations in price) and financial shocks (fluctuations in world interest rate).
2. These choices do not suggest that these four countries reflect the behaviour of all non-Franc Zone countries in SSA. Choice of Ghana and Sierra Leone is based purely on geographical location *vis-à-vis* the WAEMU countries, Nigeria on being an important oil-producing country and Kenya having a relatively well-developed manufacturing sector. Guinea–Bissau and Equatorial Guinea are excluded from the sample because of the insufficient data available for these countries.
3. The most important trading partner is based on trade volumes and value as recorded in the IMF's *Direction of Trade Statistics* (*DOTS*) Yearbooks. Data collected show that France is the most important trading partner for the Franc Zone, the UK for Ghana and Kenya and the USA for Nigeria and Belgium for Sierra Leone.
4. The discount rate is the most consistent available for the Franc Zone, but this is inappropriate as a viable measure of the cost of borrowing.
5. All variables except Δr^* are expressed as changes in the natural logarithm of these measures.
6. Although some criticism has been levelled against differencing (see Sims 1980; Doan 1992) that it 'throws away' information containing co-movements in the data, it remains a popular approach.
7. Mali, however, joined the WAEMU only in 1984.
8. There were two oil-price shocks in the 1970s and the terms of trade shocks during the 1980s, which for the Franc Zone countries was worsened by the real appreciation if the French Franc *vis-à-vis* the US Dollar.
9. Cameroon, Congo Republic and Gabon make up the oil-producing group; non-oil-producing countries in the Franc Zone include Benin, Burkina Faso, CAR, Côte d'Ivoire, Chad, Mali, Niger, Senegal and Togo.

References

Bayoumi, T. and B. Eichengreen (1994) 'Macroeconomic Adjustment under Bretton Woods and Post-Bretton Woods Float: An Impulse Response Analysis', *Economic Journal*, 104: 813–27.

Bergmann, U. M. (1996) 'International Evidence on the Sources of Macroeconomic Fluctuations', *European Economic Review*, 40: 1237–58.

Bergmann, U. M., Y. -M. Cheung and K. S. Lai (2000) 'Productivity Shocks, Monetary Shocks and the Short and Long-Run Dynamics of the Exchange Rate and Relative Prices', Lund University Working Paper 2000/4, Lund: Lund University.

Blanchard, O. and D. Quah (1989) 'Dynamic Effects of Aggregate Demand and Supply Disturbances', *American Economic Review*, 79: 655–73.

Boughton, J. M. (1991) 'The CFA Franc Zone: Currency Union and Monetary Standard', IMF Working Papers 91/133, Washington, DC: IMF.

Clement, J. A. P. (1994) 'Franc Zone Realignment is a Vital Element of New Adjustment Strategy', *IMF Survey*, Special Supplement, March.

Coleman, S. (2004) 'An Aggregate View of Macroeconomic Shocks in Sub-Saharan Africa: A Comparative Study Using Innovation Accounting', Research Paper 2004/9, Helsinki: UNU-WIDER.

Collier, P. and J. W. Gunning (1999) 'Explaining African Economic Performance', *Journal of Economic Literature*, 37(1): 64–111.

Desruelle, D., R. Kahn and R. Nord (1998) 'Impact of EMU on Selected Country Groups', IMF Occasional Paper 174, Washington, DC: IMF.

Devarajan, S. and J. de Melo (1991) 'Membership in the CFA Zone: Odyssean Journey or Trojan Horse?', in A. Chhibber and S. Fisher (eds), *Economic Reform in Sub-Saharan Africa*, Washington, DC: World Bank: 25–33.

Devarajan, S. and D. Rodrik (1991) 'Do the Benefits of Fixed Exchange Rates Outweigh their Costs? The Franc Zone in Africa', World Bank Working Papers N777, Washington, DC: World Bank.

Doan, T. (1992) *RATS User's Manual*, Evanston, IL: Estima.

Elbadawi, I. and N. Majd (1992) 'Fixed Parity of the Exchange Rate and Economic Performance in the CFA Franc Zone', World Bank Working Paper WPS 830, January.

Elbadawi, I. and N. Majd (1996) 'Adjustment and Economic Performance under a Fixed Exchange Rate: A Comparative Analysis of the CFA Zone', *World Development*, 24(5): 939–51.

Enders, W. and B.-S. Lee (1997) 'Accounting for Real and Nominal Exchange Rate Movements in the Post-Bretton Woods Period', *Journal of International Money and Finance*, 16: 233–54.

Fielding, D. and K. Shields (2001) 'Modelling Macroeconomic Shocks in the CFA Franc Zone', *Journal of Development Economics*, 66(1): 199–223.

Funke, M. and S. G. Hall (1998) 'Aggregate Demand and Aggregate Supply in UK Regions', *Journal of Economic Studies*, 25: 260–76.

Ghura, D. and M. T. Hadjimichael (1995) 'Adjustment in Sub-Saharan Africa', Appendix II in *World Economic Outlook*, a survey by the staff of the IMF, World Economic and Financial Surveys, Washington, DC: 98–107.

Ghura, D. and M. T. Hadjimichael (1996) 'Growth in sub-Saharan Africa', *IMF Staff Papers*, 43: 605–34.

Hoffmaister, A. W., J. E. Roldós and P. Wickham (1998) 'Macroeconomic Fluctuations in sub-Saharan Africa', *IMF Staff Papers*, 45(1): 132–60.

Keating, J. W. and J. V. Nye (1999) 'The Dynamic Effects of Aggregate Demand and Supply Disturbances in the G7 Countries', *Journal of Macroeconomics*, 21: 263–78.

Khalid, A. M. (1999) 'Modelling Money Demand in Open Economies: The Case of Asian Countries', *Applied Economics*, 31: 1129–35.

Kose, M. A. and R. Reizman (2001) 'Trade Shocks and Macroeconomic Fluctuations in Africa', *Journal of Development Economics*, 65: 55–80.

Leventakis, J. A. (1993) 'Modelling Money Demand in Open Economies over the Modern Floating Period', *Applied Economics*, 25: 1005–12.

Lütkepohl, H. (1991) *Introduction to Multiple Time Series Analysis*, Berlin: Springer-Verlag.
Nashashibi, K. and S. Bazzoni (1994) 'Exchange Rate Strategies and Fiscal Performance in Sub-Saharan Africa', *IMF Staff Papers*, 41(1).
Ramey, G. and V. A. Ramey (1995) 'Cross-country Evidence on the Links between Volatility and Growth', *American Economic Review*, 85: 1138–51.
Sachs, J. D. and A. M. Warner (1996) 'Sources of Slow Growth in African Economies', *Journal of African Economies*, 5 (Supplement): 335–76.
Sims, C. A. (1980) 'Macroeconomics and Reality', *Econometrica*, 48(1): 1–48.
World Bank (1994) *Adjustment in Africa, Reforms, Results, and the Road Ahead*, New York: Oxford University Press for the World Bank.

Part II

The Positive and Normative Analysis of Monetary and Exchange Rate Policy

5

Monetary Policy in the Franc Zone: Country-Level Credit Policy

Anja Shortland and David Stasavage

Introduction

The official goals of monetary policy in the Franc Zone are to maintain price stability and maintain an appropriate level of foreign reserves, which are the pooled foreign exchange reserves of the member states (IMF 2001: 17). At the Zone level the BCEAO uses a mixture of indirect policy instruments (the discount rate mechanism, a repurchase agreement facility and a system of periodic auctions of central bank bills)[1] to pursue these goals. However, the monetary policy at the Zone level will not necessarily suit all the member states in the Zone. Table 5.1 shows the cross-country correlations between some of the macroeconomic variables that the BCEAO appears to react to at the Zone level (Shortland and Stasavage 2003). It can be seen that output gaps and inflation rates are not strongly correlated within the Zone.[2] There may therefore be a need to complement the interest rate-setting at the Zone level with further policies to suit the economic situation in individual Franc Zone member countries.

In the past country-level credit planning was the main monetary policy tool in the Franc Zone (Honohan 1990: 3). The monetary programming exercise determined planned credit growth in each member country and the programme was implemented through credit ceilings on government borrowing and central bank refinancing of private sector credit. Credit growth in one country did not substantially spill over from one country to the other countries in the Zone, as the capital markets were not well integrated.

Despite the recent efforts to move towards indirect tools of monetary policy and away from credit planning, the BCEAO retains a number of policy tools, which would enable it to continue to pursue independent credit policies for each member country. The tools of credit ceilings on governments and limits on the rediscounting of bank loans have been strengthened since the late 1980s and a third potential policy tool has been introduced: reserve requirements on banks. Capital market integration also remains underdeveloped. A weak system of payments and delivery and a lack of confidence among

Table 5.1 Sample correlation coefficients

	WAEMU	Burkina Faso	Mali	Côte d'Ivoire	Senegal	Togo
Inflation						
WAEMU	1.0000					
Burkina Faso	0.7206	1.0000				
Mali	0.7213	0.4419	1.0000			
Côte d'Ivoire	0.4883	0.2018	0.1224	1.0000		
Senegal	0.4159	0.0675	0.2626	−0.1744	1.0000	
Togo	0.2329	0.1202	−0.1568	0.2668	−0.2368	1.0000
Output gap[a]						
Burkina Faso		1.0000				
Mali		0.1185	1.0000			
Côte d'Ivoire		−0.0153	0.0490	1.0000		
Senegal		0.4895	−0.0195	−0.0482	1.0000	
Togo		0.0871	0.0308	0.1423	−0.0682	1.0000
Credit to government						
Burkina Faso		1.0000				
Mali		0.8324	1.0000			
Côte d'Ivoire		0.7988	0.8035	1.0000		
Senegal		0.5945	0.6091	0.5249	1.0000	
Togo		0.7653	0.7843	0.6219	0.5423	1.0000

Note: [a] Based on Fielding, Lee and Shields (2003), quarterly GDP data.

banks about other banks' solvency prevent inter-bank lending, especially across national borders (IMF 2001: 19). Country-level credit planning is therefore still a potential monetary policy mechanism.

The policy framework for the Franc Zone is discussed in a number of recent publications (for example, Union Monétaire Ouest Africaine 1989; IMF 2001). There is also some empirical literature on monetary policy formation in the Franc Zone (for example, Fielding 2002; Savvides 1998). However, there are no recent examinations of how monetary policy is conducted at the national level: the existing studies are based on data before the devaluation of the CFA Franc (CFAF) in 1994. The aim of this study is to address the question whether a systematic country-level credit policy has been implemented since 1995.

BCEAO policy tools

The first policy tool of the BCEAO that could be used to achieve balanced money growth is the enforcement of credit ceilings on government borrowing (IMF 2001: 18). The BCEAO statutes limited central bank credit to each member government to 20 per cent of the previous year's fiscal receipts.[3] However, it is not clear to what extent the central bank could resist governments' credit demands in practice. For example the annual data provided by the IMF show that the monetary authority's claims on governments (excluding IMF loans which are administrated by the BCEAO and lent on to the national governments) exceeded 20 per cent of government revenues in Togo in 1995 and 1996 and in Côte d'Ivoire in 1994.

If the BCEAO's ability to resist government borrowing was limited, it may have restricted private sector borrowing in response to rising government borrowing, by imposing ceilings on central bank refinancing of private sector credit. The BCEAO's control over lending to the private sector has been strengthened considerably in recent years. Until 1989, the BCEAO had a statutory obligation to refinance all short-term agricultural credit granted by commercial banks, as theoretically these would be 'self-liquidating' as the harvest was sold. This law was amended in 1989, because it was found that the system was abused and the short-term credits were not repaid as expected. Since then agricultural credits have been treated in the same way as ordinary credits and a single ceiling has been applied (Union Monétaire Ouest Africaine 1989).

The third policy tool at the disposal of the BCEAO is the use of reserve requirements. Liquidity ratio rules require banks to hold a certain fraction of their assets as reserve deposits and the system of setting reserve requirements has been in place since 1993 (IMF 2001). According to the *IMF Country Report* in 2001 reserve requirements are used as a policy tool on a country-by-country basis 'taking into account the disparities in the progression of bank liquidity positions in each country' (IMF 2001: 17). However, the policy was not used actively during the 1990s. Reserve requirements were changed only infrequently (twice each in Mali and Burkina Faso, three times in Togo and four times in Senegal and Côte d'Ivoire for 1995–2000). Moreover, actual reserves and required liquid reserves are only weakly correlated. An examination of banks' liquid reserves shows that actual reserves tended to exceed required reserves, somtimes by as much as a factor of ten, but during periods of hikes in the required reserve ratio, actual reserve ratios were lower than required reserve ratios in Burkina Faso, Côte d'Ivoire, Senegal and Togo. It is possible, though, that the BCEAO used 'moral suasion' as a policy tool to influence banks' reserve levels, using the credible threat of imposing higher liquid reserve requirements.

Given that the BCEAO has a number of policy tools, which may have been used in different combinations, looking at the use of the policy tools individually may give misleading results. We therefore examine to what extent the BCEAO controls private sector credit in the Franc Zone member countries, without focusing on a particular policy tool. Did the BCEAO reduce total credit in response to emerging inflationary pressure in individual economies? Did the BCEAO sterilize foreign capital inflows and foreign borrowing?

And did the BCEAO react to increased government borrowing by restricting private sector credit?

We use data on Burkina Faso, Côte d'Ivoire, Mali, Senegal and Togo, which represent the bulk of output of the WAEMU and for which monthly data (and quarterly data on GDP) are available. The analyses are based on monthly or quarterly data from 1995 to 2000 – that is, since the devaluation of the CFAF. We exclude observations before 1995 because in the run-up to the devaluation of the CFAF monetary policy was dominated by the concern over peg stability. Moreover, most of the time-series become stationary only after the devaluation. The end date of 2000 is used because the GDP data from Fielding, Lee and Shields (2003) are available only until the end of 2000.

The chapter is structured as follows. The following section discusses two previous studies of monetary policy in developing countries, which employ a similar methodology to the one used in this chapter. We then discuss the data and methodology before examining whether the BCEAO has systematically influenced domestic credit and credit to the private sector in response to monetary policy target variables.

Previous studies of monetary policy in developing countries

There is a number of previous studies of monetary policy-making in developing countries – for example, Connolly and Taylor (1979), Kamas (1985, 1986), Fry (1993, 1995), Savvides (1998), Fielding (2002). The following discussion focuses on Fry (1995) and Savvides (1998). The (1993) and (1995) studies by Fry examined monetary policy in six Pacific Basin developing countries with a control group of twenty-one other developing countries using annual data from 1960 to 1988. Fry's monetary policy reaction function was specified as:

$$\begin{aligned}\Delta \mathbf{DC/Y} &= \beta_0 + \beta_1 \Delta \mathbf{NFAY/Y}_{it} + \beta_2 \Delta \mathbf{NFAY/Y}_{it-1} + \beta_3 (\pi - \pi^*)_{it} \\ &\quad + \beta_4 (\pi - \pi^*)_{it-1} + \beta_5 \mathbf{oilinf}_t + \beta_6 \mathbf{oilinf}_{\,t-1} + \beta_7 \Delta \mathbf{CGY}_{it} \\ &\quad + \beta_8 \Delta \mathbf{CGY}_{it-1} + \beta_{10} \mathbf{REXCHL} + u_{it}\end{aligned}$$

The dependent variable is the change in domestic credit scaled by GDP to account for size effects (Δ**DC/Y**). The dependent variables are all potential objectives of monetary policy or economic variables the central bank needs to take into account when determining domestic credit. $\Delta \mathbf{NFAY/Y}_{it}$ is the change in net foreign assets of the banking system. The variable is included to examine whether the central bank sterilizes the effects of the accumulation of foreign assets. $(\pi - \pi^*)$ is the differential between domestic and foreign inflation as inflation rates have to converge for long-run currency stability. The central bank may either accommodate or resist the effect of foreign price shocks, which are proxied by oil-price inflation (**oilinf**). The central bank may also react to increases in government borrowing (**ΔCGY**) by cutting back lending to the private sector. If the central bank completely neutralized the public sector borrowing then the coefficient on this variable would be zero, partial neutralization would result in a coefficient less than one. A further variable that the central bank may react to is the lagged real exchange rate (**REXCHL**). The impact of the variable is ambiguous. Depreciations are inflationary and therefore may necessitate a restrictive credit policy. However, real depreciations raise the cost of servicing foreign debts and may therefore increase public sector borrowing.

The estimation method is iterated 3-stage least squares (I3SLS). The I3SLS method estimates a system of structural equations where some equations contain endogenous variables. In the first stage, instrumented values of the endogenous variables are developed. The second stage obtains a consistent estimate of the covariance matrix of the equation disturbances. In the third stage, a generalized least squares-type estimation is performed using the covariance matrix estimated in the second stage and the instrumented values in place of the endogenous variables. Cross-equation restrictions were imposed on all coefficients except the intercepts. The endogenous variables are $\Delta\mathbf{NFAY/Y}_{it}$ and $(\pi-\pi^*)_{it}$. The instruments for $\Delta\mathbf{NFAY/Y}_{it}$ and $(\pi-\pi^*)_{it}$ are all exogenous variables: lagged values of the endogenous variables, as well as US inflation, the world interest rate, world economic growth, lagged values of real GNP growth and money (M2) growth.

Fry's (1995) results showed that developing country central banks react systematically to a number of economic variables. In the full sample the countries sterilized a small fraction (17 per cent) of foreign capital inflows and tended to accommodate domestic inflation and increases in oil prices. Central banks also accommodated most of the governments' credit requirement, contracting credit to the private sector by only 12 per cent of the increase in the governments' credit requirements. The Pacific Basin countries, on the other hand, sterilized 41 per cent of foreign capital inflows, were less accommodating regarding oil-price inflation and neutralized two-thirds of government borrowing.

A highly relevant application of Fry's methodology is Savvides' (1998) study of the development of domestic credit in five SSA countries including three countries in the Franc Zone.[4] Savvides (1998) estimated the following regression, also using I3SLS with annual data from 1968–91 for Côte d'Ivoire and Gabon and 1975–88 for Cameroon:

$$\begin{aligned}\Delta\mathbf{DC/Y} &= \beta_0 + \beta_1\Delta\mathbf{NFAY/Y}_{it} + \beta_2\Delta\mathbf{NFAY/Y}_{it-1} + \beta_3(\pi-\pi^*)_{it}\\ &\quad + \beta_4(\pi-\pi^*)_{it-1} + \beta_5\mathbf{oilinf}_t + \beta_6\mathbf{oilinf}_{t-1} + \beta_7\Delta\mathbf{CGY}_{it}\\ &\quad + \beta_8\Delta\mathbf{CGY}_{it-1} + \beta_{10}\mathbf{REXCHL} + \beta_{11}\mathbf{DET/Y}_{t-1} + u_{it}\end{aligned}$$

The Savvides' regression therefore uses all the explanatory variables of the Fry regressions, and also tests whether the central bank reacts to growing external indebtedness (**DET/Y**) by restricting the growth of domestic credit. Cross-country equality restrictions were imposed on all coefficients except the intercept. $\Delta\mathbf{NFAY/Y}_{it}$ and $(\pi - \pi^*)_{it}$ were treated as endogenous variables and all the exogenous variables as well as lagged values of the endogenous variables were used as instruments. Savvides' results show that there was no systematic sterilization of reserve accumulations in the Franc Zone member countries and that the (lagged) inflation differential and oil price inflation were accommodated. However private sector credit was restricted to some extent as public sector credit was expanded. With respect to rising external indebtedness the central bank action was stabilizing. Finally the BCEAO responded to a real depreciation of the CFAF by increasing domestic credit.

Data and methodology

We use the I3SLS methodology and most of the explanatory variables suggested by Fry (1995) and Savvides (1998). However, there is a number of important differences in our regressions:

(1) We use monthly data as the BCEAO makes interest rate policy decisions on a monthly basis. Therefore the analysis based on monthly data is consistent with the timing of BCEAO board meetings and it allows us to focus our examination on the period after the devaluation of the CFAF.

(2) Our data are from 1995 to 2000. The starting point of January 1995 was chosen to examine monetary policy after the devaluation of the CFAF. Moreover, several of the time-series become stationary only in 1995 or have large structural breaks in the months following the devaluation. The end-point of 2000 was dictated by the availability of the quarterly output gap data, taken from Fielding, Lee and Shields (2003), as the *IFS* records only annual GDP data.[5] All variables other than the output data are taken from the *IFS* database.

(3) We do not use domestic credit scaled by GDP (**DC/Y**) as the dependent variable, but private sector credit. The total credit series (***32 … ZF…) is calculated by the *IFS* as the sum of claims on government, claims on the private sector and claims on other financial institutions. In the Franc Zone central bank credit to the government (**CGY**) is a very large part of total credit to government, particularly because IMF credits are channelled through the BCEAO. **CGY** is therefore a major component of total credit and should not be used as an explanatory variable in the domestic credit regression. We circumvent this problem by using credit to the private sector/GDP (**PSC/Y**) as the dependent variable.[6] This still allows us to examine whether the BCEAO offsets government borrowing from the central bank, which would be indicated by a negative coefficient

for the **CGY** variable. In the **CGY** variable used in the regressions we remove the component of the monetary authorities' claims on the government that is accounted for by IMF credits, to get a purer proxy for government borrowing from the central bank.

(4) Both the Fry (1995) and Savvides (1998) regressions include a variable tracking the changes in the real exchange rate. We exclude this variable in our regressions, as the variable is not relevant for the Franc Zone countries after the devaluation of 1994. Any movement in the real exchange rate would be captured by the inflation differential.

(5) We replace the variable of the level of foreign debt/GDP (**DET/Y**) with the change in the level of foreign debt/GDP (**ΔDET/Y**), because the *DETY* series is not stationary in Senegal and Togo unless it is differenced once. All other variables suggested by Fry (1995) and Savvides (1998) are already in differences and are stationary.[7]

(6) As we cannot reject the null hypothesis of no residual autocorrelation in the regression for Togo and only marginally reject it for Côte d'Ivoire we also include a lagged dependent variable in the regressions. This corrects the problem of residual autocorrelation in all country regressions.[8]

(7) To account for potential seasonal effects in the monthly series we also include the dependent variable lagged by a year. Part of private sector credit may well be linked to the agricultural cycle and we do indeed find there to be statistically significant seasonal effects, particularly in Burkina Faso and Senegal.

(8) Lastly, we test whether the cross-equation restrictions are valid and as some of the constraints can be rejected we re-estimate the equations without the constraints on the coefficients.

There are two further variables, which are potential target variables for the BCEAO. First the BCEAO may respond to a contraction in economic activity by expanding domestic credit and vice versa. However, the only proxy for GDP data is the quarterly series constructed by Fielding, Lee and Shields (2003). A monthly interpolation of any output gap measure based on these quarterly data is unlikely to be a good proxy of the data on economic activity available to the BCEAO at its monthly meetings.[9] Unfortunately data on unemployment and industrial production, which could serve as an alternative proxy for information available to the BCEAO, are published only quarterly or annually, if at all.[10]

Second, given the constraints of the peg the BCEAO may also be sensitive to a loss of its centrally held foreign exchange reserves. BCEAO policy rules require credit restrictions whenever gross foreign assets fall below 20 per cent of sight liabilities. However, the 20 per cent ratio was not breached in the period under investigation and the variable was not significant in any specification of the regressions. We therefore do not include it in the regressions reported below.

The subsequent regression therefore tests whether the BCEAO reacts to the following monetary policy target variables: the change in banks' foreign exchange reserves/GDP, the change in the level of foreign debt/GDP, the countries' inflation differentials with France, the change in central bank credit to the government/GDP[11] and oil-price inflation:

$$\begin{aligned}\Delta\mathbf{PSC/Y} = {} & \beta_0 + \beta_1\Delta\mathbf{PSC/Y}_{it-1} + \beta_1\Delta\mathbf{PSC/Y}_{it-12} + \beta_3\Delta\mathbf{NFAY/Y}_{it} \\ & + \beta_4\Delta\mathbf{NFAY/Y}_{it-1} + \beta_5\Delta\mathbf{DET/Y}_{t-1} + \beta_6(\pi - \pi^*)_{it} \\ & + \beta_7(\pi - \pi^*)_{it-1} + \beta_8\Delta\mathbf{CGY}_{it} + \beta_9\Delta\mathbf{CGY}_{it-1} + \beta_{10}\mathbf{oilinf} + u_{it}\end{aligned}$$

Current net foreign assets and the current inflation gap are treated as endogenous variables as they are linked to domestic credit through the banks' balance sheets. All the exogenous variables as well as lagged values of the endogenous variables (lag length $t - 2$) are used as instruments. The methodology used is I3SLS.[12] The regressions are initially performed with cross-country equality restrictions on the coefficients (other than the intercepts) following Fry (1995) and Savvides (1998). We then test the validity of the constraints on the coefficients. Given that most constraints are rejected at the 5 per cent level we re-estimate the equations without the cross-country equality restrictions. The results show that there was no systematic response to target variables across the five countries.

Regressions with constrained coefficients

In the regression of the determinants of private sector credit, where the coefficients (other than on the intercepts) are constrained it appears that the BCEAO was sensitive to some monetary policy variables:

$$\begin{aligned}\Delta\mathbf{PSC/Y} = {} & \beta_0 - 0.130^{***}\Delta\mathbf{PSC/Y}_{it-1} + 0.324^{***}\Delta\mathbf{PSC/Y}_{it-12} \\ & + 0.060^{***}\Delta\mathbf{NFAY/Y}_{it} - 0.028^{*}\Delta\mathbf{NFAY/Y}_{it-1} \\ & + 1.402^{*}\Delta\mathbf{DETY}_{t-1} - 0.076^{***}(\pi - \pi^*)_{it} \\ & + 0.017(\pi - \pi^*)_{it-1} + 0.014^{***}\Delta\mathbf{CGY}_{it} + 0.002\,\Delta\mathbf{CGY}_{it-1} \\ & - 0.001\mathbf{oilinf} + u_{it}\end{aligned}$$ [13]

Only a very small fraction of increases in current foreign capital inflows are lent on to the private sector and there appears to be an attempt to sterilize lagged foreign capital inflows. The coefficients on the foreign assets variables (current and lagged) are significant at the 1 and 5 per cent level respectively. The results also show a marginally significant relationship between increases in long-term foreign debt and increasing domestic credit, contradicting the Savvides' result of a stabilizing central bank reaction to rising external indebtedness. There is evidence of a contraction in private sector credit in response to a higher current inflation differential: the coefficient on the current inflation differential is negative and the relationship is statistically significant at the 1 per cent level. However, the BCEAO does not seem to offset increases in government borrowing by reducing private sector credit, as the coefficient on this variable is positive. There is no statistically significant relationship between changes in oil prices and changes in private sector credit.

These results are in contrast with those of Savvides for the period before the devaluation of 1994. There is no longer evidence of a policy to restrict private sector credit in response to government borrowing from the central bank and no stabilizing response to rising external indebtedness. On the other hand credit does not rise to accommodate inflation or oil price shocks, but credit policy appears to be restrictive in response to rising inflation.

Regressions with unconstrained coefficients

When we test whether we can accept the constraints placed on the coefficients in the estimation, we find that we have to reject the constraints on the dependent variable with the one-year lag, the lagged changes in net foreign assets and foreign liabilities and the lagged changes in government borrowing. We therefore repeat the I3SLS regression without constraining the coefficient estimates. The results presented in Tables 5.2 and 5.3 show first that eliminating the constraints on the coefficients results in an improved fit for all the country regressions.[14] Second it appears that policy in the five countries responds differently to the independent variables and that there is no clear pattern of a BCEAO credit policy at the country level.

Burkina Faso

In Burkina Faso, there are three potential BCEAO target variables which are statistically significant. The coefficients on both current and lagged government borrowing from the central bank are positive and highly significant, showing no attempt by the BCEAO to offset the effect of increased government borrowing on total credit in the economy. Similarly foreign capital inflows feed into domestic credit. The coefficient on the inflation differential is negative as expected and but not statistically significant.

Côte d'Ivoire

In Côte d'Ivoire, current capital inflows feed into private sector credit to a much smaller extent than in Burkina Faso, Mali and Senegal and there appears to be some attempt to sterilize lagged foreign capital inflows. The central bank action regarding external indebtedness appears to be stabilizing (significant at the 10 per cent level). However, the coefficient on the inflation variable is now positive (as well as significant at the 1 per cent level), suggesting that inflation is accommodated, rather than contained. Again, there appears to be no pattern of restricting private sector credit

Table 5.2 Private sector credit regressions: I3SLS estimates with constrained coefficients

	Burkina Faso	**Côte d'Ivoire**	**Mali**	**Senegal**	**Togo**
Lagged dependent variable ($t-1$)	−0.130***	−0.130***	−0.130***	−0.130***	−0.130***
	(.0528)	(.0528)	(.0528)	(.0528)	(.0528)
Lagged dependent variable ($t-12$)	0.324***	0.324***	0.324***	0.324***	0.324***
	(.0438)	(.0438)	(.0438)	(.0438)	(.0438)
(Change in banks' net foreign assets)$_t$	0.060***	0.060***	0.060***	0.060***	0.060***
	(0.0167)	(0.0167)	(0.0167)	(0.0167)	(0.0167)
(Change in banks' net foreign assets)$_{t-1}$	−0.028**	−0.028**	−0.028**	−0.028**	−0.028**
	(0.0160)	(0.0160)	(0.0160)	(0.0160)	(0.0160)
(Change in foreign liabilities)$_{t-1}$	1.402*	1.402*	1.402*	1.402*	1.402*
	(0.7763)	(0.7763)	(0.7763)	(0.7763)	(0.7763)
$(\pi - \pi^*)_t$	−0.076***	−0.076***	−0.076***	−0.076***	−0.076***
	(0.0273)	(0.0273)	(0.0273)	(0.0273)	(0.0273)
$(\pi - \pi^*)_{t-1}$	0.017	0.017	0.017	0.017	0.017
	(0.0226)	(0.0226)	(0.0226)	(0.0226)	(0.0226)
(Change in central bank lending to government)$_t$	0.014***	0.014***	0.014***	0.014***	0.014***
	(0.0015)	(0.0015)	(0.0015)	(0.0015)	(0.0015)
(Change in central bank lending to government)$_{t-1}$	0.002	0.002	0.002	0.002	0.002
	(0.0016)	(0.0016)	(0.0016)	(0.0016)	(0.0016)
Oil price inflation$_t$	−0.001	−0.001	−0.001	−0.001	−0.001
	(0.0006)	(0.0006)	(0.0006)	(0.0006)	(0.0006)
Constant	−0.017	−0.017	−0.017	−0.017	−0.017
	(0.0089)	(0.0140)	(0.010)	(0.0077)	(0.0223)
R^2	0.6819	0.3027	0.1835	0.3396	0.2839

Note: ***, **, * significant at 1, 5 and 10 per cent respectively.

Table 5.3 Private sector credit regressions: I3SLS estimates with unconstrained coefficients

	Burkina Faso	Côte d'Ivoire	Mali	Senegal	Togo
Lagged dependent variable ($t-1$)	−0.188*	0.210*	−0.138	−0.276**	−0.384***
	(0.1091)	(0.1140)	(0.1152)	(0.1144)	(0.116)
Lagged dependent variable ($t-12$)	0.198***	−0.008	0.131	0.164**	0.080
	(0.0573)	(0.1564)	(0.1039)	(0.0773)	(0.0880)
(Change in banks' net foreign assets)$_t$	0.370***	0.033**	0.468***	0.475***	0.185
	(0.0994)	(0.0172)	(0.0987)	(0.1903)	(0.1218)
(Change in banks' net foreign assets)$_{t-1}$	−0.005	−0.039**	0.168*	0.093	−0.112
	(0.1092)	(0.0164)	(0.1003)	(0.1657)	(0.1107)
(Change in foreign liabilities)$_{t-1}$	−0.693	−3.029*	1.042	0.991	−0.503
	(0.9518)	(1.8331)	(1.6336)	(1.2686)	(2.086)
$(\pi - \pi^*)_t$	−0.049	0.148**	−0.055	−0.101***	0.288***
	(0.0331)	(0.0718)	(0.0467)	(0.0384)	(0.1148)
$(\pi - \pi^*)_{t-1}$	−0.011	0.085	0.035	−0.033	−0.079
	(0.0260)	(0.0539)	(0.0375)	(0.0309)	(0.0947)
(Change in central bank lending to government)$_t$	0.019***	0.032***	−0.003	0.007***	0.0142***
	(0.0067)	(0.0037)	(0.0052)	(0.0019)	(0.0030)
(Change in central bank lending to government)$_{t-1}$	0.015**	−0.066	−0.001	0.002	0.005
	(0.063)	(0.0048)	(0.0062)	(0.0018)	(0.0035)
Oil price inflation$_t$	−0.000	0.001	−0.000	−0.000	0.003
	(0.0007)	(0.0015)	(0.0009)	(0.0007)	(0.0026)
Constant	−0.0013	0.029*	−0.005	−0.009	0.041*
	(0.0065)	(0.0142)	(0.0095)	(0.0075)	(0.0242)
R^2	0.8795	0.5837	0.5433	0.5439	0.4992

Note: ***, **, * significant at 1, 5 and 1C per cent respectively.

in response to current government borrowing and while the coefficient on lagged government borrowing is negative it is not statistically significant.

Mali

In Mali, both current and lagged increases in banks' net foreign assets feed into private sector credit. The coefficient on the inflation differential is negative as expected, but not statistically significant. There is no statistically significant relationship between private sector credit and government borrowing from the central bank.

Senegal

In Senegal, current foreign capital inflows are reflected in increasing private sector credit. There appears to be a restrictive credit policy in response to rising inflation, and again private sector credit rises with government borrowing from the central bank. The coefficient here is, however, lower than in any of the other countries in the Zone.

Togo

In Togo, there is no evidence for a policy of sterilizing lagged foreign capital inflows and changes in the inflation differential with France appear to be accommodated rather than contained. Private sector credit again rises with increases in current government borrowing.

The estimation results based on the unconstrained coefficients therefore cast doubt on the results obtained with the constrained coefficients. There does not appear to be a systematic policy to restrict credit in response to emerging inflationary pressures. While the regressions for Burkina Faso, Mali and Senegal show the expected negative coefficient on the inflation differential, the coefficient is positive and significant in Côte d'Ivoire and Togo. Similarly there is no systematic attempt to sterilize foreign capital inflows or foreign borrowing. Increases in long-term foreign liabilities are only marginally significant in Côte d'Ivoire. The only variable that is highly significant in four out of the five regressions is the government borrowing from the central bank. But when the BCEAO is lending to the member governments it does nothing to offset its effect on domestic credit: domestic credit increases as governments borrow more. This result is in contrast to the Savvides' results for the period before the devaluation, where the BCEAO kept a tighter control on domestic credit and restricted credit to the private sector to offset advances made to governments.

Conclusions

Our results suggest that the BCEAO did not take a particularly active role in steering private sector credit in the Franc Zone member countries, although in theory it has several policy instruments at its disposal. While the first set of regressions with constrained coefficients supported a hypothesis of restrictive credit policy in response to emerging inflationary pressures, the second set of regressions showed that across the different countries there is no evidence for a systematic policy. Not only do the significance levels and the magnitude of the coefficients vary widely, but in some cases the signs on the coefficients are reversed. The only result that is consistent across all the countries is that there is no policy to restrict private credit if governments increase their borrowing from the BCEAO.

It appears therefore that the BCEAO operates interest rate policy at the Zone level, but does little to steer credit policy at the country level, at least on a monthly basis.[15] This does raise the question of why the *de jure* powers of the BCEAO to restrict domestic credit growth have been strengthened in recent years, with the restrictions imposed on the refinancing of agricultural credits, the introduction of reserve requirements and the phasing out of central bank financing of government deficits. However, the first two of the measures predate the devaluation of the CFAF in 1994 and these may have been attempts to salvage the peg rather than being intended to strengthen BCEAO monetary control during periods of peg stability. It is therefore possible that BCEAO credit policy would become more pro-active if pressures on the currency re-emerged in the future.

Notes

We gratefully acknowledge helpful comments from Professor David Fielding, Dr Kalvinder Shields, one anonymous referee and seminar participants at the UNU-WIDER Workshop on Long Term Development in the CFA Zone Countries of Sub-Saharan Africa, Helsinki, June 2003.

1. These are relatively infrequent. For example, during 2000 there were no auctions of central bank bills.
2. This is also true for the pre-1994 period, as shown by Bayoumi and Ostry (1997).
3. In September 1998 the council of ministers decided to phase out central bank financing of government budget deficits entirely by 2002, except for within-year advances to smooth cash-flows.
4. The countries in the Savvides' paper are Cameroon, Côte d'Ivoire, Gabon, Ghana and Nigeria, but a separate regression is performed for the Franc Zone countries.
5. To get a monthly data set we used the quarterly figure for the three months in the quarter.
6. *IFS* line *** 32D ... ZF ... claims on private sector from 'Monetary Survey'.
7. According to both the ADF and the Phillips–Perron tests.
8. Using a Lagrange Multiplier test (Greene 2003: 271).
9. When a measure of the output gap based on the Fielding data is included its coefficient is never significant.
10. Industrial production is available quarterly for Côte d'Ivoire and Senegal only and unemployment is available annually for Côte d'Ivoire only (*IFS*).
11. *IFS* lines *** 12A ... ZF ... minus (*** 2 ... AA.ZF ... times ***.2TL.ZF ...).
12. Qualitatively similar results are obtained if OLS is used instead of I3SLS. We report the I3SLS results because it is the more efficient estimation method and to make the results comparable to the Savvides' results.

13. See Table 5.1 for details.
14. See R^2 statistics reported in Tables 5.2 and 5.3.
15. Another interpretation of the results would be that credit planning takes place on an annual basis (which would, however, be in contrast with the monthly setting of interest rates). In this case, we would not necessarily observe credit responding to monthly variations in monetary policy target variables. However, we cannot test the response of the BCEAO to the monetary policy target variables discussed above on an annual basis with data from 1995 to 2002.

References

Bayoumi, T. and J. D. Ostry (1997) 'Macroeconomic Shocks and Trade Flows within Sub-Saharan Africa: Implications for Optimum Currency Arrangements', *Journal of African Economies*, 6: 412–44.

Connolly, M. B. and D. Taylor (1979) 'Exchange Rate Changes and Neutralization: A Test of the Monetary Approach Applied to Developed and Developing Countries', *Economica*, 46(183): 281–94.

Fielding, D. (2002) *The Macroeconomics of Monetary Union*, London: Routledge.

Fielding, D., K. Lee and K. Shields (2003) 'Modelling Macroeconomic Linkages in a Macroeconomic Union a West African Example', Presented at the UNU-WIDER Workshop 'Long Term Development in the CFA Zone Countries of sub-Saharan Africa', Helsinki, June.

Fry, M. (1993) 'Inflation and Monetary Policy in Pacific Basin Developing Countries', in K. Shigehara (ed.), *Price Stabilisation in the 1990s: Domestic and International Policy Requirements*, London: Macmillan: 137–64.

Fry, M. (1995) *Money, Interest and Banking in Economic Development*, Baltimore, MD: Johns Hopkins University Press.

Greene, W. (2003) *Econometric Analysis*, 5th edn, New Jersey: Prentice-Hall.

Honohan, P. (1990) 'Monetary Cooperation in the CFA Zone', Policy, Research and External Affairs Working Papers 389, Washington, DC: World Bank.

IMF Country Report (2001) *The West African Economic and Monetary Union: Recent Economic Developments and Regional Policy Issues*, IMF Country Report 01/193. Washington, DC: IMF.

Kamas, L. (1985) 'External Disturbances and the Independence of Monetary Policy under the Crawling Peg in Colombia', *Journal of International Economics*, 19(3/4): 313–27.

Kamas, L. (1986) 'The Balance of Payments Offset to Monetary Policy: Monetarist, Portfolio Balance and Keynesian Estimates for Mexico and Venezuela', *Journal of Money, Credit and Banking*, 18(4): 467–81.

Savvides, A. (1998) 'Inflation and Monetary Policy in Selected West and Central African Countries', *World Development*, 26(5): 809–27.

Shortland, A. and D. Stasavage (2003) 'Monetary Policy in the Franc Zone: Estimating Interest Rate Rules for the BCEAO', Presented at the UNU-WIDER Workshop 'Long Term Development in the CFA Zone Countries of sub-Saharan Africa', Helsinki, June.

Union Monétaire Ouest Africaine (1989) *La Nouvelle Politique de la Monnaie et du Crédit de la Banque Centrale des Etats de l'Afrique de l'Ouest*, Ouagadougou: UEOMA.

6
Estimating an Interest Rate Reaction Function for the BCEAO

Anja Shortland and David Stasavage

Introduction

In October 1989, the BCEAO, which is the central bank for the WAEMU, announced its intention to shift towards using indirect instruments of monetary policy, based on modifications of the central bank discount rate as the primary policy tool. There has been some question whether the BCEAO has actually begun actively to use its discount rate as a monetary policy tool (see IMF 2001 on this point). This chapter asks to what extent the BCEAO modifies its discount rate in response to changing domestic economic conditions or, alternatively, whether movements in the BCEAO discount rate are driven above all by changes in foreign interest rates. We focus in particular on the period after the January 1994 devaluation of the CFAF, considering to what extent the BCEAO reacts to changes in domestic inflation and output, to external constraints involving reserve levels and French interest rates, as well as to other relevant variables. While the BCEAO has been criticized in the past for not using its discount rate as an active policy tool, and while it is true that discount rate changes have been infrequent since 1994, we find evidence that the BCEAO does react to domestic economic variables in a limited fashion, and in particular to inflation. Our estimates are consistent with an interpretation that, in the long run, the BCEAO matches changes in French interest rates one for one, but in the short run it retains a significant freedom to react to domestic economic variables. We arrive at this conclusion using two alternative estimation methods. In the first, we estimate several extended Taylor Rules using both quarterly and monthly data. With the second method we use a multinomial logit model to estimate the probability that changes in variables such as inflation, the output gap, or foreign interest rates will lead to a discrete change in the BCEAO discount rate. This second estimation method, which we see as complementary to the first, takes account of the fact that central banks in practice modify their discount rates in discrete steps (usually of at least 25 basis points), rather than as a continuous variable.

In the remainder of the chapter we first provide a brief description of the recent evolution of monetary policy in UEMOA. We then estimate an interest rate reaction function for the BCEAO using both quarterly and monthly data, before extending this inquiry using a multinomial logit model to estimate probabilities of discrete changes in the BCEAO discount rate. We then discuss the robustness of our interest rate results, before drawing some conclusions.

Monetary policy in UEMOA, 1993–2000

In the period immediately preceding and following the January 1994 devaluation of the CFAF, monetary policy decisions were determined almost exclusively by the goal of maintaining the CFAF's peg to the French Franc. Before January 1994 BCEAO interest rates were kept high in order to offer holders of CFAF assets a risk premium. In the months immediately following the devaluation, BCEAO interest rates were raised significantly as part of the provisions of country IMF programmes.

Since 1995 BCEAO interest rates have gone through two distinct periods. During the first, from December 1994 to October 1996, the BCEAO undertook a series of stepwise rate reductions that resulted in the discount rate falling from 10 per cent to 6.5 per cent (see Figure 6.1). This was also a period of stepwise reductions in French short-term central bank rates. Between October 1996 and December 2000 BCEAO rates remained within a very narrow range

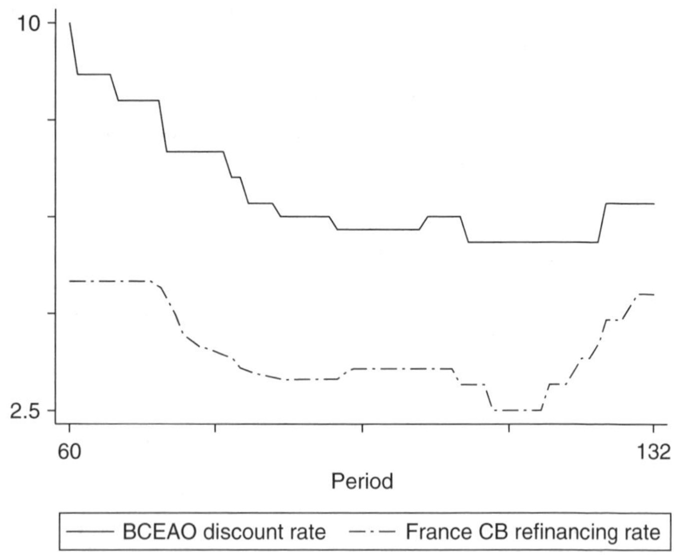

Figure 6.1 BCEAO interest rates and French interest rates, 1995–2000

(5.75–6.5 per cent), in keeping with relative stability in French interest rates, except at the end of the period.

Estimating an interest rate rule for the BCEAO

As an initial step in our empirical inquiry, we have estimated interest rate rules for the BCEAO central bank where it is assumed that the BCEAO discount rate is a continuous variable.[1] We restrict our attention to the period between January 1995 and December 2000, avoiding the period of the CFAF devaluation in 1994. We examine how BCEAO interest rates have responded to domestic inflation rates and to the output gap, as is common practice in estimates of interest rate rules for OECD countries. In addition, we consider to what extent the BCEAO authorities have responded to variables that may play more of a role in monetary policy-making in developing countries, and in particular those countries with fixed exchange rate regimes. These include foreign interest rates, levels of foreign assets and changes in central bank claims on government. Extended interest rate rules of this sort have been considered by Aron and Muellbauer (2000) for South Africa.

Specification and data

We begin by considering a basic monetary policy rule of the form adopted by Clarida, Gali and Gertler (1998) where the interest rate on the central bank's short-term lending facility r^* depends on the long-run equilibrium nominal rate $\bar{r}$, on the difference between the expectation of the inflation rate for period $t+n$ and the policy-maker's preferred rate of inflation π^*, and on the difference between the expectation of output growth for period t and the preferred rate of output growth y^*. This is a generalization of the simple interest rate rule that has been proposed by Taylor (1993):

$$r_t^* = \bar{r} + \beta_1(E_{t-1}[\pi_{t+n}] - \pi_t^*) + \beta_2(E_{t-1}[y_t] - y_t^*) \qquad (6.1)$$

Empirical estimations of (6.1) often consider both rules where the central bank reacts to forecasts of inflation in the next period ($n = 1$) and rules where it reacts to the forecast for inflation anywhere from six to twenty-four months into the future. The central bank's information set is taken to include data available in period $t-1$. Based on this assumption, one can then use instrumental variables to incorporate forward-looking expectations into the estimation. Aron and Muellbauer (2000) adopt this technique to estimate an interest rate rule for South Africa. In the case of the WAEMU, however, there is reason to believe that the appropriate estimation method may be more simple. When using information available at time $t-1$ to predict inflation at time t (based on monthly data), the only statistically significant predictor is the previous month's inflation rate. That is, when

Table 6.1 Summary statistics[a]

	Mean	Standard deviation	Minimum	Maximum
BCEAO discount	6.72	1.09	5.75	10.0
French/ECB short-term interest rate	3.64	0.80	2.50	5.00
UEMOA inflation	0.028	0.078	−0.131	0.206
Output gap	0.006	0.052	−0.157	0.100
Foreign assets/GDP	0.326	0.045	0.215	0.435
Claims on govt/GDP	0.309	0.034	0.261	0.422

Note: [a] These figures are based on monthly data, 1995–2000. Summary figures for the quarterly data set used in the chapter are similar.

we instrumented for current inflation with different lags of inflation, only the coefficient on inflation lagged one month was significant (and inflation lagged one quarter in the case of our quarterly data set). There is no available BCEAO data on inflation expectations in UEMOA, and a paper by a member of the BCEAO staff (Tenou 2002) does not include a measure of inflation expectations when estimating an interest rate rule for UEMOA. As a result, in our estimate of the BCEAO interest rate rule we assume that when setting interest rates at time t, the BCEAO reacts directly to the inflation rate and the output gap as measured at time $t-1$. As can be seen from the summary statistics in Table 6.1, monthly inflation rates in UEMOA are extremely volatile, with a standard deviation of 7.8 percentage points.[2] This volatility has potential implications for BCEAO policy-making; to the extent that inflation is volatile and difficult to forecast, the BCEAO may give this variable less weight when considering interest rate decisions.

We estimated the overall output gap for the BCEAO using a Hodrick–Prescott (HP) filter and quarterly data for GDP.[3] The paper by BCEAO staff that estimates an interest rate rule for UEMOA also uses this approach (Tenou 2002). As was true for inflation rates, the output gap in UEMOA is extremely volatile (see Table 6.1), and as a consequence, the BCEAO may give less weight to this variable in policy-making than would otherwise be the case. Given that the HP filter is known to have a number of shortcomings, particularly with accuracy deteriorating towards the end of a series, we also experimented with alternative output gap measures. One option involved calculating trend GDP by using a simple five-quarter moving average of real GDP growth. The output gap produced using this method turned out to be extremely highly correlated with our existing HP filter measure (correlation coefficient >0.95).

When considering whether the BCEAO alters interest rates in response to changes in UEMOA inflation and the output gap, we constructed each of these variables by weighting individual country inflation rates and output gaps by GDP. However, it is plausible that the decision-making process within BCEAO might result in different weightings being applied in practice. We investigated two such possibilities. First, there is a possibility that the BCEAO responds only to Ivorian economic conditions, which would be based on the interpretation that Côte d'Ivoire plays a predominant role in BCEAO decision-making. Second, it may be the case that the BCEAO responds to an unweighted average of UEMOA inflation rates and output gaps, which would be based on the interpretation that the BCEAO statutes give countries equal weight in decision making, regardless of the size of their population or their economy. Using these two alternative measures the results did not differ very significantly from those reported here.

In addition to considering the possibility that BCEAO interest rates react to current inflation and the output gap, we follow Aron and Muellbauer (2000) by examining whether interest rates are correlated with several other variables that may logically have an impact on interest rate-setting in developing countries, and the BCEAO in particular. Most importantly, given capital mobility and the maintenance of the CFAF's peg to the French Franc (and subsequently the Euro), the BCEAO can be expected to react to changes in the French central bank rate. Failure to maintain short-term interest rates at French levels (in addition to compensating for a relative risk premium for holding CFAF) will lead to a loss of exchange reserves. To the extent that the French Treasury does not unconditionally support reserve outflows, this will pose a constraint on BCEAO policy. As a result, in our empirical estimates we include the French short-term interest rate as an explanatory variable.[4]

Given the constraint imposed by the CFAF peg, the BCEAO should also logically be more likely to increase short-term interest rates in cases where the central bank's foreign assets are low. The BCEAO statutes contain a policy rule requiring credit restrictions whenever gross foreign assets of the BCEAO fall below 20 per cent of sight liabilities (*engagements à vue*).[5] In our empirical estimates we include the variable *a*, which measures the gross foreign assets of the BCEAO as a share of total UEMOA GDP.

Finally, given that the BCEAO has continued to provide a direct credit facility for governments, we also include a variable *c*, which measures total BCEAO claims on governments as a share of total UEMOA GDP. This would be justified to the extent that the facility is automatic (BCEAO cannot limit credit to governments unless this exceeds 20 per cent of annual revenues), and that there are fears that an increase in claims will have to be monetized at some point.[6] To the extent that changes in claims provide a good proxy for the overall fiscal deficit, this variable may also capture the reaction to direct inflationary effects of expansionary fiscal policy.

Results of unit root tests (reported in Table 6.2) strongly suggest that among our variables UEMOA inflation, claims on government and foreign assets are stationary over the period considered (the output gap is stationary by construction). In contrast, there is evidence that both the BCEAO discount

Table 6.2 Unit root tests of regression variables[a]

	Quarterly		Monthly	
	(no trend)	(trend)	(no trend)	(trend)
BCEAO discount	−3.82	−0.89	−3082	−1.73
	$p < 0.01$	$p = 0.96$	$p < 0.01$	$p = 0.74$
French rate	−1.49	−0.05	−1.30	0.43
	$p = 0.53$	$p = 0.99$	$p = 0.63$	$p = 0.99$
UEMOA inflation	−4.06	−4.57	−5.69	−5.85
	$p < 0.01$	$p < 0.01$	$p < 0.01$	$p < 0.01$
Claims on government/GDP	−5.40	−5.72	−4.63	−5.22
	$p < 0.01$	$p < 0.01$	$p < 0.01$	$p < 0.01$
Foreign assets/GDP	−3.86	−3.57	−3.53	−4.20
	$p < 0.01$	$p = 0.03$	$p < 0.01$	$p < 0.01$

Note: [a] Results are based on Phillips–Perron tests conducted with and without a trend.

rate and French short-term central bank rate are non-stationary. Given the theoretical relationship between the BCEAO rate and the French short-term central bank rate, one might expect that if they each have a unit root, they will also be cointegrated. If this is the case, then it makes sense to estimate an error-correction model where BCEAO rates in the long run depend exclusively on the level of French interest rates (plus a constant reflecting any risk premium), and our other explanatory variables in (6.3) (p. 109) then explain short-run deviations from this long-run tend. A likelihood ratio test based on the Johansen procedure for cointegration suggests this is indeed the case. However, the Johansen procedure is known to have poor properties in small samples, such as we have here. Tests for cointegration based on the method proposed by Engle and Granger (1987) suggested that the null of no-cointegration of French rates and BCEAO rates could not be rejected.

Based on the above tests results, which do not demonstrate unambiguously that BCEAO and French interest rates are cointegrated, we have nonetheless chosen to estimate the error-correction model reported in (6.2) and (6.3). This method produced similar results to those obtained when assuming that all variables are stationary.

$$
\begin{aligned}
r_t &= \alpha + \beta_1 r_t^{FR} + \varepsilon_1 \\
\Delta r_t &= \beta_2 + \beta_3 \Delta r_t^{FR} + \beta_4 \pi_{t-1} + \beta_5 (y_{t-1} - \bar{y}_{t-1}) \\
&\quad + \beta_6 (r_{t-1} - (\alpha + \beta_1 r_{t-1}^{FR})) + \varepsilon_2
\end{aligned} \tag{6.2}
$$

$$r_t = \alpha + \beta_1 r_t^{FR} + \varepsilon_1$$

$$\Delta r_t = \beta_2 + \beta_3 \Delta r_t^{FR} + \beta_4 \pi_{t-1} + \beta_5 (y_{t-1} - \bar{y}_{t-1}) + \beta_6 a_t + \beta_7 c_t + \beta_8 (r_{t-1} - (\alpha + \beta_1 r_{t-1}^{FR})) + \varepsilon_2 \quad (6.3)$$

Estimates using quarterly data

Models (1) and (2) in Table 6.3 report estimates of (6.2) and (6.3) using quarterly data for the period 1995–2001. We begin with a simple rule that considers the relationship between BCEAO interest rates, inflation, the output gap and French interest rates (6.2). In this regression the coefficient on French interest rates is highly significant, and given the confidence interval for this coefficient, this result is also consistent with the proposition that, in the long run, a change in French interest rates will have to be matched by a one-for-one change in BCEAO interest rates. In the short run equation the coefficient on lagged inflation is of the expected sign and quite large, but it

Table 6.3 Estimating an interest rate rule for BCEAO[a]

Regression	**(1)**	**(2)**	**(3)**	**(4)**
Long-run equation				
French rate$_t$	1.14	1.14	1.14	1.14
	(0.29)	(0.29)	(0.19)	(0.19)
Constant	2.59	2.59	2.57	2.57
	(0.89)	(0.89)	(0.61)	(0.61)
Short-run equation				
Δ French rate	0.39	0.41	0.36	0.36
	(0.16)	(0.19)	(0.18)	(0.19)
UEMOA inflation (t – 1)	0.79	−0.07	0.76	0.81
	(0.96)	(1.27)	(0.30)	(0.36)
Output gap (t – 1)	1.40	1.76	0.60	0.74
	(0.68)	(1.02)	(0.34)	(0.47)
Claims on govt/GDP		1.74		0.69
		(2.80)		(1.25)
Foreign assets/GDP		−2.85		−0.15
		(2.45)		(0.63)
Error-correction term	−0.28	−0.35	−0.14	−0.14
	(0.09)	(0.07)	(0.04)	(0.05)
Constant	−0.013	0.31	−0.06	−0.23
	(0.04)	(1.01)	(0.02)	(0.28)
N =	25	25	73	73
Frequency	Quarterly	Quarterly	Monthly	Monthly

Note: [a] Estimation by OLS with Newey–West standard errors (in parentheses).

is not statistically significant. The coefficient on the output gap is both large and statistically significant.

We next estimate an extended rule where the BCEAO interest rate also responds to changes in the level of foreign assets held by the BCEAO and to changes in central bank claims on the government (6.3). In this specification in the short-run equation the coefficient on UEMOA inflation is not significant either, but the coefficient on the output gap remains of similar magnitude and is significant at the 10 per cent level. The coefficients on the foreign assets variable and the government claims variable have the expected sign, but they are not statistically significant.

Given the results of these regressions using quarterly data, the horizon most frequently used to estimate interest rate rules, it can be suggested that the BCEAO responds strongly to changes in French interest rates, but there is also an indication that in the short run the BCEAO reacts systematically to lagged inflation and the output gap.

Estimates using monthly data

While the majority of empirical studies of interest rate rules use quarterly data, several authors have observed that it may make more sense to use monthly data for these estimates, because this is the frequency with which central bank governing boards generally meet to consider interest rate changes.[7] Among the variables used in our estimations of (6.2) and (6.3), the output gap is available only on a quarterly basis, but data for all other variables are available monthly. Models (3) and (4) from Table 6.3 report estimates of an interest rate rule for the BCEAO using monthly data.[8] In these regressions the output gap has been constructed using a simple interpolation where the output gap in each month is estimated to be equal to the measured output gap for that quarter.

In model (3) (based on (6.2)) there is again evidence that in the long run the BCEAO responds one for one to changes in French short-term interest rates. In addition, there is now more unambiguous evidence that BCEAO responds to increases in inflation with higher interest rates. A one standard deviation increase in UEMOA inflation (+0.078) is estimated to result in a short-run increase of 0.06 in the BCEAO's discount rate. The coefficient on the output gap in model (3) is also statistically significant, suggesting that a one standard deviation increase in the output gap (0.054) would be associated with a short-run increase in BCEAO rates of 0.03 percentage points. The results for model (4) (based on (6.3)) with regard to inflation and the output gap are quite similar. Once again, there is no evidence that the BCEAO responds to changes in its level of foreign assets or to changes in claims on government.

In sum, our estimates using monthly data suggest that while changes in French interest rates remain the primary factor to which the BCEAO responds when it sets its discount rate, since 1995 the BCEAO has also reacted to UEMOA inflation and the UEMOA output gap.

Estimating probabilities of interest rate changes

While standard interest rate rules are used to estimate how the level of interest rates responds to changes in macroeconomic variables such as inflation and output, and they implicitly assume that interest rates can be modified by any amount, in practice central banks face choices of whether to respond to changing economic conditions with a discrete change in interest rates, generally of at least 25 basis points. As a consequence, rather than using macroeconomic variables to predict the level of interest rates, it may also be useful to use these same variables to predict the direction of change of the central bank's discount rate (cut, no change, or increase). In this section we follow Chevapatrakul, Mizen and Kim (2001) by using a multinomial logit model to estimate the probability that the BCEAO will cut interest rates, increase rates, or hold them constant in any given month. The multinomial logit model allows us to take account of the fact that central banks are forced to choose between no change in the interest rate, a discrete increase, or a discrete decrease.[9] We view this method as complementary to the method used above for estimating the interest rate rules, as using both methods will help us to identify the extent to which assumptions about BCEAO behaviour are driven by specific assumptions about whether the BCEAO discount rate is a continuous variable.

Over the period we consider, while the level of the BCEAO's discount rate has varied significantly, changes in the level have tended to occur in large discrete jumps. Over the seventy-three months in our sample the BCEAO changed rates on ten occasions, decreasing rates eight times, and increasing rates in two instances. Seven out of these ten modifications involved changes of at least 50 basis points. This distribution of outcomes suggests that while it may be possible to predict decreases in the discount rate with some confidence, it may be quite difficult to predict rate increases very accurately. Given this distribution, one might prefer to group together cases of interest rate increases with cases where the rate was held steady and then use a standard logit or probit model to estimate the likelihood of a rate decrease. We also considered this possibility and found that the results were very similar to those obtained with the multinomial logit procedure. As a consequence, we have chosen to report the multinomial logit estimates in Table 6.4.

Table 6.4 reports the results of our multinomial logit estimates of the following three outcomes where X_t is a vector of variables that are likely to be correlated with interest rate changes.

$$\Pr(r_t - r_{t-1} < 0|X_t)$$

$$\Pr(r_t - r_{t-1} = 0|X_t)$$

$$\Pr(r_t - r_{t-1} > 0|X_t)$$

Table 6.4 Estimating probability of a change in BCEAO interest rates, multinomial logit estimates[a]

	Reduced model		Extended model	
	Cut	Increase	Cut	Increase
$\left(r_{t-1}^{BCEAO} - r_{t-1}^{FR}\right)$	5.04	−2.50	13.0	−2.70
	(1.88)	(1.43)	(3.7)	(1.17)
UEMOA inflation ($t-1$)	−13.9	8.1	−31.1	8.9
	(6.1)	(12.4)	(13.7)	(10.2)
Output gap ($t-1$)	35.2	5.10	53.0	7.88
	(17.5)	(3.76)	(18.3)	(8.63)
Claims on govt/GDP			−39.2	15.2
			(18.6)	(37.6)
Foreign assets/GDP			75.7	−4.17
			(31.6)	(19.3)
Constant	−19.5	2.91	−59.2	1.135
	(7.0)	(3.01)	(18.3)	(0.608)
$N =$	73		73	
Pr > Chi^2 – H_0: constant only	$p < 0.01$		$p < 0.01$	
Pr > Chi^2 – H_0: reduced model			$p = 0.064$	

Note: [a] Estimation by multinomial logit with heteroscedastic–consistent standard errors (in parentheses).

For the vector X_t, we use the same set of explanatory variables used to estimate (6.2) and (6.3), with one exception. Instead of using the level of French short-term interest rates, we use the difference between the BCEAO's discount rate and the French/European Central Bank (ECB) short-term rate as an explanatory variable $(r_{t-1}^{BCEAO} - r_{t-1}^{FR})$. While the level of the French rate is a likely predictor of the level of the BCEAO rate, the probability that BCEAO rates will be changed in any given month is more likely to be a function of the difference between the BCEAO rate and the French rate.

Table 6.4 reports the results of our multinomial logit estimates. In the reduced model, the coefficient on the difference between the BCEAO rate and the French rate has the expected sign for predicting both cuts in the BCEAO rate and for predicting increases, and it is statistically significant in the former case. In addition, the level of UEMOA inflation has a statistically significant effect on the probability of a rate cut: higher inflation makes a cut less probable. Contrary to intuition, the coefficient on the output gap is actually positive and significant, suggesting that when GDP is above trend the BCEAO is more likely to cut interest rates.

The 'extended model' reported in Table 6.4 adds claims on government and the level of foreign assets to the central bank's information set. In this extended model the coefficients on UEMOA inflation and on the output gap remain of similar magnitude as in the reduced model. In addition, the levels of BCEAO foreign assets and of its claims on government are significant predictors of a cut in the BCEAO's discount rate. A likelihood ratio test shows that these coefficients are jointly significant. As would be expected, when foreign assets are high and claims on government are low, the BCEAO is more likely to cut rates.

A look at the substantive magnitude of the effects from our multinomial logit estimates provides a mixed picture. Changes in French interest rates have large effects on our estimated probabilities of interest rate changes, and changes in other explanatory variables may also have sizeable effects, but only when they are quite far from their mean values. For each of our explanatory variables, Table 6.5 reports the predicted probability of a cut in BCEAO interest rates when the variable in question is set at one, two and three standard deviations away from its mean. Other variables remain set at their mean values (when all variables are set at their means the estimated probability of an interest rate cut is 0.001). The value for each of the variables listed is shifted in the direction which, according to the extended model in Table 6.4, would be associated with an increased probability of a cut in the BCEAO discount rate. From Table 6.5, it is clear that an increase in the gap between French and BCEAO interest rates by one standard deviation or more has a very large effect on the estimated probability of an interest rate cut. In contrast, the level of UEMOA inflation or the level of foreign assets only has a sizeable impact on the estimated probability of a rate cut when these variables are at least two standard deviations away from their mean. In the sample we consider, this would apply to only 2 per cent of the observations for foreign assets and 5 per cent of the observations for inflation. Finally, even very large changes in levels of claims on government have no effect on the estimated probability of a rate cut.

As a final look at the substantive predictions of our multinomial logit estimates, Figure 6.2 charts the estimated probabilities of a rate cut for each date in

Table 6.5 Predicted probability of an interest rate cut[a]

		$\Pr(r_t - r_{t-1} < 0)$		
Variable	**Variable change**	**1 std dev.**	**2 std dev.**	**3 std dev.**
Difference ($t-1$)	Above mean	0.78	0.99	0.99
UEMOA infl. ($t-1$)	Below mean	0.01	0.13	0.62
Output gap ($t-1$)	Above mean	0.02	0.24	0.83
Claims on govt/GDP	Below mean	<0.01	0.02	0.06
Foreign assets/GDP	Above mean	0.03	0.51	0.93

Note: [a] Based on extended model reported in Table 6.3. Other variables set at their means. Predicted probability when all variables are set at their means is 0.001.

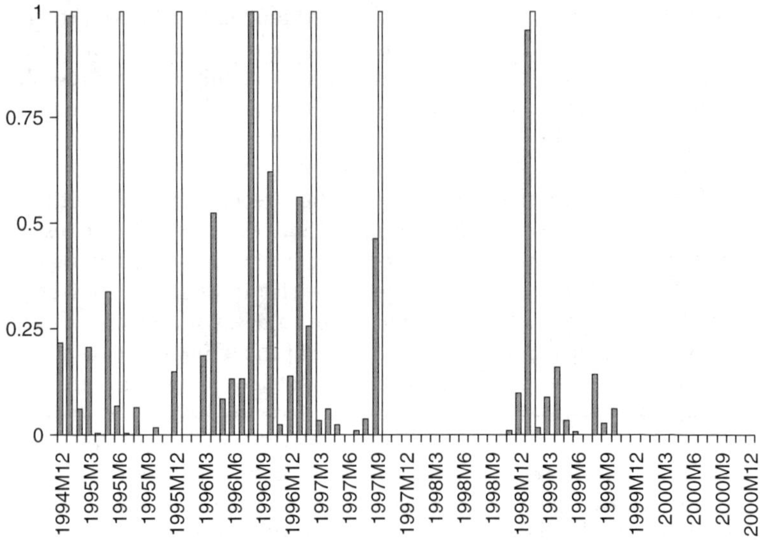

Figure 6.2 Estimated probability of a rate cut, using gap with French rates, 1994–2000 (actual cut indicated by unshaded column)

our sample (in the shaded columns), and it also indicates the dates on which the BCEAO actually chose to cut interest rates (in the unshaded columns). As can be seen, there is a reasonably close correspondence between a high predicted probability of a cut and an actual BCEAO decision to cut rates. However, a further look shows that the accuracy of the model is driven above all by the estimated effect of a change in the interest rate differential between UEMOA and France. Figure 6.3 reports the estimated probabilities from the extended model after we removed the interest rate differential variable from the regression. As can now be seen, there continues to be a correlation between a predicted change in rates and an actual change in rates, but the predicted probability of a change in rates in this model is never greater than 0.5.

Robustness of the interest rate results

Before drawing firm conclusions based on our estimates, it is worth considering to what extent these results may be influenced by serial correlation of the errors, by outliers and by the model specification we adopted. We conclude that our results are robust after considering each of these potential problems.

Standard tests for serial correlation of errors provided mixed conclusions about our Table 6.3 estimates. Based on a Durbin *h*-test, the null of no

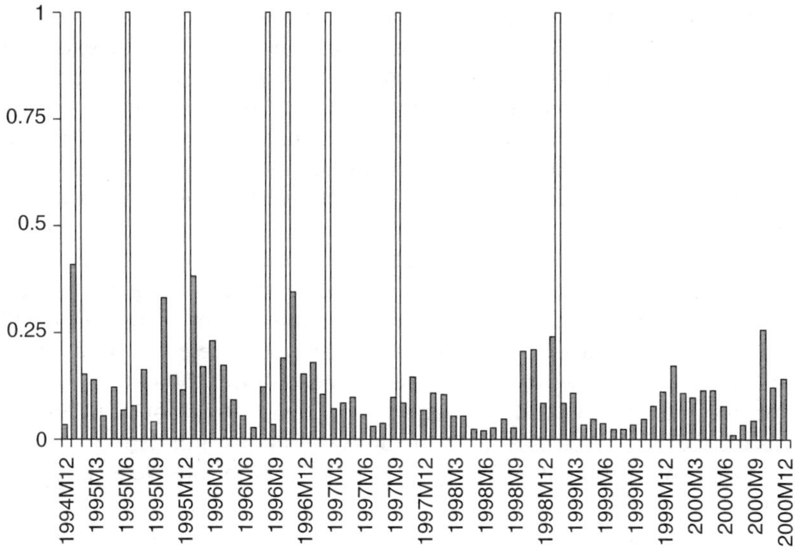

Figure 6.3 Estimated probability of a rate cut, domestic variables only, 1994–2000 (actual cut indicated by unshaded column)

first-order serial correlation could not be rejected for either the estimates using quarterly data or those using monthly data. On the other hand, results of a Breusch–Godfrey test, which can be used to test for both first-order and higher-order autocorrelation, suggested that there is first-order autocorrelation in both our quarterly and our monthly estimates, and there is also higher-order autocorrelation in the quarterly estimates. These results for the quarterly data should probably be qualified by the fact that the sample size is quite small. We examined whether inclusion of additional lags of our explanatory variables could successfully address any potential serial correlation. However, after inclusion of additional lags, the coefficients on these lag terms were not statistically significant, and tests continued to suggest that both first-order and higher-order autocorrelation might be present. As a consequence, in our Table 6.3 estimates we have reported the standard errors proposed by Newey and West (1987), which are consistent in the presence of both first-order and higher-order autocorrelation.

We also considered to what extent our empirical results are influenced by the presence of outliers. For the estimates in Table 6.3 we identified outliers using Cook's distance and then re-estimated the regressions after excluding those observations where this value was greater than $4/(n - k - 1)$. After exclusion of several outliers the results of all four regressions remained similar. For our multinomial logit estimates we identified outliers using the Delta–Beta influence statistic developed by Pregibon (1981). After exclusion of two outliers (January 1995 and June 1996) the estimates for predicting a cut in interest rates remained virtually unchanged. In contrast, in both the reduced and the extended model the estimates for an *increase* in BCEAO rates altered substantially. The coefficients on lagged inflation, the lagged output gap and claims on government were each statistically significant with the expected sign.

In addition to examining the effect of serial correlation and outliers on our results, it is also worth considering to what extent our conclusions are dependent on the particular specification adopted in our OLS and multinomial logit estimates. As a first possibility, we considered to what extent our results depend on the restrictive assumption that BCEAO does not use a forecast for inflation and the output gap when setting policy. When we re-estimated our regressions while including a forecast of inflation and output (based on instruments available at time $t-1$), the results were quite close to those reported here.

Conclusion

Our empirical results provide a nuanced picture regarding monetary policy in the WAEMU. Short-term central bank rates in France (now the Euro Zone) have continued to be the most important influence on both the level of the BCEAO's discount rate and on decisions to alter the BCEAO discount rate. This is a logical implication of the CFAF's peg to the French Franc (and now the Euro). While our estimates suggest that in the long-run the BCEAO has to match changes in the Bank of France (now ECB) lending rate on a one-for-one basis, it nonetheless appears to retain flexibility in the short-run to use interest rates to react to changes in UEMOA economic conditions. We have provided evidence that the BCEAO takes into account inflation rates, the output gap, central bank claims on government and its foreign exchange position when making interest rate decisions. It should be noted, though, that the substantive magnitude of these effects remains relatively small.

Notes

We gratefully acknowledge helpful comments from Professor David Fielding, Dr Kalvinder Shields, one anonymous referee and seminar participants at the UNU-WIDER Workshop on Long Term Development in the CFA Zone Countries of Sub-Saharan Africa, Helsinki, June 2003.

1. As in Taylor (1993), Clarida, Gali and Gertler (1998), Aron and Muellbauer (2000).
2. Inflation rates show similar volatility in quarterly data, with a standard deviation of 6.4 percentage points over the 1995–2000 period. There also remains nearly as much volatility in the series if one considers a six-month backward-looking moving average for inflation rates. Here the standard deviation is 5.0 percentage

points. A six-month moving average of this form was a poorer predictor of current inflation than was a one-month lag.
3. Quarterly data from Fielding, Lee and Shields (2004). In addition, because there was evidence of seasonality of output, we regressed the output gap on a set of seasonal dummies and then used the residual from this regression as our final output gap measure for estimation. There was no strong evidence of seasonality in other variables in our data set, nor was a set of seasonal dummies statistically significant in any of the regressions we performed.
4. Banque de France repurchase rate and subsequently the ECB marginal lending facility.
5. This includes notes and coins, sight deposits of banks, financial institutions and the Treasury, and foreign currency liabilities.
6. A similar assumption is made in Fielding (2002), chapter 3.
7. This point has been made by Clarida, Gali and Gertler (1998) as well as Chevapatrakul, Mizen and Kim (2001).
8. Given the significance of a number of variables in our regressions using quarterly data, it may make sense to include three lags of our dependent variable in our monthly regressions. We began with this specification but excluded the second and third lags after we found that they were never statistically significant.
9. For reasons of tractability we ignore the fact that the BCEAO has made discrete changes of differing magnitudes in recent years.

References

Aron, J. and J. Muellbauer (2000) 'Estimating Monetary Policy Rules for South Africa', Central Bank of Chile Working Papers 89, December.

Chevapatrakul, T., P. Mizen and Tae-Hwan Kim (2001) 'Using Rules to Make Monetary Policy: The Predictive Performance of Taylor Rules Versus Alternatives for the United Kingdom 1992–2001', University of Nottingham, mimeo.

Clarida, R., J. Gali and M. Gertler (1998) 'Monetary Policy Rules in Practice: Some International Evidence', *European Economic Review*, 42: 1033–67.

Engle, R. and C. Granger (1987) 'Co-Integration and Error Correction: Representations, Estimating, and Testing', *Econometrica*, 35: 251–76.

Fielding, D. (2002) *The Macroeconomics of Monetary Union: An Analysis of the CFA Franc Zone*, London: Routledge.

Fielding D., K. Lee and K. Shields (2004) 'Modelling Macroeconomic Linkages in a Macroeconomic Union: A West African Example', Research Paper 2004/22, Helsinki: UNU-WIDER.

International Monetary Fund (IMF) (2001) 'West African Monetary Union: Recent Economic Developments and Regional Policy Issues in 2000', IMF Country Report 01/193.

Newey, W. and K. West (1987) 'A Simple Positive Semi-Definite, Heteroscedasticity and Autocorrelation Consistent Covariance Matrix', *Econometrica*, 55: 703–8.

Pregibon, D. (1981) 'Logistic Regression Diagnostics', *Annals of Statistics*, 9: 705–24.

Taylor, J. (1993) 'Discretion Versus Policy Rules in Practice', *Carnegie–Rochester Conference Series in Public Policy*, 39: 195–214.

Tenou, K. (2002) 'La Règle de Taylor: un exemple de règle de politique monétaire appliquée au cas de la BCEAO', *Etudes et Recherches* 523, March, Dakar: BCEAO.

Part III

The Franc Zone and Poverty

7
Poverty and Growth in the WAEMU after the 1994 Devaluation

Jean-Paul Azam

Introduction

The decision to devalue the CFAF in January 1994 was probably one of the longest-awaited decisions in the modern history of adjustment policies. The exchange rate with the French Franc had not changed since 1948. While the performance of the CFA Zone economies was much better than that of the other African economies until the collapse of most commodity prices in 1986–88, the latter were undoubtedly much better at adjusting to these shocks (Devarajan and Rodrik 1992). It was probably in 1989 that the need to devalue was the most acute, after the collapse of the terms of trade in most of the Zone at the end of 1987 and the decision by president Houphouët-Boigny of Côte d'Ivoire to withdraw the whole cocoa crop from the market in 1988. He was trying single-handedly to support the world cocoa market and this ruined his country's creditworthiness (Azam and Morrisson 1994). The impact of this worsening of the macroeconomic situation on poverty, in the wake of the terms-of-trade collapse, can be analysed only in the case of Côte d'Ivoire, among the CFA Zone countries, as none of the others has two household surveys performed at the relevant dates, to compare the outcomes before and after this shock. Figure 7.1, derived from Demery and Squire (1996) shows that Côte d'Ivoire saw its poverty level increase as macroeconomic policy was deteriorating, over the 1985–88 period, contrary to the countries presented for comparison. In fact, the deterioration mainly occurred during the last year of this period. Not everybody suffered equally in this country from the downturn, which had a positive distributional effect on some groups (Grootaert and Kanbur 1995). In particular, as explained later, poverty decreased over that period in the urban informal sector, especially before the terms-of-trade crash which occurred at the end of 1987 (Grootaert 1996).

It would probably be mistaken to take Côte d'Ivoire as representative of the whole CFA Zone, although it is the leading economy of this area. It fared especially badly after 1986, as its terms of trade deteriorated catastrophically, while some unwelcome policy decisions were taken. Nevertheless, the

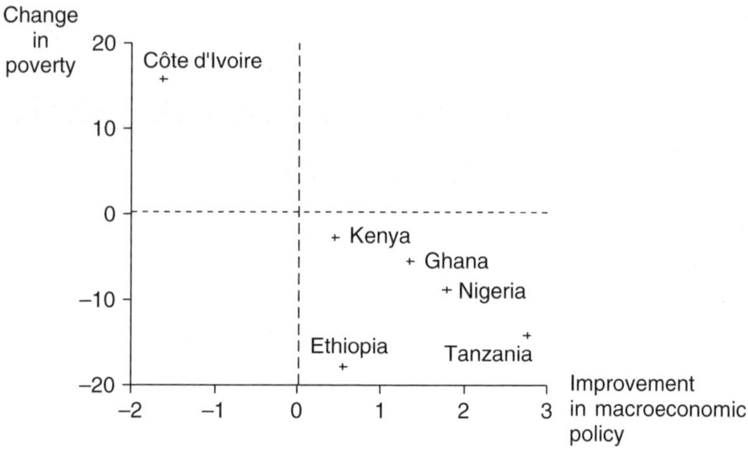

Figure 7.1 Poverty and macroeconomic policy

Source: Derived from Demery and Squire (1996).

existing analyses of the evolution of poverty over that period of deteriorating macroeconomic policies provides some clues about the relevant phenomena to look at when observing the impact of policy changes on poverty (Grootaert and Kanbur 1995; Grootaert 1996). They show the diversity of the impact on different groups of households, depending on the regions where they live, their occupation, and their socio-economic status. For example, Grootaert and Kanbur (1995) show that households from the East Forest area had a 20.4 per cent probability of improving their poverty status despite the worsening macroeconomic situation in 1987–88, while the food crop farmers had a 39.1 per cent probability of doing so over the same period. One might thus expect to meet similarly diverse effects in response to the improved macroeconomic situation that resulted from the devaluation and the accompanying measures. In fact, a much simpler picture emerges from the results presented below.

Nevertheless, despite the widespread increase in poverty in 1987–88, in the wake of the terms-of-trade crash, it was not until Houphouët's death (in December 1993) that the decision to devalue was obtained by Michel Camdessus, on behalf of the IMF, in January 1994. The theory of postponed policy reforms, developed in particular by Alesina and Drazen (1991), Fernandez and Rodrik (1991) and Casella and Eichengreen (1996), points to the uncertainty of the distributional impacts of the reforms as the main cause of delay. The results presented below, which are somehow unexpected, may provide some support to this view (see also Azam 1994). In fact, it turns out that the observed growth recovery left out many people, as poverty increased.

In the case of the CFA Zone economies, the fixed exchange rate with the FF, which has been *de facto* linked to the Deutsche Mark (DM) since 1983, together with the swings in the US dollar and in the prices of their main export commodities, had resulted in excessively high wages in the formal sector, widely recognized as such (see Van de Walle 1991). The fixed exchange rate was thus protecting 'the lucky few amidst economic decline' (Grootaert and Kanbur 1995). Therefore, many felt that the only remaining uncertainty was concerning the ability of the wage earners from the formal sector to pass on any devaluation to wage increases, thus triggering an inflationary wage–price spiral mediated by repeated devaluation. The French were wary about this and supported until the fall of 1993 the resolve of most CFA countries' rulers not to devalue, fearing probably a contagion effect on the French Franc. This did not happen, although the 1994 devaluation took place in an electoral context. Wages in the formal sector did not respond much, as shown below, and this explains the success of this policy reform, from a macroeconomic point of view.

The next section briefly presents the main impact of the devaluation on growth and inflation, focusing on the WAEMU countries. The oil-rich CEMAC countries probably require a different analysis. Growth resumed, while inflation fell short of catching up on the devaluation, leaving a high degree of effectiveness. We then look at the net effect of the devaluation package on poverty in the cases of Côte d'Ivoire and Niger, where the availability of two household surveys, before and after the devaluation, allows for some tracking of the change in poverty. Other surveys have been performed since then in other countries, mainly in the early 2000s – that is, too long after the devaluation to be really useful for the purpose at hand. The focus is put on the changes affecting the different occupational categories, which are likely to represent accurately the different segments of the labour market. A simple model will be presented to provide a theoretical framework for thinking about the way in which a cut in real formal sector wages works through the various segments of the labour market to affect the incomes of the workers in the informal sector, where most of the poor earn their living. This model is a simple dynamic analysis, which takes on board the widely observed fact that formal sector workers are generally running businesses in the informal sector, where they often hire workers from their social network (kin group, village of origin, extended family and the like). The relevance of this approach is supported by reference to some results which surprised the donor community in the late 1980s, and which square very well with the explanation presented here (Azam *et al*. 1993; Grootaert 1996).

The recovery of economic growth after the devaluation

The overvaluation of the CFAF was taking its toll on the economies of the CFA Zone before the 1994 devaluation, as can be seen by looking at their growth performance. Panels (a)–(c) of Figure 7.2 show that the most affected economy was Côte d'Ivoire, which experienced negative growth from 1987, when its terms of trade started on a steep downward slide until 1992. Most of these economies experienced some negative growth in the early 1990s, most of them in 1993 and sometimes before (such as Niger and Togo). Benin seems to have been unaffected by this phenomenon. Two main events explain the bad performance experienced in 1993 in the WAEMU. First, Côte d'Ivoire

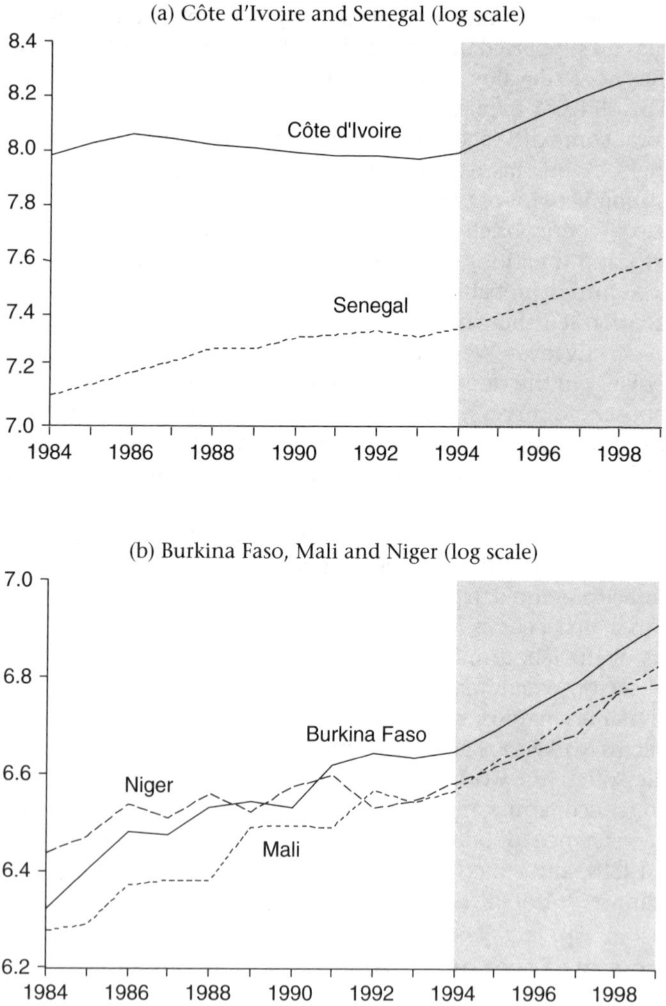

Figure 7.2 Real GDP, 1984–98

Continued

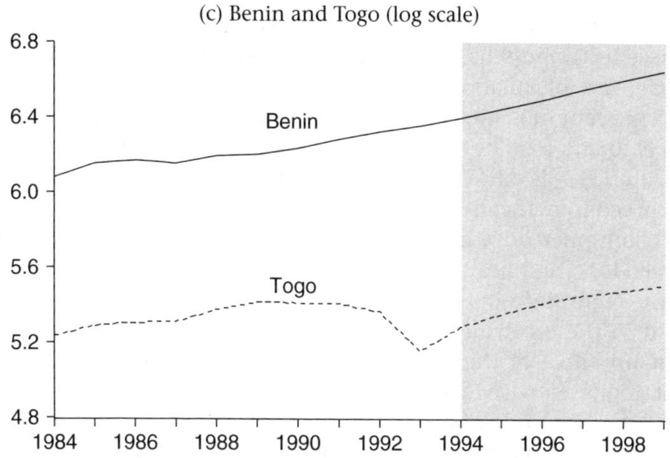

Figure 7.2 Continued

was put under sanction by the international financial institutions (IFIs), who wanted to induce its president to accept the devaluation, and the resulting lack of any external funding for supporting effective demand decimated its industrial sector; second, in August 1993, under the pressure of the French Treasury, the BCEAO suspended the external convertibility of the CFA bank notes (see Azam 1997). The cost of the resulting speculative attack, which was easily predictable from elementary open-economy macroeconomics, has been estimated at US$610 million of foreign exchange reserves. A further credit squeeze followed and made the slump more damaging. Part of the benefit of the devaluation resulted from the lifting of sanctions and from the massive loans that the countries got from outside. The IMF and the World Bank started new programmes with these governments, which relieved the self-inflicted foreign exchange shortage. With the exception of Benin, which went through 1993 without apparent trouble, growth recovered in all these countries after the devaluation and became smoother. With the exception of Benin and Senegal, all these countries saw the post-devaluation boom slow down in the year 2000, with Côte d'Ivoire, Niger and Togo going into recession.

The WAEMU countries traditionally have very low rates of inflation, for two reasons. This is due in part first to the fixed exchange rate with France, which translated into a fixed exchange rate with low-inflation Germany since 1983. It is also due, second, for some of these countries, to the fact that their consumer goods markets are largely integrated with Nigeria, through unrecorded cross-border trade, so that the fast depreciation of the naira on the parallel market entails some price deflation in some of its CFA neighbours (see Azam 1991). This is especially true of Niger. Although some of the 100 per cent devaluation was passed on to consumer prices in 1994 and the subsequent years, its effectiveness has been quite high. Between 1994 and 1996, the cumulative rate of inflation ranged between 35.6 per cent in Burkina Faso and 48.5 per cent in Benin. By 1999, this range was between 36.3 per cent in Burkina Faso and 52.6 per cent in Benin. Despite this high degree of effectiveness, the 1994 devaluation did not affect much relative consumer prices, as shown econometrically by Azam and Wane (2001). Using some disaggregated consumer price indices for Côte d'Ivoire, Niger and Senegal, they have tested for a significant change in the structure of relative prices by running some regressions on monthly prices. Only second-order effects can be identified in these consumer price series. They conclude that this cannot be the main effect of the devaluation, as no significant impact is found, for most goods. In particular, these results undermine the relevance of the view that the main role of devaluation is to affect the relative price of tradable and non-tradable goods, suggesting that this variable has been largely over-emphasized in policy debates about francophone Africa.

Figure 7.3 illustrates the main problem that faced the CFA Zone before the devaluation: too high wages in the public sector (see Van de Walle 1991; Rama 2000). In this plot, the ratio of the wage rate in the public sector to *per capita* GDP is on the *y*-axis, while the number of public agents per 1,000 inhabitants is on the *x*-axis. Figure 7.3 shows that the WAEMU countries were massively located in the north-western quarter of this space, where the average public sector wage is more than eight times larger than *per capita* GDP and more

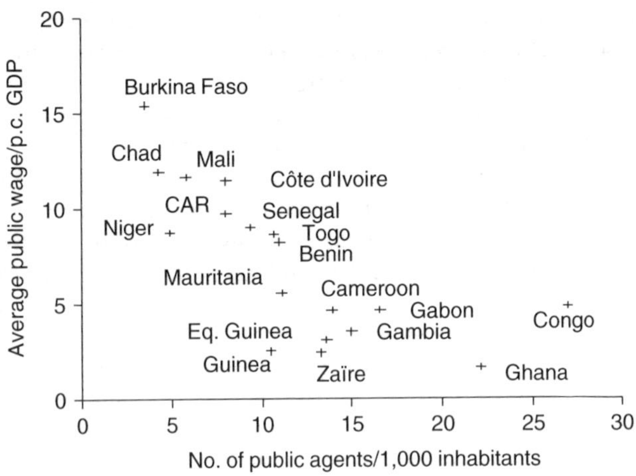

Figure 7.3 Relation between public wages and public employment, 1987

Source: Azam (1995).

than ten times so for Burkina Faso, Mali and Côte d'Ivoire. By contrast, the supply of public services, as measured by the number of public agents, is below standard. Chad and the CAR, the non-oil-exporting members of the CEMAC, are also located in the same part of the chart. This chart also suggests that wage rigidity lay at the heart of the problem, because in the lower half of this space, one finds either oil economies, where the denominator is inflated by oil revenues, or countries with a flexible exchange rate and a history of more or less rapid depreciation, that kept a check on the real wage cost of public sector employees. The non-oil fixed rates countries all suffered from excessive public sector wages, relative to the others.

Rama (2000) has analysed wage misalignment in the CFA countries and concludes that real wage rigidity is involved in the long run and not the type of nominal wage rigidity that makes devaluation work. However, the post-devaluation record shows that the catching up of public sector wages on the price level is very slow indeed. This might be due to a structural break in the real wage series, as public sector workers had long relied on France to prevent the devaluation of the CFAF and the fall in their real wages. In this interpretation, the 1994 decision came as a revelation that the former colonial power would no longer stand ready to finance any public sector deficit and therefore would not support the purchasing power of the civil servants forever. However, wages and salaries had already been cut in some countries, such as Cameroon and Senegal, and frozen in others, so that civil servants and formal sector wage earners were probably expecting that a downward adjustment of their earnings would come sooner or later, one way or another.

In any case, wage moderation in the public sector has been remarkable after the devaluation, while several electoral episodes had led some to fear some wage explosion. In particular, the 1995 elections in Côte d'Ivoire have given rise to no wage increases and this stability remained in place until the military coup of 24 December 1999, which gave rise to a large increase in the wages of military personnel. The level of public sector wages does not matter only from a budgetary point of view, as Rama (2000) has shown that it in fact affects the level of wages in the whole formal sector of the economy, by contagion. As productivity is much higher there than in the other sectors, the real cost of labour in this sector has important macroeconomic effects, insofar as it negatively affects employment and output in this sector. In Côte d'Ivoire, the hourly minimum wage rate had been CFAF 191.4 between January 1982 and February 1994, when it was increased to 212, its current value (IMF 2000a). In Senegal, it was 174.9 between April 1983 and January 1985, when it became 183.8, until July 1989, when it reached 201.1. It was then increased to 209 in December 1996 and to 209.1 in December 1997 (IMF 2000b). However, Rama's results suggest that we should not pay too much attention to this minimum wage, which does not seem to affect the wages actually paid in any sector (Rama 2000). More significant is the annual rate of change of the average wage in the central government, presented in Table 7.1,

Table 7.1 Annual rate of change of the average wage in central government, 1993–99, per cent

Year	1993	1994	1995	1996	1997	1998	1999
Côte d'Ivoire	n.a.	7.4	3.7	0.0	1.5	10.2	4.5
Senegal	−7.2	12	−5.3	3.2	−1.8	0.7	3.6

Sources: IMF (2000a), (2000b).

for the two leading economies of the WAEMU, namely Côte d'Ivoire and Senegal. It shows that wage increases have been extremely moderate in the civil service, at an annual rate below 4.6 per cent on average in Côte d'Ivoire, and below 0.8 per cent on average in Senegal, mainly because of the fall preceding the devaluation. This provides the basic stylized fact of the impact of the 1994 devaluation on the WAEMU economies: it engineered a sizeable cut in real wages in the civil service and most probably also in the whole public sector and, by contagion, in the whole formal sector. At the same time, some downsizing of the staff of the central government – by 5.1 per cent in 1994 and 1.9 per cent in 1995 – occurred in Côte d'Ivoire, although this was negligible in Senegal.

This fall in real wages in the formal sector certainly contributed to the resumption of GDP growth, both by restoring the fiscal situation, allowing public investment to recover, and by restoring the profits of the modern sector firms, boosting their incentive to invest and expand their activity. This explains the growth recovery seen above, which was fuelled by this boost of the competitiveness and profitability of the formal sector firms. However, this leaves unexplained the increase in poverty that took place at the same time. The latter is presented in detail in the next section.

Deepening poverty in Côte d'Ivoire (1993–95) and Niger (1994–95)

In this section, some results are presented on the decomposition of poverty among different socio-economic groups in Côte d'Ivoire and Niger (from Azam and Wane 2001). These two countries performed household surveys at two successive dates close to 1994, that can help shed some light on the short-run impact of the devaluation on poverty. It should be emphasized that the resulting sample is not a panel, so that a transition analysis as performed by Grootaert and Kanbur (1995) is not possible. It is thus impossible to disentangle in the observed change in the distribution of income, as measured by consumption expenditures, what is due to the impact of the devaluation from what is due to a sampling problem, such that this distribution would be different even if the devaluation had not taken place. This remark is especially relevant for Côte d'Ivoire, whose two samples are different in obvious ways, as described below. It is therefore, important to check the validity of our results by going beyond the global figures and looking at the 'before–after' changes using different decompositions of the samples, in order to check that the results seem robust in this respect. However, this does not seem to be so relevant for Niger.

Only the Côte d'Ivoire surveys are really suitable for this exercise, as one took place just before the devaluation, in 1993, followed by a second one in 1995, after a full year in the post-devaluation era. However, even this pair of surveys raises problems, which have always stood in the way of a fully satisfactory analysis of poverty in Côte d'Ivoire, despite its large number of household surveys. As emphasized by Grootaert and Kanbur (1995) and by Grootaert (1996), this country has long had a deficient price index. The consumer price index collected by the statistical office has long been restricted to Abidjan and it is only recently that a more comprehensive price index, covering some information about the countryside, has been collected. It became operational for the analysis of the 1998 household survey (see Kouadio *et al.* 2000). Here, the deflator used comes from the World Bank's (1997) tables, from which an inflation of 44 per cent can be computed, over the two years. It is probably an overestimate, as prices might possibly have increased more slowly outside Abidjan. The 1993 survey was a so-called 'priority survey' on the social dimensions of adjustment, and interviewed a total of 10,080 households. In fact, 1,680 households from Abidjan were actually surveyed in 1992, and another 480 in 1993, while all the other households were surveyed in 1993 (see Ouattara 1997). The 1995 survey was a living standards survey, with a more complete questionnaire, but a much smaller sample. Only 1,200 households were surveyed in this round, 1,000 picked fully at random and 200 among the households surveyed in 1993. This drastic difference in sample size between the two dates may legitimately raise some suspicion about how representative the second one is. This problem does not arise with the surveys of Niger.

Table 7.2 presents the contributions of different groups to poverty, using the 'FGT' measure (Foster, Greer and Thorbecke 1984). These computations are done with respect to the poverty line $z = 144{,}800$ CFAF suggested by the World Bank, for Côte d'Ivoire. Three measures of poverty are presented: the headcount ratio (P_0), the poverty gap (P_1) and the FGT2 (P_2). They are all derived from the so-called 'FGT family' (Foster, Greer and Thorbeke 1984). Its general formula is:

$$P_\alpha = \frac{1}{n}\sum_{i\leq q}\left(\frac{z - y_i}{z}\right)^\alpha \tag{7.1}$$

Table 7.2 Côte d'Ivoire: contribution to poverty of different groups before and after the devaluation, 1993–95, per cent

	Poverty line z = CFAF 144,800					
	Headcount P_0		Poverty gap P_1		FGT P_2	
	1993	1995	1993	1995	1993	1995
Socio-economic category						
Unknown	44.5	55.4	1.73	2.96	0.105	0.252
Self-employed	65.4	75.8	3.23	5.04	0.237	0.472
Unskilled employee	40.9	57.0	1.57	2.51	0.100	0.167
Traders	38.1	57.4	1.43	2.74	0.086	0.186
Skilled employees	17.6	36.1	0.498	1.40	0.025	0.085
Others	36.1	52.5	1.56	2.69	0.108	0.203
Sector of activity						
Unknown	44.5	55.4	1.73	2.96	0.105	0.253
Primary	70.3	76.3	3.58	5.17	0.266	0.490
Public	18.9	39.5	0.56	1.47	0.028	0.086
Secondary	34.2	45.2	1.20	1.78	0.069	0.107
Commerce	37.6	54.7	1.46	2.58	0.092	0.176
Transportation	38.1	40.0	1.28	1.57	0.074	0.079
Others	31.0	56.9	1.08	2.49	0.066	0.161
Education level						
None	60.0	72.6	2.83	4.51	0.201	0.409
Primary	47.2	61.4	2.00	3.48	0.133	0.281
At least secondary	20.5	41.0	0.71	1.72	0.045	0.109
Farm						
None	51.3	74.1	2.29	4.63	0.157	0.419
Exporting	49.5	46.0	2.26	2.29	0.159	0.174
Food crop	49.7	48.1	2.33	2.19	0.169	0.150
Non-farm enterprise						
Yes	47.3	62.9	1.99	3.34	0.133	0.260
No	52.7	63.0	2.52	3.85	0.181	0.349
Region						
Abidjan	12.7	38.7	0.27	1.71	0.01	0.112
Other cities	44.6	58.7	1.73	2.73	0.10	0.189
East Forest	62.2	72.2	2.66	4.01	0.17	0.338
West Forest	70.3	76.2	3.77	5.47	0.29	0.531
Savannah	77.7	80.0	4.26	5.56	0.33	0.539
Ethnic group						
Akan	42.5	62.4	1.60	3.31	0.09	0.266
Krou or Voltaic	59.0	65.3	2.99	4.10	0.22	0.372
Mande	56.6	59.4	2.85	3.59	0.22	0.315
Non-Ivoirian	46.7	63.5	2.02	3.56	0.13	0.296
Aggregate poverty	50.4	62.9	2.29	3.65	0.16	0.313

where z is the poverty line, y_i is individual is income, usually measured by consumption. The individuals are assumed to be ranked from the poorest to the richest, with i running from 1 to n, and q being the index of the individual whose income is just at the poverty line. This poverty measure has two attractive characteristics, that explain its widespread use. First, it is decomposable, in that it can be computed for different sub-groups of the population without changing the total. Second, it encompasses several widely used measures, depending on the value chosen for α. When $\alpha = 0$, it is in fact the headcount ratio q/n – that is, the ratio of the number of poor to the total population. When $\alpha = 1$, we find the headcount ratio multiplied by the average income gap – that is, the average distance of the incomes in the group of the poor to the poverty line, which can be written as follows, defining $\bar{y}$ as the average income of this group:

$$P_1 = \frac{q}{n}\frac{z - \bar{y}}{z} \tag{7.2}$$

Both of these versions of the FGT measure treat all the persons below the poverty line equally. The headcount ratio is the most widely used index, but it does not take into account the depth of poverty. The weighted poverty gap P_1 does this, but does not take into account the inequality among the poor, which it treats equally. For example, a mean-preserving spread of the income distribution among the poor, with some of them coming closer to the poverty line, while others would move into deeper poverty, would not affect it. Hence, some authors prefer to choose $\alpha = 2$, which amounts to weighting each person's poverty gap by itself, thus giving more weight to the poorest of the poor. Table 7.2 shows the values of these three measures for Côte d'Ivoire, computed from the 1993 and the 1995 surveys, according to different partitions of the population. Notice that the use of 1993 as the base year for this comparison is likely to reduce the observed deterioration of the poverty situation, compared to a normal year, because this was an especially bad year, owing to sanctions inflicted on Côte d'Ivoire by the IFIs.

The first partition in Table 7.2 aims at bringing out the different impact on different occupations. It shows that poverty increased in all the occupational categories, whichever measure is used. In relative terms, it is undoubtedly the skilled employees, a typical formal sector category, who suffered the hardest blow. The second partition presented looks at the impact by industry. Here again, poverty goes up, according to all the measures. However, it is clear that poverty went up more strongly among the public sector workers and in the commerce sector. Transportation was more or less unaffected. The sector labelled 'secondary' involves manufacturing industry and mining, and also displays a deterioration of the poverty situation.

The criterion of education in Table 7.2 provides also some interesting information. The incidence of poverty increased the most, in relative terms, among the persons with at least a secondary education level, in relative terms. Here again, this criterion points at the formal sector, as few educated persons work in the informal sector. People without any education were less affected by the deterioration, in terms of headcount. However, the use of the distribution-sensitive measures shows that all were affected. The next partition shows that people involved in farming were somehow protected from the increase in poverty. This is true for the headcount index and for the poverty gap measure, as far as the food crop growers are concerned. But it is not true for the last measure. By contrast, the fact of owning a non-farm enterprise has no discriminating power.

The next partition in Table 7.2 is especially interesting. Here, the geographic criterion is used, decomposing the population first according to the urban–rural distinction and then among the rural people, according to the most relevant regional division: Savannah, in the north, and East and West Forest zones, in the south. While the rural people have not been shielded from the increase in poverty, whichever measure is used, it is clear that urbanites suffered the strongest deterioration. Abidjan, in particular, saw its situation deteriorate massively. The West Forest and the Savannah zones had a much softer impact. The East Forest zone, the traditional Akan area, where cocoa and coffee have been grown since the beginning, saw also a non-negligible increase in poverty. Even among the relatively protected groups, in terms of headcount, the data show that the deterioration is worse the more distribution-sensitive is the measure used.

The last partition in Table 7.2 also gives some interesting clues. It is the traditionally dominant group, the Akan, who paid the largest price, in terms of deteriorating poverty. Incidence is then even larger than among the Mande, a northern group from the Savannah. In fact, the Akan have been politically dominant between independence and the 1999 military coup. They were the most numerous in the public sector and other segments of the formal sector (Azam and Morrisson 1994).

The data are therefore consistent with a story where the formal sector workers, and in particular those from the public sector, have seen their poverty situation deteriorate, and have brought down with them the living standards of other urbanites, mainly in the commerce sector, but in other sectors as well. Then, some spillover from the worsened urban situation to the rural one, in the Harris–Todaro spirit, probably followed, as the rural–urban migration probably slowed down, or even in some cases reversed itself (Harris and Todaro 1970).

Concerning the dates at which the household surveys have been performed, the data for Niger are not as suitable as the Ivorian ones, as they took place in 1994 and 1995, so that the post-devaluation era has been observed *en route*. On the other hand, their sample size is more balanced, as the 1994 survey provides a sample of 3,823 households and the 1995 one 4,067. Because the post-devaluation adjustment was already in process when the first survey was done, the inflation rate between the two rounds is smaller, namely 10.9 per cent. This might be an under-estimation of the true average increase in consumer prices that affected the sample households, because it refers to the change in prices between the two dates, at the end of the year. This is at variance with the Côte d'Ivoire case, where we might suspect an over-estimation. Moreover, the price index for Niger suffers from the same drawback as that from Côte d'Ivoire, namely that it reflects only prices in the capital city. Nevertheless, the two before–after comparisons provide roughly the same picture. In fact, Table 7.3 suggests that the increase in poverty in the wake of the devaluation is larger and deeper in Niger than in Côte d'Ivoire. Only the private sector employees, whichever the poverty measures used, and the administrative staff for P_2, seem to have seen their poverty situation improve. All the other socio-economic categories have seen poverty go up among their members, much as in Côte d'Ivoire. In relative terms again, it is in the urban sector that the blow hit the hardest. But here, even the farmers saw their poverty situation worsen.

The next section presents a simple model that helps us to think about the way in which this type of real wage cut works through the various segments of the labour market, to affect the earnings of the workers in the informal sector.

A model of informal sector wage dynamics in the shadow of the devaluation

In order to go further in the analysis, we need to take into account the type of labour market rigidity that can be observed in many developing countries: the wages in the formal sector are higher than in the other sectors and do not respond flexibly to the fluctuations of the demand for – and supply of – labour. The first authors to have drawn some consequences from this observation were Harris and Todaro (1970). In their model, the workers are facing a trade-off between working in the rural sector, where full employment prevails, or in the urban sector, where there is some unemployment, on the one hand and a formal sector with a rigid wage, on the other. The migration equilibrium is found where the mathematical expectation of the urban wage, which is equal to the formal sector wage multiplied by the probability of finding a job there, is equal to the rural wage. This model has been criticized by Jamal and Weeks (1993) as giving a distorted picture of the working of the typical African labour market, putting too much emphasis on the rural–urban wage gap, related to the so-called 'urban bias' (Lipton 1977), while wage inequalities within the urban sector are probably more significant.

The model presented here does not fall under this criticism and it takes on board the typical stratification of African labour markets. It used to be widely said, before the devaluation, that formal sector workers supported on average more than forty people with their earnings. Nowadays, people are citing

Table 7.3 Niger: contribution to poverty of different groups before and after the devaluation, 1994–95, per cent

	Poverty line z = CFAF 150,000					
	Headcount P_0		Poverty gap P_1		FGT P_2	
	1994	1995	1994	1995	1994	1995
Socio-economic category						
Idle	61.9	83.3	5.89	8.81	0.92	1.48
Management and professional	12.4	32.6	0.42	1.47	0.03	0.13
Administrative staff	23.4	52.7	1.96	2.30	0.33	0.16
Service staff	40.3	73.1	2.71	5.61	0.36	0.64
Unskilled workers	56.1	76.3	3.37	4.74	0.34	0.46
Traders	50.3	78.3	3.26	6.25	0.37	0.73
Craftsmen	47.3	77.0	3.52	7.12	0.47	0.97
Marabouts and other religions	63.2	84.8	5.43	7.94	0.83	1.15
Farmers	84.7	96.2	8.02	13.5	1.14	2.47
Status in occupation						
Unknown	63.0	92.6	6.06	12.8	0.96	2.38
Entrepreneur	45.3	54.5	2.80	3.96	0.32	0.50
Self-employed	70.8	88.0	6.22	9.96	0.87	1.58
Public sector employees	26.4	55.6	1.22	3.13	0.10	0.28
Private sector employees	84.1	63.0	7.31	4.40	0.82	0.53
Family helpers	50.0	91.4	4.20	11.7	0.75	2.13
Others	56.6	78.6	3.16	6.94	0.23	0.99
Education level						
None	70.8	91.0	6.22	11.1	0.87	1.89
Primary	43.0	79.6	2.51	6.82	0.26	0.96
At least secondary	18.2	46.8	0.90	2.68	0.09	0.26
Farming						
None	55.9	74.7	4.64	6.34	0.66	0.84
Yes	77.8	95.2	6.76	13.0	0.89	2.37
Non-farm enterprise						
None	57.1	82.2	7.10	10.1	0.77	1.82
Yes	63.9	87.4	5.17	9.60	0.68	1.50
Region						
Urban	46.7	77.8	2.80	6.66	0.29	0.84
Rural	84.2	96.4	8.90	14.4	1.39	2.79
Aggregate poverty	61.3	85.3	5.17	9.82	0.71	1.63

more generally the number of twenty. Most of the time, the relatively well off formal sector workers provide jobs for members of their social network (extended family, kin group, village of origin, etc.), either at home as domestic helpers, or in some businesses that they are running in the informal sector (taxis, small shops, garment production, food processing, etc.). These businesses also provide an outlet for their savings, which they rarely deposit with formal financial institutions. The banking crisis of the late 1980s suggests that their distrust of the banking sector was based on rational expectations. In fact, in the words of Aryeetey and Udry (1997): 'the conclusion of virtually all studies of informal finance in both rural and urban Africa is that a substantial majority of lending occurs among friends, family and neighbours.' Azam *et al*. (2001) support this view, using a sample of manufacturing firms in Côte d'Ivoire. They show that this is the cheapest way of getting funding for the firms who have access to this type of credit, while the formal banking sector caters for those who have no access to the informal sector, or who want to finance very large investment projects. Conversely, African savers invest most of their money in informal sector businesses, or even in small and medium-sized enterprises (SMEs) of the formal sector.

The formal sector workers are supposed to earn a wage w^F and to run simultaneously a small business in the informal sector. The production function for the latter is denoted $f(k, \ell)$, and is supposed to be well behaved, with constant returns to scale, and positive and decreasing marginal returns. Assume that the informal sector labour market is competitive, with a ruling wage w^I. The representative formal sector worker, assumed infinitely lived, seeks to maximize:

$$\int_0^\infty u(c)e^{-rt}dt \tag{7.3}$$

where c denotes consumption and t is time, subject to the following budget constaint:

$$dk/dt = w^F + f(k, \ell) - w^I \ell - c \tag{7.4}$$

Applying Pontryagin's Maximum Principle, one can easily derive the following three optimality conditions, where subscripts represent again partial derivatives:

$$f_\ell(k, \ell) = w^I \tag{7.5}$$

$$f_k(k, \ell) = r + \varepsilon d \log c/dt \tag{7.6}$$

and

$$\lim_{t\to\infty} u'(c)ke^{-rt} = 0 \tag{7.7}$$

Condition (7.5) simply says that the informal sector firm will hire labour up to the point where its marginal productivity is equal to the ruling wage. Condition (7.6) is the standard Keynes–Ramsey formula, equating the marginal product of capital in the informal sector, which measures the real rate of interest for the representative saver analysed here, with the subjective rate of interest. Here

$$\varepsilon = \frac{-cu''(c)}{u'(c)}$$

is the relative degree of risk aversion, more appropriately called here aversion to change. Lastly, (7.7) is the transversality condition.

Given the condition on the marginal productivity of labour, and assuming a given supply of labour $\tilde{\ell}$, equilibrium on the informal sector labour market allows us to define the profit function as:

$$\pi(k, \tilde{\ell}) = f(k, \tilde{\ell}) - \tilde{\ell} f_{\ell}(k, \tilde{\ell}) \tag{7.8}$$

Moreover, after substituting the labour supply in (7.5), one can easily derive that the equilibrium wage rate in the informal sector is an increasing function of the capital stock, by differentiating it. This yields:

$$\frac{\partial w^I}{\partial k} = f_{\ell k}(k, \tilde{\ell}) > 0 \tag{7.9}$$

There is therefore a one-to-one correspondence between the dynamics of the informal sector wage rate and that of the capital stock invested in this sector. It is more convenient to focus now on the latter.

The dynamics of the model is governed by the following pair of differential equations:

$$\frac{dc}{dt} = \frac{c}{\varepsilon}(f_k(k, \tilde{\ell}) - r) \tag{7.10}$$

and

$$\frac{dk}{dt} = w^F + \pi(k, \tilde{\ell}) - c \tag{7.11}$$

Notice that the function $\pi(k, \tilde{\ell})$ is most likely to be increasing and concave in k. It is so for the CES production function, for example, and is assumed to hold below. However, this requires some conditions on second and third derivatives, that need not detain us here, as the precise properties of this function do not affect much the dynamic analysis.

For any given value of w^F, one can draw the phase diagram of Figure 7.4. The vertical line is the locus $dc/dt = 0$, where the marginal product of capital in the informal sector is equal to the rate of time preference of the representative saver. Consumption is moving upwards for all points located on the

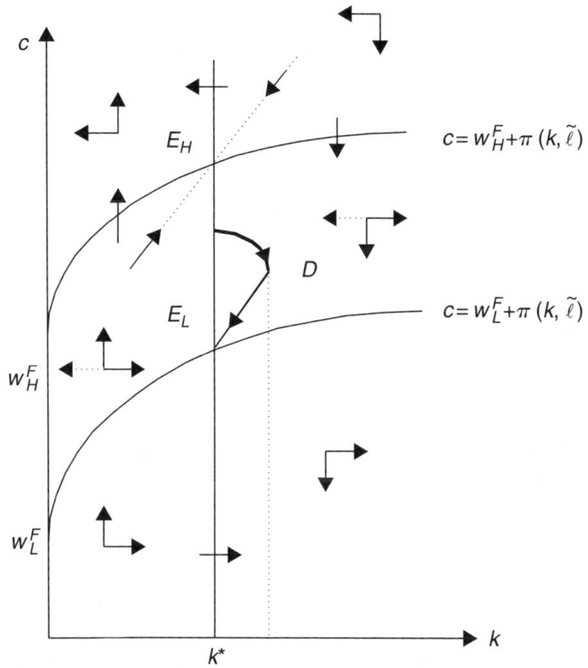

Figure 7.4 Dynamic response to anticipated devaluation

left-hand side of this vertical line, where the real rate of interest is higher than the rate of time preference, and it is moving downwards on the right-hand side. The upward sloping concave curve is the locus $dk/dt = 0$. Above it, consumption is too high, and the capital stock falls. Below it, the agent is saving, and capital is moving upwards. The arrows drawn in the different zones of the phase space represent these dynamics.

If w^F was constant, then the agent would select the saddle path of the phase diagram of Figure 7.4, drawn with a dotted line. However, we are interested here in the case where the agent is predicting that w^F will fall in the future, either because of a devaluation, or because of any other adjustment policy. Assume that the representative agent has reached initially the steady state corresponding to $w^F = w_H^F$, labelled E_H in Figure 7.4. Now, he understands at date zero, for whatever reason, that his wage will be cut at a future date T. How is he going to respond? In order to deal with this question, assume that w^F follows the following path:

$$w^F = w_H^F, \quad \text{for } t < T \tag{7.12}$$

and

$$w^F = w_L^F < w_H^F, \quad \text{for } t \geq T \tag{7.13}$$

In this case, the locus $dk/dt = 0$ shifts downwards exactly at date T and stays there for ever after. As usual with this type of model, we must work backward to find the right trajectory. It is clear that the agent must choose a consumption path which lies on the saddle path after date T, aiming at the steady state E_L, for the usual reasons. The arbitrage condition (7.6) rules out any discontinuity in the trajectory of c at any future period. Therefore, one will immediately cut their consumption at date zero, in order to follow a trajectory heading to the south-east of the phase space and reaching the saddle path at exactly date T. Such a trajectory is represented in Figure 7.4 by the curvilinear downward sloping curve, heading to the south-east. This is a divergent trajectory relative to the steady state labelled E_H, according to the dynamics prevailing prior to T. It reaches the saddle path heading to E_L at point D.

In other words, in this dynamic model, the prospect of a future cut in his formal sector wage induces the representative formal sector worker to start saving as soon as they form this prediction, for the sake of consumption smoothing. He invests these increased savings in informal sector business, with a positive impact on the wages prevailing there, and will gradually deplete this extra capital when the wage cut occurs – that is, in this case, in the wake of the devaluation – in order to slow down the fall in consumption.

The capital stock thus increases prior to the devaluation, as soon as the formal sector worker starts predicting the future wage cut and decreases gradually after its occurrence. We know from (7.9) that the informal sector wage rate will follow suit, going up in the pre-devaluation phase, starting when the prediction of the future wage cut arises, and going down in the post-devaluation phase. This analysis thus predicts that the informal sector thrives in the shadow of the devaluation, leading to the so-called 'informalization' of the economy, but begins to suffer when the light resumes.

Casual observation suggests that the process of 'informalization' just described occurred in most CFA Zone countries as soon as the structural adjustment programmes started. In the case of Niger, Azam *et al.* (1993) have described the expansion of the informal sector in the city of Niamey in the wake of the adoption of a structural adjustment programme (SAP) in 1982. This was made possible thanks to a pair of surveys of the informal sector performed by the local Statistical Office with the support of the ILO, in 1981, just before the change in policy, and in 1988. A point that was regarded by many as contentious at the time was that the wages in the informal sector firms were going up by about 20 per cent between these two dates, in real terms. The number of established informal sector firms – that is, disregarding street vendors, door-to-door craftsmen, etc. – in Niamey increased by 125 per cent over this period, while the population increased by about 33 per cent. The average number of employees per firm increased from 1 to 1.4. The local donor community was puzzled. The model just presented offers a neat interpretation of this observation: as formal sector workers perceived their position in the formal sector under threat, especially in various state-owned enterprises (SOEs), they increased their savings and investment in informal sector firms. This had a positive impact on wages there.

I am not aware of similar data for Côte d'Ivoire, where only indirect evidence is available. The 'informalization' process is nevertheless highly plausible there as well, in view of the existing evidence. According to Grootaert (1996), informal sector employment grew steadily between 1980, at the beginning of the adjustment process, and 1992 (Grootaert 1996: 81). It increased over this twelve-year period by 153 per cent, while it increased in the whole country by only 52 per cent. Moreover, there is some evidence of rural – urban migration over this period, as employment in agriculture only grew by 38 per cent. This suggests that earnings in the informal sector became more attractive than in agriculture over that period. In the meantime, employment in the 'modern sector' fell by 14 per cent, reflecting the effects of the two waves of adjustment programmes (Azam and Morrisson 1994). Another indirect look at this process can be derived from the CILSS (Côte d'Ivoire Living Standard Survey), which took place in four rounds in 1985–88. It shows that the incidence of extreme poverty fell in the informal sector, for both employees and self-employed, between 1985 and 1987 (Grootaert 1996: 81). Then, it increased abruptly in 1988, in the wake of the terms-of-trade crash that occurred at the end of 1987. Nevertheless, the self-employed in this sector remained better off in 1988 than in 1985, according to this criterion.

Conclusion

This chapter has analysed the effects of the 1994 devaluation of the CFAF on growth and poverty in the WAEMU, with a medium-run horizon. Examination of the data has first shown that the crucial channel of impact is the fall in the real wages of the formal sector workers, which had not been achieved by any other means in most CFA Zone countries. Labour markets are known to be segmented in African economies, between the rural and the urban sector, on the one hand and, within the latter, between the formal and the informal sector, on the other. This is what the classic Harris–Todaro (1970) model is meant to capture. I did not follow this path here and modelled instead the stratification of the labour market between formal and informal sectors. The crucial link is through the fact that formal sector workers, who are much more affluent than the other workers in most countries of the CFA Zone, are running businesses in the informal sector. They invest their savings in small firms, where they generally employ people from their social network.

Then, it is the increase in saving induced by the prospect of a future wage cut, because of an expected devaluation or other reasons, that drives the predicted dynamics of the model. For the sake of smoothing consumption, formal sector workers begin to increase their saving in anticipation of the cut in their purchasing power, and invest more in their informal sector firms. This entails an increase in informal sector wages, in the pre-devaluation period, as capital intensity increases in equilibrium. However, when the cut comes, as it did after the 1994 devaluation, then savers are gradually running down their assets and informal sector wages go down. It is thus a medium-run model of a stratified labour market, as it takes into account capital accumulation and decumulation, while it does not take on board longer-term processes such as technical progress and the accumulation of human capital. In particular, it does not take into account the improvement in public finance that resulted from the policy change and which in due course will improve the supply of health and education services.

This provides a rationale for an observation which at first seems puzzling, namely that poverty increased a lot in the wake of the 1994 devaluation in Côte d'Ivoire and Niger, and most probably also in other CFA Zone countries. The designers of this measure were expecting a response in the other direction, hoping that the depreciation would mainly entail an improvement in agricultural prices, boosting the incomes of the rural poor. The results found by looking at the change in various standard measures of poverty before and after the devaluation in Côte d'Ivoire and Niger show, in fact, a marked deepening of poverty, despite the resumption of GDP growth. Only the people somehow related to agriculture got some relative protection from the cut in living standards in Côte d'Ivoire. Preliminary results using the 1998 survey by Kouadio *et al.* (2000) and by Grimm (2001), while using different approaches, confirm that urban poverty increased in Côte d'Ivoire in the wake of the devaluation, while they show that some recovery took place in the rural sector, especially among food crop farmers and export crop farmers from the West Forest area. This was in part the result of the improvement in world prices for export crops. While unexpected at the time of the decision, this type of de-linking of growth and poverty is not unheard of. Deaton (2001: 125) concludes: 'Thus economic growth, as measured, has at best a weak relationship with poverty, as measured.' The story presented here suggests that the standard favourable impact of a devaluation, mediated by the recovery of economic growth, should be expected only from an unexpected devaluation.

These results are not perfectly satisfactory, in so far as the data are not ideally suited for this exercise. In both countries, there are problems with the CPI, while the 1995 survey in Côte d'Ivoire has a small sample and the 1994 survey in Niger was performed while the devaluation was already in process. The convergent results of these two before–after comparisons, for two very different countries, at a drastically different level of income *per capita*, suggest either of two conclusions: (1) the labour earnings of the poor really have fallen behind the devaluation-induced price rises, entailing a fall in their real incomes, or (2) we have a more fundamental methodological problem, namely that consumption expenditures are in this case a misleading indicator of incomes, because despite some increase in labour earnings, households have decided to reduce consumption in order to restore the level of their assets. After all, the real balance effect is one of the standard mechanisms whereby a devaluation is supposed to help cutting absorption, in standard open-economy macroeconomics. Only a detailed study of the evolution of earnings in different segments of the labour market, which falls outside the scope of the present chapter, can hope to shed some light on this issue. Nevertheless, it seems unlikely that the poor held a lot of nominal assets whose real value was cut by the devaluation, beside the wages of their relatives working in the formal sector.

Note

This paper was presented at the UNU-WIDER Project Meeting: Long Term Development in the CFA Zone Countries of Sub-Saharan Africa, Helsinki, 27–28 June 2003. Useful comments by Lambert N'Galadjo Bamba, Jean-Claude Berthélemy, David Fielding, Moubarack Lo and Anja Shortland are gratefully acknowledged. This chapter uses some statistical results initially presented in 'The 1994 Devaluation and Poverty in the WAEMU' (Azam and Wane 2001). It has benefited from comments by Lionel Demery, and by participants at an IDS/World Bank meeting in Brighton, UK in April 1999. The interpretation of these results, and the analytical model that supports it, are new. The views expressed are those of the author, and do not necessarily represent those of the World Bank. Special thanks are due to Idrissa Ouattara.

References

Alesina, A. and A. Drazen (1991) 'Why Are Stabilizations Delayed?', *American Economic Review*, 81(5): 1170–88.

Aryeetey, E. and C. Udry (1997) 'The Characteristics of Informal Financial Markets in Sub-Saharan Africa', *Journal of African Economies*, 6(1): 161–203.

Azam, J.-P. (1991) 'Niger and the Naira: Some Monetary Consequences of Cross-Border Trade with Nigeria', in A. Chhibber and S. Fischer (eds), *Economic Reform in sub-Saharan Africa*, Washington, DC: World Bank: 66–75.

Azam, J.-P. (1994) 'The Uncertain Distributional Impact of Structural Adjustment in sub-Saharan Africa', in R. van der Hoeven and F. van der Kraaij (eds), *Structural Adjustment and Beyond in sub-Saharan Africa: Research and Policy Issues*, DGIS, London: James Currey and Heinemann: 100–13.

Azam, J.-P. (1995) 'L'Etat auto-géré en Afrique', *Revue d'économie du développement*, 4: 1–19.

Azam, J.-P. (1997) 'Public Debt and the Exchange Rate in the CFA Franc Zone', *Journal of African Economies*, 6(1): 54–84.

Azam, J.-P., B. Biais, M. Dia and C. Maurel (2001) 'Informal and Formal Credit Markets and Credit Rationing in Côte d'Ivoire', *Oxford Review of Economic Policy*, 17(4): 520–34.

Azam, J.-P., C. Bonjean, G. Chambas and J. Mathonnat (1993) *Le Niger: La pauvreté en période d'ajustement*, Paris: L'Harmattan.

Azam, J.-P. and C. Morrisson (1994) *The Political Feasibility of Adjustment in Côte d'Ivoire and Morocco*, Paris: OECD, Development Centre Studies.

Azam, J.-P. and W. Wane (2001) 'The 1994 Devaluation and Poverty in the WAEMU', Washington, DC: World Bank, unpublished.

Casella, A. and B. Eichengreen (1996) 'Can Foreign Aid Accelerate Stabilisation?', *Economic Journal*, 106(436): 605–19.

Deaton, A. (2001) 'Counting the World's Poor: Problems and Possible Solutions', *World Bank Research Observer*, 16(2): 125–47.

Demery, L. and L. Squire (1996) 'Macroeconomic Adjustment and Poverty in Africa: An Emerging Picture', *World Bank Research Observer*, 11: 39–59.

Devarajan, S. and D. Rodrik (1992) 'Do the Benefits of Fixed Exchange Rates Outweigh their Costs: The CFA Zone in Africa?', in I. Goldin and L.A. Winters (eds), *Open Economies: Structural Adjustment and Agriculture*, Cambridge: Cambridge University Press: 66–92.

Fernandez, R. and D. Rodrik (1991) 'Resistance to Reform: Status Quo Bias in the Presence of Individual-Specific Uncertainty', *American Economic Review*, 81(5): 1146–55.

Foster, G., J. Greer and E. Thorbecke (1984) 'A Class of Decomposable Poverty Measures', *Econometrica*, 52: 761–6.

Grimm, M. (2001) 'A Decomposition of Inequality and Poverty Changes in the Context of Macroeconomic Adjustment: A Microsimulation Study for Côte d'Ivoire', WIDER Discussion Paper 2001/91, Helsinki: UNU-WIDER.

Grootaert, C. (1996) *Analyzing Poverty and Policy Reform*, with contributions from L. Demery and R. Kanbur, Aldershot: Avebury.

Grootaert, C. and R. Kanbur (1995) 'The Lucky Few Amidst Economic Decline: Distributional Change in Côte d'Ivoire as Seen Through Panel Data Sets, 1985–88', *Journal of Development Studies*, 31(4): 603–19.

Harris, J.R. and M.P. Todaro (1970) 'Migration, Unemployment, and Development: A Two-Sector Analysis', *American Economic Review*, 60: 126–42.

IMF (2000a) 'Côte d'Ivoire: Selected Issues and Statistical Appendix', Washington, DC: IMF, unpublished.

IMF (2000b) 'Senegal: Recent Economic Developments', Washington, DC: IMF, unpublished.

Jamal, V. and J. Weeks (1993) *Africa Misunderstood or Whatever Happened to the Rural–Urban Gap?*, London: Macmillan.

Kouadio, A. K., M. N'Zi, D. N'Guessan and I. Ouattara (2000) 'Ajustement monétaire et pauvreté alimentaire en Côte d'Ivoire, rapport d'étape révisé', CREA-AERC, University of Abidjan, Cocody, mimeo.

Lipton, M. (1977) *Why Poor People Stay Poor: A Study of Urban Bias in World Development*, London: Temple Smith.

Ouattara, I. (1997) *Profil de pauvreté en Côte d'Ivoire 1993 et 1995, résultats définitifs*, Abidjan: Institut national de statistiques.

Rama, M. (2000) 'Wage Misalignment in CFA Countries: Were Labour Market Policies to Blame?', *Journal of African Economies*, 9(4): 475–511.

Van de Walle, N. (1991) 'The Decline of the Franc Zone: Monetary Politics in Francophone Africa', *African Affairs*, 90: 383–405.

World Bank (1997) *African Development Indicators*, Washington, DC: World Bank, diskette.

8

Economic Growth, Income Distribution and Poverty: Time-Series and Cross-Country Evidence from the Franc Zone Countries of Sub-Saharan Africa

Michael Bleaney and Akira Nishiyama

Introduction

This chapter focuses on growth in the Franc Zone countries since the 1960s, and also addresses issues of income distribution and poverty alleviation. In particular, we investigate whether recent growth models can explain the growth of Franc Zone countries and, if so, what variables account for Franc Zone growth performance. We also investigate the trends and major fluctuations in Franc Zone growth since 1971, and consider the evolution of income distribution, the share of the poorest 20 per cent in total income and the growth of the average incomes of the poorest 20 per cent. We use cross-country regressions instead of the panel-data method, as while the panel-data method is useful for deducing the short-term relationship between variables, the cross-country method reveals long-term relationships more accurately. Our interests here are the latter rather than the former.

Growth performance in an international context

The Franc Zone countries are distinctive because of their exchange rate regime and monetary arrangements. Previous research has not uncovered any clear relationship between exchange rate regimes and growth. For example, although Ghosh, Gulde and Wolf (2002: Chapter 6) find that intermediate regimes tend to have significantly faster growth than pegged or floating regimes in a large sample of 147 countries over the period 1970–99, the result is not significant once country fixed effects are included, which suggests that faster-growing countries just happen to have a particular type of exchange rate regime, without any causality necessarily being involved. Nevertheless it is interesting to investigate whether or not growth in CFA countries is adequately explained by conventional growth regressions.

Table 8.1 Regional average of economic measures

Variable	Developing countries (excl. SSA)	SSA (excl. CEMAC and UEMOA)	CEMAC	UEMOA
Economic growth 1965–90 (%)	2.05	0.97	0.82	0.18
Initial GDP per capita (log), 1965	8.09	7.31	7.46	7.17
Openness, 1965–90	0.26	0.09	0.00	0.04
Initial life expectancy (log), 1965	4.02	3.77	3.75	3.67
Central government savings, 1970–90	2.80	2.98	7.81	5.84
Tropical climate	0.57	0.87	1.00	1.00
Institutional quality, 1980	4.89	4.44	4.91	4.66
Primary product exports/GDP, 1970	0.17	0.21	0.15	0.13
Labour force growth minus population growth, 1965–90	0.38	−0.04	−0.25	−0.18
Democracy, 1975	0.41	0.27	0.17	0.06
Male schooling (secondary + higher), 1965	0.77	0.22	0.67	0.08
Terms-of-trade growth, 1965–90	0.69	−1.15	2.71	−0.38

Note: See Table A8.3 for details.

Table 8.1 shows regional averages of some economic measures for all developing countries, sub-Saharan Africa (SSA) (excluding the Franc Zone), CEMAC and UEMOA. It is obvious that UEMOA Zone countries experienced rather poor economic performance in growth rates, even relative to the rest of SSA, and the CEMAC Zone's economies also grew slightly more slowly than the average of the rest of SSA. Central government savings are much higher in CEMAC and UEMOA not only than the rest of the SSA but also than the rest of the developing countries. Since most developing countries have had substantially more inflation than the Franc Zone countries, this statistic probably reflects the much lower levels of seigniorage revenue in the Franc Zone. The difference between labour force growth and population growth is negative for the CEMAC Zone and UEMOA Zone countries, which indicates that demographic developments have been unfavourable for these countries' economic performance. While the CEMAC countries experienced higher terms-of-trade growth than the average of developing countries, that of the UEMOA countries was negative but better than the average of the rest of SSA.

Table 8.2 shows the results of re-estimating two growth models – Bleaney and Nishiyama (2002) and Sachs and Warner (1997) – with dummy variables

Table 8.2 Growth models and the dummies for the African regions (dependent variable: annual average growth rate of PPP-adjusted real GDP *per capita*, 1965–90)

	BN^b + SSA	BN + CEMAC + UEMOA + NCFASSA	SW^b + SSA	SW + CEMAC + UEMOA + NCFASSA
	(1)	(2)	(3)	(4)
Constant	−23.91**	−21.56*	−64.83	−22.95
	(−2.24)[a]	(−1.97)	(−1.60)	(−0.59)
Per capita income (*Y*)	4.78*	4.43	−1.48***	−1.42***
	(1.81)	(1.67)	(−5.82)	(−6.05)
Per capita income^2	−0.43***	−0.40**		
	(−2.68)	(−2.49)		
Openness	1.53***	1.55***	11.27***	12.04***
	(5.02)	(4.99)	(3.81)	(4.39)
Openness times *Y*			−1.14***	−1.23***
			(−3.16)	(−3.70)
Land-lockedness			−0.42	−0.16
			(−1.54)	(−0.59)
Life expectancy[c]	3.13***	2.88***	35.80*	14.93
	(3.65)	(3.20)	(1.73)	(0.75)
Life expectancy^2			−4.14	−1.58
			(−1.57)	(−0.62)
Central government savings	0.071***	0.070***	0.12***	0.085***
	(2.81)	(2.78)	(5.08)	(3.65)
Tropical climate[d]	−0.67***	−0.64**	−0.62**	−0.70**
	(−2.70)	(−2.52)	(−2.14)	(−2.56)
Institutional quality	0.35***	0.35***	0.36***	0.35***
	(4.09)	(4.00)	(3.72)	(3.91)
Primary product exports/GDP	−4.50***	−4.88***	−4.02***	−4.28***
	(−5.00)	(−5.22)	(−3.82)	(−4.35)
Labour force growth – population growth	0.97***	1.04***	0.82*	1.27***
	(2.71)	(2.68)	(1.94)	(3.07)
Democracy	4.10***	3.69***		
	(3.70)	(3.26)		
Democracy^2	−3.35***	−3.04***		
	(−3.23)	(−2.90)		
Male schooling	0.38***	0.35**		
	(2.71)	(2.39)		
Terms-of-trade growth	0.21***	0.20***		
	(3.85)	(3.32)		
SSA dummy	−0.18		−0.26	
	(−0.46)		(−0.60)	
CEMAC dummy		0.10		1.51**
		(0.16)		(2.35)
UEMOA dummy		−0.78		−0.79
		(−1.43)		(−1.41)

Continued

Table 8.2 Continued

	BN[b] + SSA	BN + CEMAC + UEMOA + NCFASSA	SW[b] + SSA	SW + CEMAC + UEMOA + NCFASSA
	(1)	(2)	(3)	(4)
NCFASSA[e]		−0.11		−0.41
		(−0.27)		(−1.03)
Adjusted R^2	0.896	0.897	0.835	0.859
Standard error	0.617	0.613	0.797	0.737
No. of observations	70	70	84	84

Notes:
[a] Figures in parentheses are *t*-statistics.
[b] Regressions labelled BN reproduce the model of Bleaney and Nishiyama (2002), and those labelled SW reproduce the model of Sachs and Warner (1997).
[c] For life expectancy, we use log of life expectancy in 1965 in order to minimize any possible endogeneity problems, while we use the 1970 value for the SW model as they did in their paper.
[d] For tropical climate, we use our own variable which amended measurement errors in Sachs and Warner's original. A full list of the amendments is available from the authors on request.
[e] NCFASSA = Non-Franc Zone SSA.
*, **, *** designate statistical significance at the 10 per cent, 5 per cent and 1 per cent levels, respectively.

for SSA regions. The SSA dummy is statistically insignificant at the 10 per cent level in the Bleaney–Nishiyama model. Likewise, decomposing the SSA dummy into the CEMAC Zone, the UEMOA Zone, and the rest of SSA, none of these regional dummies is statistically significant at the 10 per cent level. This body of evidence suggests that the independent variables included in the Bleaney–Nishiyama model – at least statistically – explain the regional uniqueness in economic growth rates of sub-sets of SSA as well as the whole SSA. In columns (3) and (4), this exercise is repeated for the Sachs–Warner model. This model also fits SSA well, but the estimated coefficient on the CEMAC Zone dummy is statistically significant at the 5 per cent level.

Table 8.3 shows the contribution of each independent variable to economic growth in OECD and SSA, *relative to other developing countries*. We use the Bleaney–Nishiyama growth model to estimate the contribution of each independent variable to economic growth in the Franc Zone countries compared with the rest of SSA and other developing countries. Each independent variable was regressed on a constant, an OECD dummy and a SSA dummy.[1] The coefficients of these dummies indicate how the average level of each variable differs between the OECD, SSA and other developing countries. The estimated coefficient on each regional dummy was then multiplied by the coefficient of each regressor in the Bleaney–Nishiyama model to derive the estimated growth effect. Then, to decompose SSA, we also regressed each independent variable in the Bleaney–Nishiyama model on a constant, dummy variables for

Table 8.3 Explaining regional difference in growth rates[a]

	OECD	SSA	NCFASSA[b]	CEMAC	UEMOA
Comparative *per capita* GDP growth	+0.63	−1.25	−1.07	−1.23	−1.87
Independent variable					
Per capita income	−2.78	+1.43	+1.41	+1.24	+1.64
Openness	+1.04	−0.31	−0.28	−0.42	−0.35
Life expectancy	+0.74	−0.87	−0.80	−0.86	−1.11
Central government savings	−0.17	+0.09	+0.01	+0.03	+0.02
Tropical climate	+0.38	−0.24	−0.21	−0.30	−0.30
Institutional quality	+1.36	−0.12	−0.15	+0.01	−0.08
Primary product exports/GDP	+0.46	−0.03	−0.15	+0.11	+0.23
Labour force growth minus population growth	−0.15	−0.49	−0.44	−0.66	−0.58
Democracy	+0.05	−0.30	−0.20	−0.28	−0.62
Male schooling	+0.31	−0.20	−0.21	−0.04	−0.26
Terms of trade growth	−0.50	−0.26	−0.38	+0.42	−0.22

Notes:
[a] All numbers are relative to the omitted region (that is, developing countries except for SSA). Figures reflect the data for the full sample of countries (more than 100 for each variable, not just those used in the regression).
[b] NCFASSA = Non-Franc Zone SSA.

OECD, Non-Franc Zone SSA (NCFASSA), the CEMAC Zone and the UEMOA Zone, and repeated the same calculation. Thus, for example, the +1.43 for *per capita* income for SSA indicates how much faster SSA is predicted to grow than other developing countries (because of its low initial *per capita* income level). SSA has a strong advantage in initial low *per capita* income through the convergence effect (since there is a well-evidenced tendency that the lower the initial income, the faster the subsequent economic growth). On average, the convergence effect adds 1.5 percentage points to economic growth of SSA. Budget management, proxied by central government savings, is better in SSA than in the other developing countries, and this adds 0.1 percentage points to SSA's economic growth. However, SSA performs very poorly in terms of the other explanatory variables, which offset good potential for rapid economic growth through the convergence effect. The low degree of democracy, the limited openness to international trade and negative terms-of-trade growth each reduce growth by 0.3 percentage points. SSA does not suffer much from specialization in primary product exports or from low institutional quality, although these factors are important to OECD countries in offsetting the disadvantage of their high initial *per capita* incomes. The geographical disadvantage of SSA is evident in the effects of tropical climate, which takes 0.25 percentage points off the annual economic growth rate. The low stock of human capital, represented by male schooling, costs 0.2 percentage points in SSA's annual growth rate. The greatest disadvantage for Africa's economic growth is poor health, proxied by life expectancy, and large non-working population, proxied by labour force growth minus population growth. While the former reduces annual economic growth by 0.87 percentage points, the latter takes off 0.5 percentage points.

The last two columns of Table 8.3 enable us to scrutinize the CEMAC Zone and the UEMOA Zone countries. For most independent variables, the estimated figures of the CEMAC and UEMOA regions are very close to those of the mean for SSA, suggesting that the CEMAC Zone countries, the UEMOA Zone countries and the rest of SSA confront similar socio-economic problems in achieving faster economic growth. However, there are some notable differences between those three regions. For the CEMAC Zone countries, the relative contributions of institutional quality, primary product exports and terms-of-trade growth are positive, while those for the average of SSA are negative. This is, however, more than offset by more negative openness and labour force growth. On the other hand, the growth rate of the UEMOA Zone countries is pulled down by poor performance in life expectancy, institutional quality and democracy, while their low dependence on primary product exports relative to the other developing countries is estimated to have added 0.23 percentage points to their annual economic growth rate.

In general, what these results show is that the Franc Zone countries are not very different from the rest of SSA in the dimensions which seem to be important in determining growth rates. Although the growth rates of Franc Zone countries have tended to be slightly inferior to the SSA average, the difference is sufficiently small that the econometric models estimated on a large sample of countries also fit Franc Zone countries.

Trends and fluctuations in growth rates

In this section of the chapter we use data on real GDP growth in the six Franc Zone countries for which a continuous series is reported in *International Financial Statistics* from 1971 to 2000. The six countries are Benin, Burkina Faso Cameroon, the Congo Republic, Senegal and Togo. Although other sources give annual growth data for more Franc Zone countries, the presumption must be that these data are less accurate.

The most important single macroeconomic event during this period was the devaluation of January 1994. This was the only change of parity during the period, but it was a large one: the external value of the CFAF was halved. Consequently prices rose rapidly during 1994 (34 per cent on average), but also stabilized quickly (inflation was down to 13 per cent in 1995 and under 5 per cent in 1996). It would appear that the currency was substantially over-valued in the years prior to devaluation, and that the devaluation achieved a significant corrective real exchange rate depreciation. Another potentially significant period was the late 1970s and early 1980s, when the prices of coffee, cocoa and oil moved up particularly sharply. Although cocoa prices fell rapidly after their peak in 1977, coffee and oil prices stayed high until the mid-1980s.

In order to get a feel for how growth rates have evolved in the Franc Zone, we regress the unweighted mean GDP growth rate of these six countries for each year on a constant, a time trend and dummies for each complete five-year period. These five-year periods are constructed to run up to years ending in '3' and '8', so that the pre-devaluation period 1989–93 constitutes one period and the immediate post-devaluation period 1994–98 another. The results of this regression are shown in Table 8.4. The first column shows the complete regression, in which only the dummies for 1979–83 (+) and 1989–93 (−) are significant (plus the constant). After sequentially eliminating the least significant variables, starting with the time trend, we end up with the second column, which still includes the insignificant 1994–98 dummy, and finally with the third column. This regression suggests that the growth rate

Table 8.4 GDP growth of Franc Zone countries,[a] 1971–2000

Dependent variable	**Unweighted six-country mean annual GDP growth (%)**		
Independent variables			
Constant	3.36	3.12	3.42
	(2.73)[b]	(6.37)	(2.99)
Time trend	0.0037		
	(0.06)		
Dummy 1974–78	−0.399		
	(−0.30)		
Dummy 1979–83	2.82	3.11	2.80
	(2.21)	(3.17)	(2.93)
Dummy 1984–88	−0.471		
	(−0.37)		
Dummy 1989–93	−3.72	−3.40	−3.70
	(−2.71)	(−3.47)	(−3.87)
Dummy 1994–98	0.877	1.22	
	(0.57)	(1.25)	
R^2	0.550	0.547	0.540
Standard error	2.01	1.90	1.92

Notes:
[a] The six countries are: Benin, Burkina Faso, Cameroon, Congo Republic, Senegal and Togo.
[b] Figures in parentheses are *t*-statistics.

Table 8.5 Growth regressions for individual countries, 1971–2000

	Dependent variable: annual GDP growth 1971–2000 (%)				
Independent variable	**Constant**	**Dummy 1974–78**	**Dummy 1989–93**	R^2	**Standard error**
Country					
Benin	3.85	1.80	−1.33	0.05	3.98
	(4.32)[a]	(0.90)	(−0.67)		
Burkina Faso	5.50	−3.73	−4.32	0.25	3.71
	(5.35)	(−1.78)	(−2.21)		
Cameroon	3.46	5.96	−7.18	0.50	4.23
	(3.57)	(2.77)	(−3.34)		
Republic of Congo	1.60	13.6	−0.18	0.49	5.45
	(1.31)	(4.99)	(−0.07)		
Senegal	3.03	0.97	−2.61	0.06	4.66
	(2.84)	(0.41)	(−1.12)		
Togo	3.98	−3.84	−7.48	0.25	5.22
	(3.37)	(−1.47)	(−2.86)		

Note: [a] Figures in parentheses are *t*-statistics.

of GDP has been fairly constant over the period, except for a period of exceptionally fast growth during the commodity boom of 1979–83, and a period of exceptionally slow growth immediately before devaluation (1989–93). If exchange rate over-valuation was the cause of this slow growth in the early 1990s, then devaluation was definitely expansionary for the Franc Zone countries.

Table 8.5 shows the same regression as in the third column of Table 8.4 for the six countries individually. Several points stand out. One is that the growth rate of the individual countries is much more variable than that of the unweighted mean (the standard error of these regressions is more than twice as large in five out of six cases). This suggests that there are substantial uncorrelated output shocks across the Franc Zone, which one would expect given the weight of agricultural production in the region. A second point is that all six countries have negative coefficients for the 1989–93 dummy, although the size of the coefficient varies widely. Finally, there is not the same consistency in the sign of the 1979–83 dummy, which is positive for four countries but quite substantially negative for two.

The main conclusions of this section are the following. The Franc Zone countries have experienced roughly constant growth (though with substantial year-to-year fluctuations) since 1970, except for a period of fast growth around 1980 and slow growth in the early 1990s. The latter shows up more consistently across countries, and was probably caused by real exchange rate over-valuation that was corrected by the devaluation of

January 1994. The period of exceptionally fast growth was evident only in some countries and was most likely associated with commodity price booms.

Poverty alleviation and income inequality

In this section, we investigate poverty and inequality in the Franc Zone countries in the cross-country framework. We first construct an empirical model of the growth rate of the income of the poor. The most serious problem here, as elsewhere, is lack of data for the Franc Zone countries. This problem is particularly serious for the quintile shares of income and the Gini coefficient, which we use in our investigation. Therefore, instead of seeking SSA models or Franc Zone models, we construct cross-country models from global data of poverty and income inequality, which explain the characteristics of Franc Zone countries as well.

Our investigation in this section uses two types of income inequality data: (1) the Gini coefficients of income distribution, and (2) the poorest quintile's income shares of the total income of the economy. The most popular measure of income inequality is the Gini coefficient, which represents the entire distribution of income. The most comprehensive cross-country data of the Gini coefficients are perhaps the UNU-WIDER WIID (World Income Inequality Database). We use version 1.0 which was last updated on 12 September 2000.[2] This database incorporates Deininger and Squire's (1996) data set of income inequality (the Gini coefficients of income distribution), which is another popular data set. The WIID covers a large number of countries within a reasonable time period. Yet, it is a collection of data from various data sources rather than a synthesized data set. In some cases the data set provides multiple data for an identical country for an identical year with several data definitions, but for other country samples it includes a large number of blanks. Therefore, even for the identical country for the identical year, the choice of numbers depends on researchers' purposes and sensitivity (see Table 8A.3).[3] The WIID database differentiates 'reliable' data from 'less reliable' data: we always chose 'reliable' data were they available. To maintain consistency, we also always chose data of national coverage and ignored those of rural or urban coverage only.

We are aware that the comparison between data of different definitions (for example, income-based or expenditure-based) is far from ideal. Because of redistribution through taxation, expenditure-based Gini coefficients (Table 8A.1) give the impression of less inequality than income-based data. Nevertheless gross income data are most frequently used in international comparison because of their wider availability, and we give preference to these data for the same reason. In the absence of gross income data, we use data based on net incomes. Expenditure data were least willingly accepted.

Deininger and Squire (1996: 582) report that, from reliable data, the 'mean difference between income-based and expenditure-based Gini coefficients is about 6.6', while the difference between other reference units is not significantly important. This is not fully satisfactory, but there is no obvious alternative.[4]

The other data on income inequality that we use are the poorest quintile's share of total income. Since the UNU-WIDER WIID does not provide data on income shares, we derive them from Deininger and Squire's 1997 database. This data set is an updated version (by adding more data from African countries) of their original data set (Deininger and Squire 1996). Just like the Gini coefficients in WIID, the data on income shares in Deininger and Squire (1997) do not measure the same dimension of inequality in every country. Therefore, the choice of data, again, depends on the researchers' purposes and decisions. The criteria that we employed are basically the same as those for the Gini coefficients (see Table A8.2). No data adjustment was made for the income shares data since no reliable method of transformation for income shares of different data units exists. Observations of the closest years to 1965 and 1990 were chosen for our data set.[5]

Note that a high (low) value in the Gini coefficient of income distribution means more (less) inequality, while a high (low) value in the income share of the poorest 20 per cent of the population indicates a less (more) unequal society. In a given empirical model specification, the expected sign of coefficients on these two measures are opposite to each other. To make the signs of coefficients on these inequality measures more consistent, we constructed an *income equality index* by subtracting the Gini coefficients (in a 100-point scale) from 100. Therefore, both the income equality index and the income share of the poorest 20 per cent of the population score higher in a more equal society compared to a less equal society. Thus, hereafter, we use the income equality index – rather than the Gini coefficients – and the income shares of the poorest quintile as our two measures of income inequality.[6] Furthermore, in constructing the change variables (annual average growth rates of the income equality index and of the income share of the poor) for our period 1965–90, the actual difference in years between the initial observation and the final observation was used, instead of simply assuming the difference was twenty-five years for all countries.

We define the 'poor' as the lowest quintile group and calculate the income of the poor and its growth rate as follows. If Y is the total income of an economy with population N, and YP is the aggregate income of those defined as 'poor', whose population is NP, then the average income of a poor person may be decomposed as follows:

$$\left(\frac{YP}{NP}\right) = \left(\frac{YP}{Y}\right) \times \left(\frac{N}{NP}\right) \times \left(\frac{Y}{N}\right) \tag{8.1}$$

Equation (8.1) says that the average income of the poor equals their share of total income, divided by their share of population, multiplied by average *per capita* income. If the share of the poor in total population is defined to be constant over time (as here), then taking logarithms and differentiating with respect to time, we get:

$$d\left[\ln\left(\frac{YP}{NP}\right)\right]/dt = d\left[\ln\left(\frac{YP}{Y}\right)\right]/dt + d\left[\ln\left(\frac{Y}{N}\right)\right]/dt \qquad (8.2)$$

which says that the rate of growth of the average incomes of the poor equals the rate of growth of their income share plus the rate of growth of average *per capita* incomes. We take (N/NP) to be 0.2, and use data on the other two terms in (8.1) for 1965 and 1990 (or dates as close as possible to these in the case of YP/Y) to calculate the growth rate of YP/Y.

In Table 8.6, in order to investigate poverty and inequality in the Franc Zone countries, we first constructed a cross-country model of the growth rate of the income of the poor. The first column shows our preferred model. The coefficient on the income share of the poorest quintile is statistically significant and has a negative sign, suggesting that the lower the initial income share of the poor, the faster the growth of their income. Equally interestingly, initial *per capita* income has a significant and negative coefficient, indicating that poorer countries tend to improve the income of the poor faster than richer countries. The estimated coefficient on openness to international trade is positive and significant at the 1 per cent level. This effect most likely reflects the strong correlation between openness and economic growth, so that the poor benefit from openness through economic growth. Life expectancy, measured at the beginning of the period, is positive and highly significant. This suggests that investment for health in hygiene and hospitals is an effective policy to combat poverty. Central government savings, which is a key determinant of growth as shown in Table 8.2, helps the poor improve their income by enlarging the whole economy. Tropical climate and the size of primary product exports (measured as the ratio to GDP) have negative coefficients. This most likely reflects findings in Sachs and Warner (1997) and Bleaney and Nishiyama (2002) that countries under a tropical climate and with high dependency on primary product exports experience slow economic growth. An interesting result is that the estimated coefficient on ethno-linguistic diversity, which was found to have a negative correlation with economic growth in Easterly and Levine (1997), has a small but positive coefficient here.[7] Our speculative explanation for this is that ethnically diverse countries are more likely to distribute their wealth in order to maintain political stability. Further, four diagnostic tests have been conducted. The model passes serial correlation, normality and heteroscedasticity tests, but fails the functional form test. However, since inequality-related data are deemed to be subject to large measurement errors, one should not be over-sensitive to the test results here. In columns (2) and (3), a dummy variable for SSA and a dummy for the Franc Zone countries are added to our preferred model. These two dummies are, respectively, not significant even at the 10 per cent level, suggesting that this model statistically explains

Table 8.6 Growth rate of the income of the poor (dependent variable: annual average growth rate of PPP-adjusted real GDP *per capita* of the poor, 1965–90)

	(A)	(A) + SSA	(A) + Franc Zone
Constant	−23.86***	−17.72**	−24.49***
	(−3.45)[a]	(−2.29)	(−3.13)
Income share of the poorest quintile	−3.27***	−3.25***	−3.28***
	(−8.14)	(−8.26)	(−7.99)
Initial *per capita* income	−3.09***	−2.95***	−3.12***
	(−8.46)	(−8.01)	(−7.78)
Openness	3.05***	3.07***	3.03***
	(5.29)	(5.44)	(5.17)
Initial life expectancy (log)[c]	9.78***	8.02***	9.98***
	(4.75)	(3.51)	(4.23)
Central government savings	0.19***	0.19***	0.19***
	(3.03)	(3.12)	(2.97)
Tropical climate	−1.68***	−1.73***	−1.70***
	(−3.59)	(−3.77)	(−3.52)
Primary product exports/GDP	−4.31**	−3.62*	−4.26**
	(−2.23)	(−1.87)	(−2.16)
Ethno-linguistic diversity	0.012*	0.014*	0.012*
	(1.75)	(1.95)	(1.73)
SSA dummy		−1.03	
		(−1.63)	
Franc Zone dummy			0.15
			(0.18)
Adjusted R^2	0.784	0.792	0.778
Standard error	1.100	1.078	1.114
No. of observations	49	49	49
Diagnostic Tests			
Serial correlation	$F(1,39) = 0.0008$		
	[0.98][b]		
Functional form[d]	$F(1,39) = 6.76$		
	[0.01]		
Normality	$\chi^2(2) = 1.52$		
	[0.47]		
Heteroscedasticity	$F(1,47) = 1.85$		
	[0.18]		

Notes:
[a] Figures in parentheses are *t*-statistics.
[b] Figures in square brackets are *p*-ratios.
[c] For life expectancy, we use log of life expectancy in 1965 in order to minimize any possible endogeneity problems.
[d] Ramsey's RESET is used to test the Functional Form.
*, **, *** designate statistical significance at the 1 per cent, 5 per cent and 10 per cent levels, respectively.

Table 8.7 Change in the income share of the poor (dependent variable: annual average change in the income share of the poorest quintile, 1965–90)

	(B)	(B) + SSA	(B) + Franc Zone
Constant	0.76***	0.86***	0.77***
	(4.37)	(4.88)	(4.38)
Initial income share of the poor	−0.031***	−0.032***	−0.031***
	(−7.74)	(−8.20)	(−7.64)
Per capita income	−0.049***	−0.059***	−0.050***
	(−3.22)	(−3.77)	(−3.25)
Central government savings	0.0056*	0.0069**	0.0061*
	(1.70)	(2.13)	(1.81)
Initial fertility ratio (log)	−0.15***	−0.16***	−0.15***
	(−4.06)	(−4.48)	(−4.06)
Ethno-linguistic diversity	0.00063**	0.00091***	0.00069**
	(2.04)	(2.77)	(2.16)
SSA dummy		−0.052*	
		(−1.98)	
Franc Zone dummy			−0.027
			(−0.74)
Adjusted R^2	0.548	0.577	0.543
Standard error	0.054	0.052	0.054
No. of observations	49	49	49
Diagnostic Tests			
Serial correlation	$F(1, 42) = 0.26$		
	[0.61]		
Functional form	$F(1, 42) = 0.27$		
	[0.61]		
Normality	$\chi^2(2) = 2.09$		
	[0.35]		
Heteroscedasticity	$F(1, 47) = 7.00$		
	[0.01]		

Notes: See Table 8.6 for notes.

differentials in the growth rate of the income of the poor in SSA and the Franc Zone countries.

In Table 8.7, we constructed an empirical model to investigate the change in the income share of the poor. The estimated coefficients on the initial income share of the poor and *per capita* income are negative. They show that the more unequal and the poorer the country is, the faster the income share of the poor increases. Central government savings have a positive and significant coefficient. Sound management of government budgets probably reflects a dimension of capability of the government, which may influence efficient policy management to handle income inequality. The coefficient on the initial fertility ratio is negative, indicating that high fertility is a more serious obstacle for the poor than the rich in improving their standard of living. Ethno-linguistic diversity is positively correlated with change in the income share of the poor, suggesting that an ethnically diverse society is more enthusiastic over income distribution. The model passes three out of four diagnostic tests, but does not succeed in the heteroscedasticity test. If a dummy for SSA is added to the regression, it is significant but only at the 10 per cent level (p-ratio = 0.054). The model is robust to the addition of the Franc Zone dummy.

As shown in (8.1), the growth rate of the income of the poor is decomposable into the growth rate of the income share of the poorest 20 per cent and the growth rate of *per capita* GDP. The results in Table 8.7 can therefore be regarded as a combination of these two factors – the growth rate of the economy as a whole and changes in income distribution. In Table 8.8, we show

Table 8.8 Changes in the equality index (dependent variable: annual average change in the equality index, 1965–90)

	(C)	(C) + SSA	(C) + Franc Zone
Constant	2.34***	2.44***	2.39***
	(6.55)	(7.03)	(6.62)
Initial equality index	−0.029***	−0.031***	−0.029***
	(−6.97)	(−7.61)	(−7.05)
Tropical climate	−0.22*	−0.19*	−0.23**
	(−1.92)	(−1.79)	(−2.05)
Initial fertility rate(log)[a]	−0.39***	−0.34***	−0.40***
	(−2.95)	(−2.66)	(−3.02)
SSA dummy		−0.25**	
		(−2.47)	
Franc Zone dummy			0.19
			(1.01)
Adjusted R^2	0.401	0.443	0.401
Standard error	0.304	0.293	0.304
No. of observations	71	71	71
Diagnostic Tests			
Serial correlation	$F(1,66) = 0.12$		
	[0.73]		
Functional form	$F(1,66) = 0.85$		
	[0.36]		
Normality	$\chi^2(2) = 4.19$		
	[0.12]		
Heteroscedasticity	$F(1,69) = 6.83$		
	[0.01]		

Notes: See Table 8.6 for notes.
[a] For fertility ratio, we use log of fertility ratio in 1965 in order to minimize any possible endogeneity problems.

an empirical model which explains international differences in changes in income inequality between 1965 and 1990, as measured by Gini coefficients (rather than the share of the poorest 20 per cent of the population). Tropical climate and initial fertility are the only significant independent variables. The estimated coefficients on tropical climate and initial fertility are both negative, suggesting that countries under a tropical climate and with high fertility rates tend to experience slower improvement in income equality. The model passes three diagnostic tests, but does not pass the heteroscedasticity test. The model is robust to the addition of the Franc Zone dummy but not to the addition of the SSA dummy.

Conclusions

The main conclusion from this chapter is that existing growth models are capable of explaining the growth of Franc Zone countries, as well as of other SSA countries. The factors which contribute to the slow growth of the Franc Zone over the 1965–90 period are much the same as for other SSA countries. There is no significant trend in Franc Zone growth rates since 1970, but there have been periods of particularly high growth (around 1980) and slow growth (in the years before the January 1994 devaluation). Cross-country models of the growth of the income of the poorest 20 per cent of the population, and the change in equality (or the poor's income share) fit the Franc Zone as well, in the sense that a Franc Zone dummy is insignificant when added to these regressions.

Data Appendix

Table 8A.1 Gini coefficients

Country	Gini c.1965	Data description Gini c.1965[c]	Gini c.1990	Data description Gini c.1990[c]
Argentina	42 (1961)[a]	G, P, ?, AP	48 (1989)	G, P, M, AP
Australia	32 (1967)*,[b]	G, P, AA, AP	41.72 (1990)*,[b]	G, H, AA, AP
Austria	29.3 (1970)*	G, P, AA, IR	31.6 (1987)*	SPDS[d]
Bahamas	48.41 (1970)*	G, H, AA, AP	41.83 (1991)*	G, H, AA, AP
Bangladesh	34.34 (1966)*	G, H, AA, AP	37 (1986)*	G, H, AA, AP
Barbados	36.2 (1962)	I, P, AA, T	NA	
Belgium	36.37 (1969)*	G, H, AA, T	31.9455 (1992)*	G, H, AA, AP
Benin	42 (1959)	G, P, AA, AP	NA	
Bolivia	53 (1968)*	G, P, AA, AP	42.04 (1990)*	E, P, AA, AP
Botswana	57.4 (1971)	I, P, AA, EA	54.21 (1986)*	E, H, AA, AP
Brazil	57.61 (1970)*	G, H, AA, AP	60.6 (1990)*	G, HC, AA, AP
Bulgaria	22.23 (1965)*	G, P, AA, AP	24.53 (1990)*	SPDS
Canada	31.61 (1965)*	G, H, AA, AP	35.0807 (1991)*	G, H, AA, AP
Chad	35 (1958)	G, P, AA, AP	NA	
Chile	45.64 (1968)*	G, H, AA, AP	54.7 (1990)*	G, H, AA, AP
China	30.5 (1964)*	G, H, AA, AP	34.6 (1990)*	G, P, AA, AP
Colombia	62 (1964)*	G, P, AA, AP	51.32 (1991)*	G, P, AA, AP
Costa Rica	50 (1969)*	G, P, AA, AP	46 (1989)*	G, P, AA, AP
Côte d'Ivoire	51.7 (1970)	I, P, AA, EA	36.9 (1988)*	E, HC, AA, AP
Cuba	28.114 (1962)	G, P, AA, IR	NA	
Czechoslovakia	22.6 (1965)*	N, HC, AA, AP	20.1 (1988)*	SPDS
Denmark	24.908 (1966)*	G, H, AA, AP	39 (1990)*	G, H, AA, AP
Dominican Republic	45.5 (1969)	G, P, AA, AP	51 (1989)*	G, P, AA, AP
Ecuador	38 (1968)*	G, P, AA, AP	50 (1993)*	G, P, AA, AP
Egypt	40 (1965)*	E, H, AA, AP	32 (1991)*	E, HC, AA, AP
El Salvador	53 (1965)*	G, P, AA, AP	53 (1994)*	G, P, AA, AP
Fiji	46 (1968)*	G, P, AA, AP	NA	
Finland	34.2 (1966)*	G, H, AA, AP	25.5 (1990)*	G, H, AA, AP
France	47 (1965)*	G, H, AA, AP	37.2 (1984)*	G, HC, AA, AP
Gabon	64 (1960)*	G, P, AA, AP	NA	
Germany, West	38 (1964)*	N, H, AA, AP	26 (1990)*	N, H, AA, AP
Greece	44.1 (1965)	I, P, AA, T	35.16 (1988)*	E, H, AA, AP
Guatemala	29.96 (1966)	I, H, R, IR	59.06 (1989)*	G, P, AA, AP
Honduras	61.88 (1968)*	G, H, AA, AP	54 (1990)*	G, P, AA, AP
Hong Kong	49 (1966)*	G, H, AA, AP	45 (1991)*	G, H, AA, AP
Hungary	22.91 (1967)*	N, P, AA, AP	20.42 (1991)*	N, HC, AA, AP
India	31.14 (1965)*	E, P, AA, AP	29.69 (1990)*	SPDS
Indonesia	33.3 (1964)*	E, P, AA, AP	33.18 (1990)*	E, P, AA, AP

Continued

Table 8A.1 Continued

Country	Gini c.1965	Data description Gini c.1965	Gini c.1990	Data description Gini c.1990
Iran	41.88 (1969)*	E, P, AA, AP	42.9 (1984)	E, P, AA, AP
Ireland	36.7 (1973)	N, H, AA, AP	35.2 (1987)*	SPDS
Israel	37.08 (1961)*	I, P, AA, T	45.3 (1992)*	I, P, AA, AP
Italy	40 (1967)*	N, H, AA, AP	32.5 (1991)*	SPDS
Jamaica	41.272 (1971)	E, H, AA, AP	41.1 (1991)*	E, HC, AA, AP
Japan	34.8 (1965)*	G, H, AA, AP	35 (1990)*	G, H, AA, AP
Kenya	63 (1964)	I, P, AA, T	57.5 (1992)*	E, HC, AA, AP
Korea, South	34.34 (1965)*	G, H, AA, AP	33.64 (1988)*	G, H, AA, AP
Lebanon	55 (1960)*	G, P, AA, AP	NA	
Madagascar	53 (1960)*	G, P, AA, AP	46 (1993)*	E, HC, AA, AP
Malawi	45.2 (1969)	I, P, AA, IR	62 (1993)*	E, P, AA, AP
Malaysia	48.3 (1967)*	G, H, AA, AP	48.35 (1989)*	G, P, AA, AP
Mexico	55.5 (1963)*	G, H, AA, AP	53.09 (1989)*	G, P, AA, AP
Morocco	50 (1965)	G, P, AA, AP	39.2 (1991)*	E, HC, AA, AP
Myanmar	35 (1958)	G, P, AA, AP	NA	
Netherlands, The	35.4 (1967)*	N, H, AA, T	29.3846 (1991)*	N, HC, AA, AP
New Zealand	57.7 (1965)	I, P, AA, T	40.21 (1990)*	G, H, AA, AP
Niger	34 (1960)*	G, P, AA, AP	36.1 (1992)*	E, HC, AA, AP
Nigeria	57.94 (1970)*	N, P, AA, T	41.15 (1992)*	E, P, AA, AP
Norway	36.04 (1967)*	N, H, AA, AP	33.31 (1991)*	SPDS
Pakistan	35.51 (1966)*	G, H, AA, AP	32.38 (1988)*	G, H, AA, AP
Panama	48 (1969)*	G, P, AA, AP	57 (1989)*	G, P, AA, AP
Peru	61 (1961)*	G, H, AA, AP	46.43 (1991)*	G, H, AA, AP
Philippines	50.5 (1965)*	G, H, AA, AP	47.7 (1991)*	SPDS
Poland	26 (1965)	I, P, AA, AP	31 (1990)*	G, H, AA, AP
Portugal	40.58 (1973)	N, H, AA, AP	36.76 (1990)*	N, H, AA, AP
Puerto Rico	52.32 (1969)*	G, H, AA, AP	50.86 (1989)*	SPDS
Senegal	56 (1960)*	G, P, AA, AP	54.12 (1991)*	E, P, AA, AP
Sierra Leone	56 (1968)*	G, P, AA, AP	62.9 (1989)*	E, HC, AA, AP
Singapore	49.83 (1966)*	G, P, AA, EP	39 (1989)*	G, H, AA, AP
South Africa	56 (1965)	I, P, AA, AP	63 (1990)*	G, HC, AA, AP
Spain	31.99 (1965)*	G, H, AA, AP	32.99 (1991)*	G, H, AA, AP
Sri Lanka	47 (1963)*	G, H, AA, AP	46.7 (1987)*	SPDS
Sudan	38.72 (1968)*	G, H, AA, AP	NA	
Surinam	30 (1962)*	G, P, AA, AP	NA	
Sweden	37.9242 (1967)*	G, H, AA, AP	31.112 (1992)*	SPDS
Taiwan	32.43 (1966)*	N, P, AA, AP	30.11 (1990)*	SPDS
Tanzania	54 (1964)*	G, P, AA, AP	59.01 (1991)*	E, P, AA, AP
Thailand	42.9 (1968)*	G, H, AA, AP	48.8 (1990)*	G, H, AA, AP
Trinidad and Tobago	53.9 (1971)	G, H, AA, AP	40.3 (1992)	I, HC, AA, AP
Tunisia	42.3 (1965)*	E, P, AA, AP	41 (1990)*	E, P, AA, AP
Turkey	56 (1968)*	G, H, AA, AP	44.09 (1987)*	G, H, AA, AP
Uganda	40.7 (1970)	I, P, AA, AP	40.78 (1992)*	E, P, AA, AP
Ukraine	24.6 (1968)*	I, P, AA, EP	24.4 (1989)*	I, P, AA, EP
United Kingdom	24.3 (1965)*	N, H, AA, AP	32.3 (1990)*	SPDS
United States	34.64 (1965)*	G, H, AA, AP	37.8 (1990)*	SPDS

Continued

Table 8A.1 Continued

Country	Gini c.1965	Data description Gini c.1965	Gini c.1990	Data description Gini c.1990
Uruguay	44.9 (1967)	I, H, AA, AP	NA	
USSR	26.2 (1968)*	I, P, AA, EP	27.2 (1989)*	I, P, AA, EP
Venezuela	42 (1962)	G, P, AA, AP	44.4 (1990)*	G, P, AA, AP
Yugoslavia	30.6 (1965)*	G, P, AA, IR	31.88 (1990)*	SPDS
Zambia	79.5 (1970)	I, P, AA, IR	43.51 (1991)*	E, P, AA, AP
Zimbabwe	66.27 (1968)	I, P, AA, IR	56.83 (1990)*	E, P, AA, AP

Notes:

[a] Figures in parentheses are the years of observations.

[b] In the second and the fourth columns, * indicates that the data are categorized as reliable data in our data set. Data were categorized as reliable in our data set if they satisfied both of the two criteria: (1) data are categorized as 'reliable data' *in the WIID*; (2) A gap between the year of observation and the year of concern (1965 or 1990) is no more than five years.

[c] In columns of data description, income definition, reference unit, area coverage and *population coverage* are shown in order. (1) Income definition: G = Gross income; N = Net income; I = other income, or no information on the type of income is available; E = Expenditure. (2) Reference unit: H = Household; P = Person; HC = Household *per capita*. (3) Area coverage: AA = All area; M = Metro Area; R = Rural area; ? = no information given. (4) Population coverage: AP = All population; IR = Income recipients; T = Tax payers; EA = Economically active population; EP = Employed population.

[d] In the fifth column, SPDS means that the data around 1990 are from the Same Primary Data Source of the data around 1965 and also the data share the identical data definition with the data employed for 1965. When data c.1990 are available and data c.1965 are not available, such country samples were not included in our data set for the nature of our analysis. The figures shown are pre-adjustment values. For our analysis, +6.6 was added to the figures shown, if income definition is expenditure. Our income equality indices were constructed by [100 – Gini coefficient]. As for the change variables, which we created for the dependent variables, only if all the data used in the calculation are reliable data, the created figures were categorized as reliable data; otherwise, the created figures were included only in the largest possible sample.

Table 8A.2 The poorest quintile's income share of the total income

Country	Poorest quintile's income share c.1965	Data description[a]	Poorest quintile's income share c.1990	Data description[a]
Argentina	0.0700 (1961)	I, P, AA	NA	
Australia	0.0699 (1969)*	G, H, AA	0.0460 (1990)*	SPDS
Austria	0.0680 (1970)	G, P, AA	0.0690 (1987)	SPDS
Bahamas	0.0288 (1970)*	G, H, AA	0.0389 (1991)*	G, H, AA
Bangladesh	0.0690 (1963)*	G, H, AA	0.0950 (1989)*	E, P, AA
Benin	0.0800 (1959)	G, P, AA	NA	
Bolivia	0.0350 (1968)	G, P, AA	0.0562 (1990)*	E, P, AA
Brazil	0.0320 (1960)*	G, H, AA	0.0248 (1989)*	G, P, AA
Bulgaria	0.1036 (1965)*	G, P, AA	0.1054 (1990)*	SPDS
Canada	0.0713 (1965)*	G, H, AA	0.0754 (1990)*	G, H, AA
Chad	0.0800 (1958)	G, P, AA	NA	
Chile	0.0450 (1968)*	G, H, AA	0.0370 (1989)*	I, P, AA
Colombia	0.0698 (1970)*	G, H, AA	0.0360 (1991)*	G, P, AA
Costa Rica	0.0620 (1961)*	G, H, AA	0.0400 (1989)*	G, P, AA
Côte d'Ivoire	0.0800 (1959)	G, P, AA	0.0678 (1988)*	E, P, AA
Czechoslovakia	0.1010 (1965)*	N, P, AA	0.1086 (1991)*	G, P, AA
Denmark	0.0500 (1963)	G, P, AA	0.0548 (1992)*	G, H, AA
Ecuador	0.0630 (1968)	G, P, AA	0.0536 (1994)*	E, P, AA
El Salvador	0.0550 (1965)	G, P, AA	NA	
Fiji	0.0400 (1968)	G, P, AA	NA	
Finland	0.0780 (1966)*	N, P, AA	0.0778 (1991)*	N, H, AA
France	0.0190 (1962)	G, P, AA	0.0658 (1984)	G, H, AA
Gabon	0.0200 (1960)	G, P, AA	NA	
Germany	0.1053 (1963)*	N, H, AA	0.0659 (1984)	G, H, AA
Greece	0.0900 (1957)	G, P, AA	0.0619 (1988)*	E, H, AA
Honduras	0.0160 (1968)*	G, H, AA	0.0384 (1992)*	G, P, AA
Hong Kong	0.0570 (1971)	G, H, AA	0.0489 (1991)*	G, H, AA
Hungary	0.1010 (1967)*	N, P, AA	0.0667 (1991)*	N, H, AA
India	0.0880 (1965)*	E, P, AA	0.0910 (1990)*	SPDS
Iraq	0.0200 (1956)	G, P, AA	NA	
Ireland	0.0480 (1973)	N, H, AA	0.0493 (1987)*	N, H, AA
Jamaica	0.0470 (1958)	G, H, AA	0.0598 (1990)*	E, P, AA
Japan	0.0662 (1965)*	G, H, AA	0.0590 (1982)	SPDS
Korea, North	0.0900 (1966)	G, P, AA	NA	
Korea, South	0.0580 (1965)*	G, H, AA	0.0739 (1988)*	G, H, AA
Lebanon	0.0300 (1960)	G, P, AA	NA	
Madagascar	0.0390 (1960)	G, P, AA	0.0585 (1993)*	E, P, AA
Malaysia	0.0400 (1970)*	G, H, AA	0.0458 (1989)*	G, P, AA
Mexico	0.0360 (1963)*	G, H, AA	0.0320 (1989)*	G, P, AA
Morocco	0.0710 (1965)	G, P, AA	0.0657 (1991)*	E, P, AA
Myanmar	0.1000 (1958)	G, P, AA	NA	
Netherlands, The	0.0400 (1962)	G, P, AA	0.0692 (1991)*	N, H, AA
New Zealand	0.0680 (1973)	G, H, AA	0.0458 (1990)*	SPDS
Niger	0.0780 (1960)	G, P, AA	0.0748 (1992)*	E, P, AA
Nigeria	0.0700 (1959)	G, P, AA	0.0660 (1992)*	E, P, AA
Norway	0.0556 (1967)*	N, H, AA	0.0540 (1991)*	SPDS

Continued

Table 8A.2 Continued

Country	Poorest quintile's income share c.1965	Data description[a]	Poorest quintile's income share c.1990	Data description[a]
Pakistan	0.0916 (1969)*	E, H, AA	0.0840 (1991)*	E, P, AA
Panama	0.0180 (1970)*	G, H, AA	0.0200 (1989)*	G, P, AA
Peru	0.0400 (1961)	G, P, AA	0.0620 (1986)*	E, P, AA
Philippines	0.0350 (1965)*	G, H, AA	0.0520 (1988)*	G, P, AA
Portugal	0.0575 (1973)	N, H, AA	0.0570 (1990)*	N, H, AA
Puerto Rico	0.0180 (1969)*	G, H, AA	0.0290 (1989)*	SPDS
Senegal	0.0300 (1960)	G, P, AA	0.0350 (1991)*	E, P, AA
Sierra Leone	0.0276 (1968)	G, H, AA	NA	
South Africa	0.0190 (1965)	G, P, AA	0.0202 (1993)*	G, H, AA
Spain	0.0715 (1965)*	G, H, AA	0.0839 (1989)*	E, H, AA
Sri Lanka	0.0445 (1963)*	G, H, AA	0.0892 (1990)*	E, P, AA
Sudan	0.0824 (1968)*	G, H, AA	NA	
Surinam	0.1070 (1962)	G, P, AA	NA	
Sweden	0.0420 (1967)*	N, H, AA	0.0740 (1990)*	N, H, AA
Taiwan	0.0784 (1966)*	N, P, AA	0.0776 (1990)*	SPDS
Tanzania	0.0480 (1964)	G, P, AA	0.0685 (1993)*	E, P, AA
Thailand	0.0800 (1962)*	G, H, AA	0.0400 (1990)*	G, H, AA
Trinidad	0.0194 (1971)	G, H, AA	NA	
Tunisia	0.0570 (1965)*	E, P, AA	0.0586 (1990)*	E, P, AA
Turkey	0.0300 (1968)*	G, H, AA	0.0524 (1987)*	G, H, AA
United Kingdom	0.0987 (1965)*	N, P, AA	0.0778 (1990)*	SPDS
United States	0.0520 (1965)*	G, H, AA	0.0460 (1990)*	SPDS
Venezuela	0.0360 (1971)	G, P, AA	0.0361 (1990)*	I, P, AA
Yugoslavia	0.0821 (1963)*	G, H, AA	0.0733 (1990)*	G, P, AA
Zambia	0.0630 (1959)	G, P, AA	0.0557 (1991)*	E, P, AA

Notes: See Table 8A.1, except: data are categorized as 'reliable data' in *Deininger and Squire (1997)*; [a] In columns of data description, income definition, reference unit, and area coverage are shown in order. (1) Income definition: G = Gross income; N = Net income; I = other income, or no information on the type of income is available; E = Expenditure. (2) Reference unit: H = Household; P = Person. (3) Area coverage: AA = All area. No information on population coverage is available from Deininger and Squire (1997).

Table 8A.3 Descriptions of variables and data sources[a]

Variable	Data source	Variable designation in source
[Largest possible sample] Annual average change in the income equality index for 1965–90, 100 scale	Authors, created from Deininger and Squire (1997)	CQ1HLP
[Largest possible sample] Initial income share of the poor, c.1965, 100 scale	Authors, created from Deininger and Squire (1997)	Q1HLP
[Largest possible sample] Annual average growth rate of the income of the poor for 1965–90	Authors, created from Deininger and Squire (1997) and Sachs and Warner (1997)	GRPILP
[Largest possible sample] Initial income of the poor c.1965 (log)	Authors, created from Deininger and Squire (1997)	LPI65LP
[Largest possible sample] Annual average change in the income equality index for 1965–90, 100 scale	Authors, created from UNU-WIDER *WIID*	CEQLP
[Largest possible sample] Initial income equality, c.1965, 100 scale	Authors, created from UNU-WIDER *WIID*	EQ65LP
Central government savings/GDP, 1970–90	Sachs and Warner (1997)	CGB7090
Tropical climate	Authors, based on TROPICS in Sachs and Warner (1997)	CLIMATE
Democracy, 1975	Barro (1997)	DEMOCRACY75
Fertility rate, 1965 (log)	Barro and Lee (1994)	FERT65L
Annual growth rate of PPP-adjusted real GDP *per capita* for 1965–90	Sachs and Warner (1997)	GR6590
PPP-adjusted real GDP *per capita* 1965 (log)	*Penn World Tables 5.6*	LRGDPC65
Openness to international trade, 1965–90	Sachs and Warner (1997)	OPEN6590
Life expectancy, c.1965 (log)	Barro and Lee (1994)	LLIFE65
Institutional quality, 1980	Sachs and Warner (1997)	ICRGE80
Primary product exports/GDP, 1970	Sachs and Warner (1997)	SXPR
Labour force growth minus population growth, 1965–90	Sachs and Warner (1997)	GEAP-POP
Male schooling (secondary plus higher), 1965	Barro and Lee (1996)	SHM25 (= SYRM25 + HYRM25)

Continued

Table 8A.3 Continued

Variable	Data source	Variable designation in source
Terms-of-trade growth, 1965–90	Authors, constructed from World Bank (2000). For missing data, *World Tables* 1992 and 1994 were used for TOT70 and TOT90, respectively	TOTGR
Ethno-linguistic diversity	Sachs and Warner (1997)	ETHLING
Financial depth average, 1965–90	Barro and Lee (1994)	LLY

Note: [a] We amended Sachs and Warner's (1997) tropical climate variable so that it more accurately represents the proportion of the country that falls between the Tropics of Cancer and Capricorn. This involves some significant reclassifications including Hong Kong as 1 (not 0), Egypt as 0.2 (not 1) and Bangladesh as 0.5 (not 0.1), and rectifying some omissions in the Sachs and Warner's data set for this variable.

Notes

1. In Bleaney and Nishiyama (2002), we included dummy variables for Latin America and Caribbean, and for East Asia as well as the OECD dummy and the SSA dummy; these regions were therefore compared with the rest of the world. However, in this investigation, we focus on values of economic measures for the Franc Zone countries of SSA, relative to developing countries other than SSA.
2. A revised version of the World Income Inequality Database (WIID2 Beta) was released on 3 December 2004, with a further update in June 2005, http://www.wider.unu.edu/wiid/wiid.htm.
3. As a consequence, empirical studies (Knowles 2001; Odedokun and Round 2001; Sylwester 2000, 2001) on income inequality provide appendixes of the actual figures of inequality data used in the research, as we do.
4. The UNU-WIDER WIID (2000) contains a *WWW Guide* (http://www.wider.unu.edu/wiid/wiiddoc.htm) which reports that 'Gini coefficients of gross incomes are roughly 5–10 points higher than Gini coefficients of net (disposable) incomes, and Gini coefficients of (net) earnings may be roughly 5 points higher than Gini coefficients of (net) expenditure. Gini coefficients of disposable incomes may also be roughly 5 points higher than Gini coefficients of expenditure.' However, it is not clear whether these estimates are based on actual calculation or just casual observation. Further, it is not mentioned whether these estimates were derived from reliable data only or from all data including less reliable data.
5. For some countries, however, available points of time are not abundant. We allowed the data of the Gini coefficients and of the income share of the poor to have up to a seven- and eight-year margin, respectively, before or after each of the years concerned (1965 and 1990). These allowances are justified, considering that the Gini coefficients and income shares do not dramatically change over time

and that losing observations due to an intolerance of time lag would be equally inappropriate.

6. Equivalently, one can call these variables measures of income *equality*.
7. The statistical significance of ethno-linguistic diversity is not because many poor countries are ethnically divided. Such an effect is captured by a variable of *per capita* income since it is included in the regression.

References

Barro, R. J. (1997) *Determinants of Economic Growth: Cross-Country Empirical Study*, Cambridge, MA: MIT Press.

Barro, R. J. and J. W. Lee (1994) 'Data Set for a Panel of 138 Countries', http://www.columbia.edu/~xs23/data/readme.txt.

Barro, R. J. and J. W. Lee (1996) 'International Measures of Schooling Years and Schooling Quality', *Papers and Proceedings of American Economic Review*, 86(2): 218–23.

Bleaney, M. and A. Nishiyama (2002) 'Explaining Growth: A Contest Between Models', *Journal of Economic Growth*, 7(1): 43–56.

Deininger, K. and L. Squire (1996) 'A New Data Set Measuring Income Inequality', *World Bank Economic Review*, 10(3): 565–91.

Deininger, K. and L. Squire (1997) 'Deininger and Squire Data Set: A New Data Set Measuring Income Inequality', http://www.worldbank.org/research/growth/dddeisqu.htm.

Easterly, W. and R. Levine (1997) 'Africa's Growth Tragedy: Policies and Ethnic Divisions', *Quarterly Journal of Economics*, 112: 1203–50.

Ghosh, A. R., A. -M. Gulde and H. C. Wolf (2002) *Exchange Rate Regimes: Choices and Consequences*, Cambridge, MA: MIT Press.

Knowles, S. (2001) 'Inequality and Economic Growth: The Empirical Relationship Reconsidered in the Light of Comparable Data', CREDIT Research Paper 01/03, Centre for Research in Economic Development and International Trade, University of Nottingham. Published in (2005) *Journal of Development Studies*, 41(1): 135–159.

Odedokun, M. O. and J. L. Round (2001) 'Determinants of Income Inequality and its Effects on Economic Growth: Evidence from African Countries', Paper presented at WIDER Development Conference on Growth and Poverty, UNU-WIDER, Helsinki, 25–26 May.

Sachs, J. D. and A. M. Warner (1997) 'Sources of Slow Growth in African Economies', *Journal of African Economies*, 6(3): 335–76.

Sylwester, K. (2000) 'Income Inequality, Education Expenditures, and Growth', *Journal of Development Economics*, 63: 379–98.

Sylwester, K. (2001) 'Can Education Expenditures Reduce Income Inequality?', Southern Illinois University, mimeo.

UNU-WIDER WIID (2000) World Income Inequality Database V1.0 (12 September), UNU-WIDER, Helsinki, http//:www.wider.unu.edu.

World Bank (1992) *World Tables 1992*, Maryland, MD: Johns Hopkins University Press.

World Bank (1994) *World Tables 1994*, Maryland, MD: Johns Hopkins University Press.

World Bank (2000) *Terms of Trade Data*, Washington, DC: World Bank.

9

How does Monetary Policy Affect the Poor? Evidence from the West African Economic and Monetary Union

David Fielding

Introduction

In this chapter we shall explore the impact of monetary policy interventions on poverty in the West African Economic and Monetary Union (WAEMU, UEMOA). Most papers in applied monetary economics are concerned with aggregate macroeconomic data, and ignore the possible consequences of monetary policy interventions for income distribution and poverty. This is true not only of those about OECD countries, but also of those about developing economies. There are some exceptions. Romer and Romer (1998) and Easterly and Fischer (2000) look at the cross-country correlation between aggregate inflation and the well being of the poor, finding that on average low inflation enhances welfare. Similar conclusions arise from the case studies in Ganuza and Taylor (1998). Another group of papers, including Cardoso (1992), Cobham (2001) and Azam (Chapter 7 in this volume), look at the impact of different types of macroeconomic policy reform – such as orthodox stabilization packages, capital account liberalization and nominal exchange rate devaluation – on poverty.

A common theme in many of these papers is an emphasis on extreme contrasts (such as the difference between countries with hyperinflation and those with moderate inflation) or on the extreme policy interventions associated with macroeconomic policy reform that were so common in developing countries in the 1980s and 1990s. They have less to say about the impact of 'day-to-day' monetary policy on poverty. In countries that now have a relatively low and stable rate of inflation, and a manageable budget deficit, how do alternative types of monetary policy intervention affect the poor? Often, when looking at large, secular changes in the inflation rate, the focus of attention is on the adjustment of wages and on unemployment. But alternative short-term stabilization policy rules that impact on the prices of different commodities in different ways could also have very different consequences for the welfare of the poor. Even at very short horizons, over which wages are fixed, variations in prices could have a substantial impact on welfare. For example, some types of policy could be associated with relatively high variation in the prices of commodities (such as food) that make up a large fraction of the consumption of poorer households.

Why might this be so? Consider the possible differences between the impact of a change in interest rates and a change in the volume of currency in circulation. (The central bank of the UEMOA has direct control over the base interest rate and indirect control over the volume of currency in circulation, via a reserve assets ratio and quantitative controls on bank credit. The practicalities of monetary policy intervention are outlined in Fielding 2004: Appendix 1.) Manipulating M0 is still a potentially effective monetary policy strategy in countries where financial markets are under-developed and cash makes up a large fraction of the total money stock. But the impact of a change in M0 on prices is not necessarily uniform. Suppose, for example, that there is a reduction in the reserve assets ratio for a given interest rate. This is likely to lead to a rise in M0, *ceteris paribus*. The extra liquidity will put upward pressure on prices, but the prices of some goods are likely to rise more quickly than others. This could be because the market for some goods is relatively competitive, or because short-run changes in expenditure on some commodities are relatively easy. Food products, which are relatively homogeneous and sold in small-value units, might well experience relatively large price changes in the short run. Even if the prices of different commodities are cointegrated in the long run, inertia in the price convergence process might mean that short-run asymmetries of this kind are substantial.

The picture becomes even more complex if increases in liquidity stimulate a positive agricultural supply response in the short run, and cause an initial *reduction* in food prices. On the one hand, an increase in M0 is likely to correspond to an increase in credit and consumer expenditure, pushing up agricultural prices. But an increase in money and credit could also generate a positive agricultural supply response, if farmers are credit-constrained. This would make the sign of the short-run agricultural price response ambiguous *a priori*.

It is quite possible that alternative types of monetary policy intervention that have the same aggregate effect – on for, example, the aggregate CPI – have very different types of effect on the components of this index, and therefore on the volatility of prices faced by different income groups. By a similar argument, there could be substantial regional asymmetries in the effects of different types of policy.

The UEMOA is a suitable area in which to address these questions because it has a history of a low and stable rate of inflation. The currency of the monetary union, the CFAF issued by the BCEAO, has long been pegged to the FF (and now the Euro) at a fixed rate, with only a single devaluation since 1948. This devaluation (of 100 per cent) occurred in January 1994, and

1 Euro is now worth 657 CFAF. Aside from the first few months of 1994,[1] inflation in the member states of the UEMOA has been comparable with that of France.[2] Commitment to the fixed peg by a trans-national central bank makes a low long-run rate of monetary expansion a time-consistent policy. The questions about poverty surrounding the comparison of low- and high-inflation regimes are not relevant here. But the formulation of welfare-enhancing short-term monetary policy ought to be informed by the impact of such policy on the poor. Moreover, the relatively high-quality monetary data provided by the BCEAO makes such a study feasible.

In addition, the existence of regional price data within the UEMOA makes it possible to determine whether there are any regional asymmetries in the impact of monetary policy. The area has a single central bank issuing a single currency; but regional differences in, for example, the magnitude of short-run price inertia might mean that a monetary policy intervention has very different effects in different regions.

These issues will be addressed by fitting a time-series model of regional food and non-food prices to data from the UEMOA. The structure of this model is elaborated in the following section.

Conceptual overview

The aim of this chapter is to trace the impact of monetary policy interventions on the price of the food and non-food components of the retail price index (RPI) for urban consumers in different locations in the UEMOA. In this way, we can examine the effect of policy changes on the cost of living of different hypothetical income groups, among whom food consumption makes up a different proportion of total expenditure.

BCEAO monthly price statistics (discussed in more detail in the next section) are available for the principal cities of seven out of the eight countries that make up the UEMOA: Benin, Burkina Faso, Côte d'Ivoire, Mali, Niger, Senegal and Togo.[3] (Data for Guinea–Bissau, which joined the monetary union in 1997, are not available.) We should note here that data availability forces us to focus on urban consumer prices. Rural prices are not recorded on a monthly basis, and there remains a pressing need to model consumer prices in rural areas. Our econometric model will make use of these data. We shall focus on the post-devaluation period (1994–2002). The 100 per cent devaluation of the CFAF in January 1994 represented a substantial structural break in the data generating process for prices across the UEMOA, and it turned out not to be possible to fit a model with stable parameters to a data set incorporating the break period.

In this section, we provide an overview of the modelling framework to be employed. This framework is based on several key assumptions.

The first underlying assumption of the model (which will later be tested) is that there is long-run cointegration between the logarithms of food and non-food prices (p^f and p^r) in each country i, each of which is integrated $I(1)$. Moreover, there is long-run cointegration between the price of food in country i and the price of food in any of the other countries; the same is true of the non-food aggregate. However, prices differ from each other in the short run because they are subjected to shocks (ε_{it}^z, $z = (f, r)$) that are not perfectly correlated.[4] These shocks include local variations in productivity and in the cost of imports (the share of different commodities in total imports varying from one country to another).

The process of equilibrium correction could take a number of forms. In the UMEOA, one country (Côte d'Ivoire) is very much larger than the rest, and there is a substantial amount of migration between many of the smaller countries and Ivorian cities.[5] We will assume that Côte d'Ivoire is a 'lead' country, in the sense that prices in other countries all eventually converge on those in Côte d'Ivoire, but Ivorian prices are not affected by prices in the smaller countries, at least in the long run. (This assumption will be tested later.) In the absence of any changes in income, the money supply or interest rates, prices in each of the smaller countries (i) evolve according to an equilibrium correction process of the form:

$$\beta_i^f(L)\Delta p_{it}^f = \mu_{it}^f + \sum_z \sum_{j \neq i} \theta_j^{zf}(L)\Delta p_{jt-1}^z + \theta_i^f(L)\Delta p_{it-1}^r - \gamma_{i0}^f\left[p_{it-1}^f - p_{it-1}^r\right]$$
$$- \gamma_{i1}^f\left[p_{it-1}^f - p_{CIVt-1}^f\right] - \gamma_{i2}^f\left[p_{it-1}^r - p_{CIVt-1}^r\right] + \varepsilon_{it}^f \qquad (9.1)$$

$$\beta_i^r(L)\Delta p_{it}^r = \mu_{it}^r + \sum_z \sum_{j \neq i} \theta_j^{zr}(L)\Delta p_{jt-1}^z + \theta_i^r(L)\Delta p_{it-1}^f - \gamma_{i0}^r\left[p_{it-1}^f - p_{it-1}^r\right]$$
$$- \gamma_{i1}^r\left[p_{it-1}^f - p_{CIVt-1}^f\right] - \gamma_{i2}^r\left[p_{it-1}^r - p_{CIVt-1}^r\right] + \varepsilon_{it}^r \qquad (9.2)$$

where the $\beta_i(L)$ and $\theta_i(L)$ terms are lag operators and the μ_{it} terms represent the deterministic components in the process, an intercept and linear trend. The time domain t is measured in months. We expect the signs and sizes of the γ parameters to be consistent with the long-run stability of the system with full price convergence, but do not impose any structure on the short-run dynamics captured by the $\beta_i(L)$ and $\theta_i(L)$ terms. In the short run, prices in country i could be especially sensitive to prices in one or more of the other countries. Equations (9.1)–(9.2) can also be re-parameterized as:

$$\beta_i^f(L)\Delta p_{it}^f = \mu_{it}^f + \sum_z \sum_{j \neq i} \theta_j^{zf}(L)\Delta p_{jt-1}^z + \theta_i^f(L)\Delta p_{it-1}^r$$
$$- \eta_{i0}^f\left[p_{CIVt-1}^f - p_{CIVt-1}^r\right] - \eta_{i1}^f\left[p_{it-1}^f - p_{CIVt-1}^f\right]$$

$$- \eta^f_{i2}\left[p^r_{it-1} - p^r_{CIVt-1}\right] + \varepsilon^f_{it} \tag{9.3}$$

$$\beta^r_i(L)\Delta p^r_{it} = \mu^r_{it} + \sum_z \sum_{j \neq i} \theta^{zr}_j(L)\Delta p^z_{jt-1} + \theta^r_i(L)\Delta p^f_{it-1}$$

$$- \eta^r_{i0}\left[p^f_{CIVt-1} - p^r_{CIVt-1}\right] - \eta^r_{i1}\left[p^f_{it-1} - p^f_{CIVt-1}\right]$$

$$- \eta^r_{i2}\left[p^r_{it-1} - p^r_{CIVt-1}\right] + \varepsilon^r_{it} \tag{9.4}$$

where the first equilibrium correction term includes only Ivorian prices. Note that in the 'lead' country, Côte d'Ivoire, only the first equilibrium correction term enters into the price equations. The last two equilibrium correction terms are equal to zero by construction.

How do changes in monetary policy affect prices? In this chapter we consider the possible influence of two policy instruments, the (log) stock of currency in circulation in the UEMOA (m) and the BCEAO base interest rate (r).

It is important to note at this point that the BCEAO has the power to manipulate both r and m independently. The UEMOA is a small open economy with a fixed exchange rate, and there is (probably) a long-run interest parity condition with the EMU. But in the short run there are variations in the BCEAO interest rate around the corresponding ECB rate, which is feasible because capital is not perfectly mobile in the short run. Note that the French Treasury guarantees to exchange CFAF for Euro at a fixed rate, so r does not have to be used to target the exchange rate. (The CFAF is not pegged to the Euro: rather, the Euro is pegged to the CFAF.) The recent history of interest rate policy is discussed by Shortland and Stasavage in Chapter 5 in this volume. They also discuss BCEAO credit policy. For a given r, the central bank has the power to manipulate private sector credit (and therefore, indirectly, the volume of private sector liquidity) by means of a minimum reserve assets ratio and by means of quantitative controls on private sector credit, the *accords de classement*. They find that this second type of monetary policy intervention has been used less frequently in recent years than interest rate interventions. Nevertheless, they point out that the legislative framework of the UEMOA provides the BCEAO with all it needs to use both types of monetary policy in a pro-active way. In this chapter, we are not directly concerned with modelling past BCEAO policy, but rather with providing counterfactual estimates of the impact that different types of monetary policy intervention are likely to have. There is enough sample variation in r and m to do this.

The impact of changes in m on prices will depend on its interaction with other monetary aggregates. There is some evidence that there is a stable real M1 demand function (that is, demand for m plus checking deposits) across the monetary area, if we allow for an exogenous structural break in the devaluation year, 1994. This is the consensus of Rother (1999) and Sugimoto (2001). Moreover, there are few legal restrictions on checking deposits. So, if checking deposits are a close substitute for currency, any increase in m will (at least partially) be offset by a reduction in deposits, *ceteris paribus*. In this case, there will be no stable long-run relationship between the real value of currency and the determinants of demand for M1 (real income and interest rates).

This appears to be the case.[6] If we use annual data for the pre-devaluation period (1964–93), it is not possible to reject the hypothesis that there is no long-run relationship between the real value of currency, income and the interest rate. We conducted a test for the existence of such a relationship using real GDP as an income measure for the seven UEMOA countries (excluding Guinea–Bissau), and constructing an aggregate UEMOA price series as the GDP-weighted average of national GDP deflators. (CPIs are not available for all countries before 1970.) The test follows the method of Pesaran, Shin and Smith (2001), which does not require *a priori* knowledge about the order of integration of the series. It is constructed as an F-statistic for the joint significance of the θ parameters in the regression:

$$\begin{aligned}\beta(L)\Delta(m-p)_t &= \alpha_0 + \alpha_1 \cdot t + \gamma(L)\Delta y_t + \delta(L)\Delta r_t \\ &\quad - \theta_0 \cdot (m-p)_{t-1} + \theta_1 \cdot y_{t-1} + \theta_2 \cdot r_{t-1} + u_t\end{aligned} \tag{9.5}$$

where p_t is the aggregate deflator, y_t is aggregate real income, r_t is the (base) interest rate and u_t a residual. There is a range of critical values for the F-statistic, depending on the (unknown) order of integration of the different series. Using a lag order of one (which optimizes the Hannan–Quinn and Akaike Information Criteria for the regression), our computed F-statistic is 2.90, which falls below the lower bound of these critical values. In other words, regardless of the order of integration of the series, we cannot reject the null that there is no long-run relationship.[7] If the sample is extended beyond 1993, there is still no evidence for a long-run relationship, and the regression parameters become unstable.

For this reason, we model the impact of monetary policy on prices in the post-devaluation period *without* cointegration between $(m-p)$ and the determinants of demand for real M1. We allow for the possibility that changes in m or r have an immediate direct impact on prices. But in the long run there is no stable relationship between the price level and the level of currency.

More formally, we amend (9.3)–(9.4) as follows:

$$\begin{aligned}\beta_i^f(L)\Delta p_{it}^f &= \mu_{it}^f + \sum_z \sum_{j\neq i} \theta_j^{zf}(L)\Delta p_{jt-1}^z + \theta_i^f(L)\Delta p_{jt-1}^r \\ &\quad + \phi_i^f \Delta m_{t-1} + \psi_i^f \Delta r_{t-1} - \eta_{i0}^f\left[p_{CIVt-1}^f - p_{CIVt-1}^r\right] \\ &\quad - \eta_{i1}^f\left[p_{it-1}^f - p_{CIVt-1}^f\right] - \eta_{i2}^f\left[p_{it-1}^r - p_{CIVt-1}^r\right] + \varepsilon_{it}^f\end{aligned} \tag{9.6}$$

$$\beta_i^r(L)\Delta p_{it}^r = \mu_{it}^r + \sum_z \sum_{j \neq i} \theta_j^{zr}(L)\Delta p_{jt-1}^z + \theta_i^r(L)\Delta p_{jt-1}^f$$
$$+ \phi_i^r \Delta m_{t-1} + \psi_i^r \Delta r_{t-1} - \eta_{i0}^r \left[p_{CIVt-1}^f - p_{CIVt-1}^r\right]$$
$$- \eta_{i1}^r \left[p_{it-1}^f - p_{CIVt-1}^f\right] - \eta_{i2}^r \left[p_{it-1}^r - p_{CIVt-1}^r\right] + \varepsilon_{it}^r \qquad (9.7)$$

where m_t is the value of the stock of currency in circulation at the *end* of month t, and r_t is the base interest rate at the *end* of month t. Note that a permanent change in m can have a permanent impact on the price level. If the BCEAO engineers an increase in M0 through a fall in the reserve assets ratio, then *ceteris paribus* prices will start to rise and deposits will start to fall. (But there is likely to be inertia in both.) Given the initial rise in prices, and a fixed real demand for M1, the eventual fall in deposits will be less than the initial increase in M0. So the long run will see a larger total nominal money stock and higher prices, but the price increase is less than proportional to the initial M0 increase. There is no stable long-run ratio of the volume of cash to the price level, even when we condition on determinants of money demand such as the interest rate.

One important caveat in the interpretation of the fitted model is that there is no variable in (9.6)–(9.7) to capture changes in real income. GDP data for the UEMOA countries are reported only on an annual basis, and we will be fitting a monthly model. However, over the relatively short period of eight years that we will be considering, it is likely that variations in monthly income are dominated by the seasonal agricultural cycle. No large income shocks appear in the annual GDP data for the period. So the seasonal and trend components of μ_{it}^z in the regression equations ought to be a reasonable proxy for the income variable.

The policy variables m and r appear in the regression equations with a lag: they represent the value of the variable at the end of the month before the price index is observed. The values of policy variables are determined by the BCEAO on a monthly basis, and the raw data for the price indices are collected on a monthly basis (the process of data collection is often stretched over several weeks within the month). So the frequency of observations in the model matches the frequency with which the variables are observed. Since m_{t-1} and r_{t-1} are predetermined variables, they are weakly exogenous to prices at t, and the parameters ϕ_i and ψ_i can be estimated consistently without recourse to an instrumental variables estimator. Of course they may not be strictly exogenous, since BCEAO policy interventions may well depend on observed inflation. Fielding (1999) and Shortland and Stasavage (2003) explore this issue.

One potential problem in interpreting a model of the kind represented by (9.6) and (9.7) is that the estimated effect of Δm on prices may be partly due to a correlation between Δm and public expenditure. For example, one may worry that food subsidies (such as those introduced in many UEMOA countries in the wake of the devaluation) are correlated with public spending, which is in turn correlated with money creation. In this case there is no straightforward interpretation of the estimated effect of Δm on prices. However, the BCEAO has a number of financial instruments (for example, foreign liabilities) with which it can sterilize the impact of short-run fluctuations in government borrowing on money creation (Fielding 1999). The correlation coefficient for deseasonalized Δm and the deseasonalized rate of growth of BCEAO claims on governments in our sample period (1994m4–2002m7) is only 0.178.[8] So we can be reasonably sure that the estimated coefficient on Δm does not suffer from any substantial bias from a correlation between Δm and public spending.

Having fitted the model represented by (9.6)–(9.7) to our monthly data, we will be in a position to map the way in which individual prices series respond to a change in m or r. Before explaining how this is done, it should be noted that our aim is to explore the impact of changes in policy on prices, rather than to model policy and prices simultaneously. We will use the fitted model parameters to compute the impact of a change in a policy variable on prices, conditional on the assumption that the policy variable does not change again in response to the price changes. In this sense, the policy variable changes we explore are not intended to represent 'typical' historical policy episodes. Rather, we investigate the consequences of monetary policy interventions from the point of view of the policy-maker, treating the policy change as a strictly exogenous event.[9]

In the penultimate section, we will first present the fitted model of prices. We will then examine the implications of the model for the way in which food and non-food prices in each country evolve in response to changes in the currency stock or in the base interest rate. The focus of attention will be on the first twelve months after the change in policy, since we think it unlikely that any policy-maker will work with a time horizon longer than a year. Though the pattern of food and non-food price responses is of interest in itself, one way of expanding on the implications of the results is to plot out the response of aggregate price indices of different kinds. The share food in the consumption of households with higher incomes is likely to be lower than that of lower-income households. We will construct price response profiles for hypothetical households with different shares of food expenditure in total consumption. In this way, we can explore the possibility that households at different income levels are affected by monetary policy changes in an asymmetric way. We can also explore any regional asymmetries in the effects of changes in m and r.

The data[10]

Overview

Monthly data for the fourteen price series p_{it}^{z} are reported in the BCEAO publication, *Indices Harmonisés des Prix à la Consommation des États de l'Union Économique et Monétaire Ouest Africaine*. These are sub-components of the harmonized index of consumer prices (HICP). The weights given to the two components in the HICP vary from one country to another, but always sum to unity. The largest weight on food prices (0.5001) is in Mali; the lowest (0.3221) is in Côte d'Ivoire. This reflects a substantial difference in *per capita* GDP between the two countries: 0.166 million CFAF in Mali (€255) and 0.421 million CFAF (€640) in Côte d'Ivoire in 2001. The effect of the 1994 devaluation is very marked in many of the inflation series, particularly in Δp_{it}^{r}, and the distribution of inflation over a sample including early 1994 is markedly leptokurtic. We do not attempt to model the devaluation episode, and our sample period begins in 1994m4 and ends in 2002m7. It can be seen from the figures that over this period food prices have been markedly more volatile than non-food prices. We will see whether this difference is associated with varying degrees of sensitivity to monetary policy.

Monthly data for m_t and r_t are taken from the IMF *International Financial Statistics*, lines 14A and 60, respectively. Note that r_t is the monthly annualized interest rate. The IMF reports M0 figures for each individual country, because CFA notes are issued by national branches of the BCEAO. But these notes differ only by serial number, and circulate freely in all countries of the UEMOA. The m_t series used in the fitted model is the logarithm of the sum of these 'national' currency stocks.[11] Figure 9.1 illustrates the two series. It can be seen that there is a great deal of seasonal variation in m_t; this is because cash is one of the principal financial assets used by farmers to smooth consumption over the agricultural cycle. The BCEAO allows the stock of currency in circulation to vary over the year to match the seasonal variations money demand. For this reason the seasonal component of μ_{it}^{z} explains a large part of the variation in prices conditional on m_t. As Figure 9.1 shows, the seasonal pattern is very regular. There is also a marked break in the m_t series after the devaluation in January 1994: since the devaluation, the money stock has been allowed to expand at a much faster rate.

Time-series properties of the data

Table 9.1 reports ADF unit root statistics for the series of interest. For the inflation series, we will make inferences about orders of integration on the basis of panel unit root test statistics. It is highly improbable that

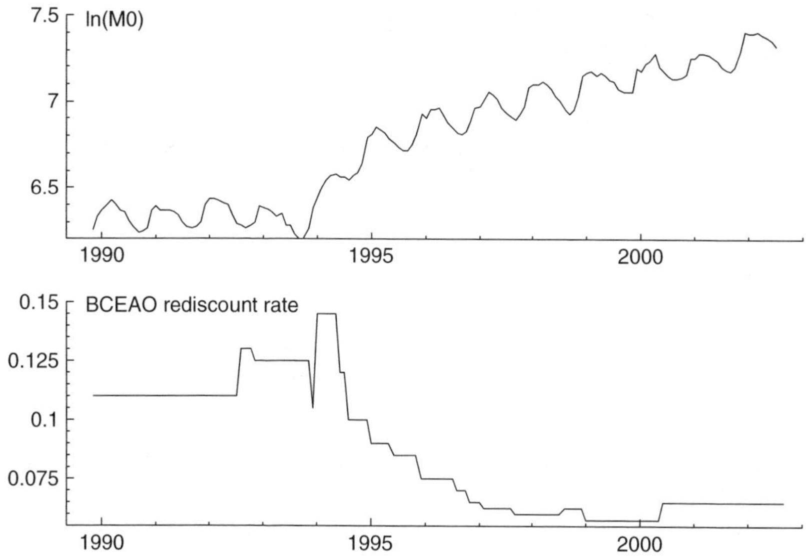

Figure 9.1 BCEAO nominal M0 and base interest rate, 1990–2002

the food price inflation series will have different orders of integration in the different UEMOA countries; the same is true for non-food price inflation. The first part of Table 9.1 shows individual ADF *t*-ratios for the Δp^f_{it} and Δp^r_{it} variables, and corresponding *t*-bar panel unit root statistics (Im, Pesaran and Shin 2003). The null that the series are $I(1)$ can be rejected at the 1 per cent level in both cases. For Δm_t and Δr_t the univariate unit root tests also indicate rejection of the null at the 1 per cent level.

Our model also assumes that the various price series are cointegrated. We test this assumption by conducting panel unit root tests for three sets of equilibrium correction terms corresponding to those in (9.1): $[p^f_{it-1} - p^r_{it-1}]$, $[p^f_{it-1} - p^f_{CIVt-1}]$ and $[p^r_{it-1} - p^r_{CIVt-1}]$. The bottom panel of Table 9.1 reports the results of these tests. In all three cases, the null that the series are $I(1)$ can be rejected at the 1 per cent level, although in the case of $[p^f_{it-1} - p^f_{CIVt-1}]$ and $[p^r_{it-1} - p^r_{CIVt-1}]$ this is true only when the alternative allows for a deterministic linear trend. In other words, we can assume that prices across the different countries of the UEMOA are cointegrated as long as we accept that there are secular trends in the relative price series.

On the basis of the results in Table 9.1, the variables appearing in the model outlined in the previous section will all be treated as $I(0)$ variables.

Table 9.1 Tests for stationarity

Individual ADF t-statistics for differenced variables

	Δp^f		Δp^r	
	ADF *t*	**Lag order**	**ADF *t***	**Lag order**
Benin	−8.6815	1	−7.4676	1
Burkina Faso	−9.9153	0	−13.945	0
Côte d'Ivoire	−8.1660	0	−4.1312	2
Mali	−10.253	0	−8.5581	1
Niger	−8.3761	0	−6.0275	1
Senegal	−8.2441	1	−10.382	0
Togo	−8.6025	0	−7.4531	2
t-bar	−8.8912		−8.2806	
(1% cv = −2.27)				
	Δm		Δr	
BCEAO	−9.7693	0	−6.6028	1
(1% cv = −3.50)				

Individual ADF *t*-statistics for *ecmf* ($p^f(i) - p^f(CIV)$) and *ecmr* ($p^r(i) - p^r(CIV)$)

	ecmf		***ecmr***	
	ADF *t*	**Lag order**	**ADF *t***	**Lag order**
Benin	−3.7748	0	−3.2111	0
Burkina Faso	−3.2758	0	−4.2054	0
Mali	−2.8399	0	−5.3792	0
Niger	−3.1084	0	−3.6263	0
Senegal	−2.2512	0	−3.9618	0
Togo	−3.1127	0	−4.2757	0
t-bar	−3.0605		−4.1099	
(1% cv = −2.91)				

Individual ADF *t*-statistics for ($p^f(i) - p^r(i)$)

	ADF *t*	**Lag order**
Benin	−2.7272	0
Burkina Faso	−2.3758	0
Côte d'Ivoire	−2.1599	1
Mali	−2.1682	2
Niger	−1.5541	2
Senegal	−2.7111	0
Togo	−3.0353	0
t-bar	−2.3902	
(1% cv = −2.27)		

Notes: The sample is 1994(4)–2002(9) for prices; 1994(4)–2002(7) for *m* and *r*. ADF regressions include seasonal intercepts but no trend.

The fitted model

Parameter estimates

The parameters of model represented by (9.7)–(9.8) for the seven countries are estimated by FIML. (OLS is not efficient because the regression residuals are correlated with each other.) The full fitted model is reported in Fielding (2004: Table A1); the lag order in this model (one) is favoured by the Hannan–Quinn and Akaike Information Criteria. The deterministic components of the model are a seasonally varying intercept and a linear trend. Two alternative estimates are reported. The first is an unrestricted version and the second incorporates a set of parameter restrictions, some coefficients being set to zero so as to minimize the Hannan–Quinn information criterion. The response profiles discussed below are based on the restricted model, though the general stylized facts presented are also true if we use the unrestricted model.

As reported in Fielding (2004: Table A2, the summary statistics Table in Appendix 2), the equilibrium correction terms are jointly significant in the unrestricted model at the 5 per cent level in all equations except those for Côte d'Ivoire. Note that in the case of Côte d'Ivoire there is a single equilibrium correction term, reflecting the assumption that Ivorian prices are not affected by prices elsewhere in the UEMOA in the long run. If any of the other pairs of equilibrium correction terms ($[p^f_{it-1} - p^f_{CIVt-1}]$, $[p^r_{it-1} - p^r_{CIVt-1}]$) are included in the Ivorian equations, the coefficients on them are not significantly different from zero. Neither are they jointly significant when all are added simultaneously. In fact, the Ivorian equilibrium correction term $[p^f_{CIVt-1} - p^r_{CIVt-1}]$ is significant only at the 10 per cent level in the Δp^f_{CIVt} equation, and not significant at all in the Δp^r_{CIVt} equation. Nevertheless, the Hannan–Quinn criterion indicates the inclusion of the equilibrium correction term in the Δp^f_{CIVt} equation, and the response profiles discussed below do incorporate internal price convergence in Côte d'Ivoire. The whole system is dynamically stable, and a temporary shock to any one variable does not cause a permanent change in any of the variables in the model.

Fielding (2004: Table A2) also reports Chow test statistics for parameter stability. These are constructed by fitting the model to a sample that excludes the last n observations, which are then used as a forecast period. The statistics reported are for $n = 6$ to $n = 42$ (that is, for six months to three-and-a-half years).[12] The forecast errors are not significant at the 5 per cent level, except for forecast periods restricted to the last year of the sample. So there is some concern that there is a structural break in the last year of the sample period. However, fitting the model to a data set ending in 2001 does not substantially alter either the parameter estimates or the response profiles discussed below.

We do not dwell in any detail on the parameter estimates in Fielding (2004: Table A1). However, a few points about the fitted model are worthy of note. First, changes in the interest rate r_t do not have any significant effect in the

Ivorian price equations, and the interest rate coefficients are set to zero in the restricted model. Because Ivorian prices are not affected by other prices in the long run, this means that permanent changes in r_t have only a short-run effect on prices in the system. However, changes in the currency stock m_t do have a substantial and significant impact in the Ivorian price equations, so permanent changes in m_t do lead to permanent changes in prices across the UEMOA. Second, all the lagged inflation terms have a significant impact in at least one of the other equations, so the short-run evolution of prices is the result of a complex web of interactions between food and non-food prices in the different countries.

The response profiles for food and non-food prices

Figures 9.2–9.5 illustrate the response of food and non-food prices in the seven countries' prices to a hypothetical permanent 1 per cent change in the currency stock, m_t, over the first twelve months after the change. Figures 9.2–9.5 also show profiles for the response of prices to a 1 percentage point change in the interest rate, r_t. The hypothetical change in m_t is positive and the hypothetical change in r_t is negative, because across the UEMOA increases in m_t are mostly inflationary, and increases in r_t are either

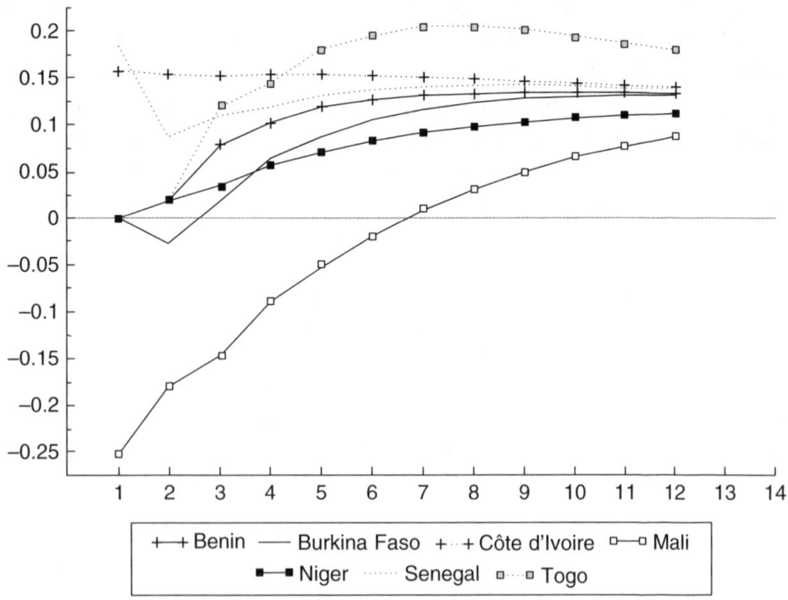

Figure 9.2 Response of p^f to a 1 per cent increase in m, months 1–12 (the vertical axis measures price variations in per cent)

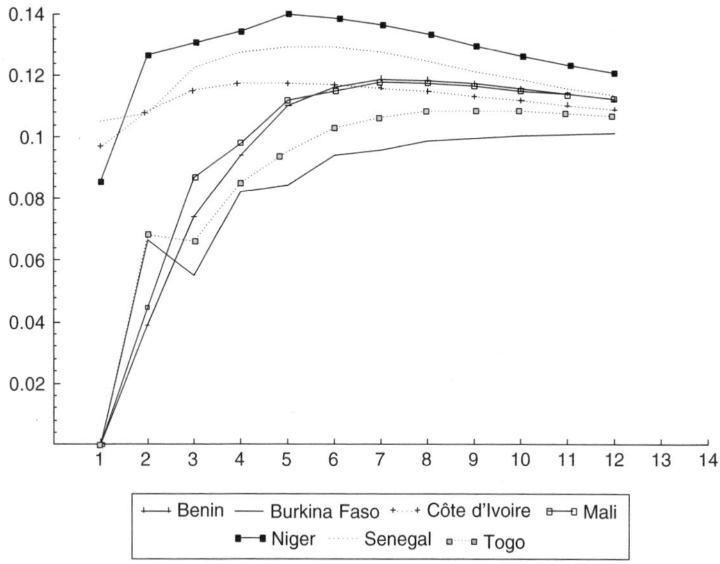

Figure 9.3 Response of p^r to a 1 per cent increase in m, months 1–12 (the vertical axis measures price variations in per cent)

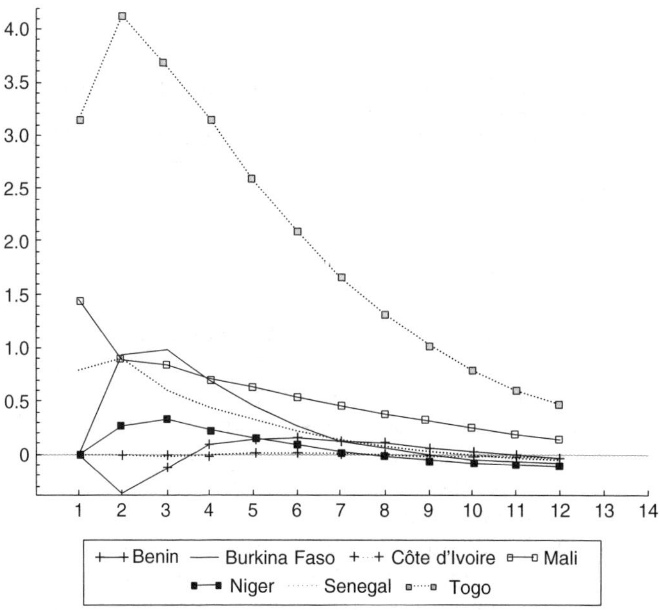

Figure 9.4 Response of p^f to a 1 per cent decrease in r, months 1–12 (the vertical axis measures price variations in per cent)

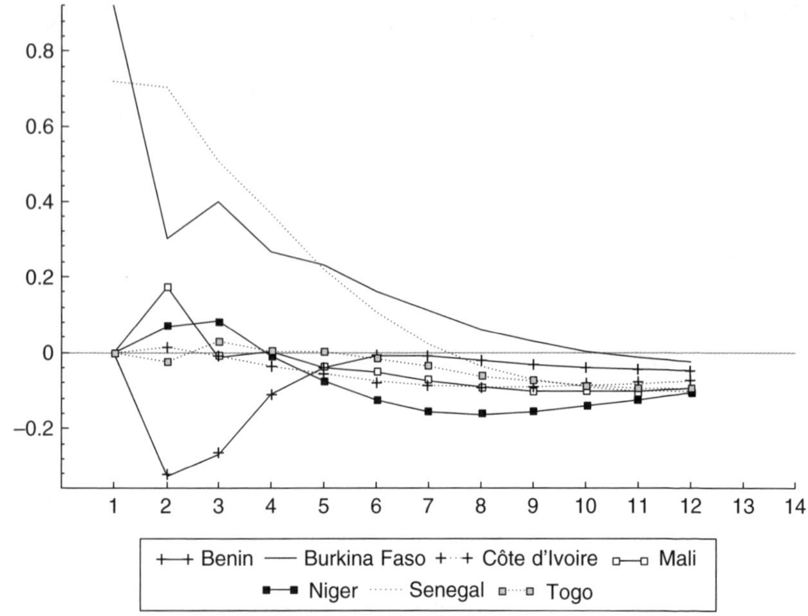

Figure 9.5 Response of p^r to a 1 per cent decrease in r, months 1–12 (the vertical axis measures price variations in per cent)

Table 9.2 Summary statistics for BCEAO M0 growth and base interest rate

	Mean (%)	**Std dev. (%)**	**Minimum (%)**	**Maximum (%)**
Δm (monthly)	0.78	4.37	−7.74	15.66
Δr (monthly)	−0.08	0.37	−2.50	0.75

deflationary or have little effect on prices. The figures correspond to the data recorded in Table 9.3 (p. 181), which reports the average monthly inflation rate for each price series at four and twelve months after the 1 per cent change in each instrument. Table 9.3 also shows a standard deviation around this average, because – as can be seen in Figures 9.2–9.5 – prices do not adjust to their new long-run level at a constant rate. Tables 9.2–9.3 report statistics for inflation rates because the price series are $I(1)$ variables. But Figures 9.2–9.5 depict price levels, in order to show the speed of price convergence.

It is important to remember that the inflation rates in Tables 9.2–9.3 are computed on a monthly basis. (If a 1 per cent inflation monthly rate were sustained for a whole year, the annual inflation rate would be a little over

Table 9.3 Simulated average values of *monthly* food/non-food price inflation in response to a 1 per cent increase in *m*/a percentage point decrease in *r*, for four and twelve months after the change

	p_f with r	p_r with r	p_f with m	p_r with m
Twelve-month figures				
Benin	−0.00241	−0.00376	0.01096	0.00935
	(0.15379)	(0.11329)	(0.01751)	(0.01485)
Burkina Faso	−0.00667	−0.00209	0.01084	0.00845
	(0.31385)	(0.33845)	(0.02022)	(0.02035)
Côte d'Ivoire	−0.00276	−0.00622	0.01170	0.00911
	(0.01157)	(0.01395)	(0.04581)	(0.02799)
Mali	0.01239	−0.00796	0.00719	0.00936
	(0.47404)	(0.07953)	(0.08382)	(0.01674)
Niger	−0.00874	−0.00866	0.00922	0.01005
	(0.09569)	(0.04453)	(0.00719)	(0.02683)
Senegal	−0.00431	−0.00850	0.01143	0.00946
	(0.26583)	(0.23720)	(0.06183)	(0.03059)
Togo	0.03927	−0.00772	0.01492	0.00890
	(1.06060)	(0.02218)	(0.03040)	(0.01966)
Four-month figures				
Benin	0.02021	−0.02747	0.02550	0.023505
	(0.28808)	(0.20990)	(0.02488)	(0.017741)
Burkina Faso	0.17199	0.06641	0.01603	0.020488
	(0.53062)	(0.64004)	(0.03579)	(0.034752)
Côte d'Ivoire	−0.00196	−0.00867	0.03845	0.029352
	(0.01882)	(0.02026)	(0.07914)	(0.045291)
Mali	0.17661	0.00149	−0.02238	0.024517
	(0.87713)	(0.14975)	(0.15421)	(0.022423)
Niger	0.05771	−0.00295	0.01428	0.033702
	(0.15251)	(0.06865)	(0.00979)	(0.038759)
Senegal	0.11220	0.09245	0.02961	0.031990
	(0.47789)	(0.42352)	(0.11531)	(0.049094)
Togo	0.78888	0.00098	0.03620	0.021365
	(1.71620)	(0.03764)	(0.04422)	(0.032684)

Notes: Figures are in per cent; standard deviation in parentheses.

12 per cent.) It is also important to note that the typical change in deseasonalized Δm_t is somewhat larger than the hypothetical 1 per cent change used in the figures and tables. As Table 9.2 shows, the standard deviation of Δm_t is about 4 per cent, though changes in m_t as large as 16 per cent are observed. On the other hand, Table 9.2 shows that a typical change in r_t is around 0.4 percentage points, although changes as large as 2.5 percentage points have been known.

Figures 9.2–9.3 show the response of prices to a change in m_t. There is a lot more cross-country variation in the response of food prices (p^f_{it}) than in that of non-food prices (p^r_{it}). In the case of p^f_{it}, the response of prices on impact is insignificantly different from zero in four of the countries. But in the two largest countries, Côte d'Ivoire and Senegal, the response to a 1 per cent increase in m_t on impact is a price increase of over 0.15 per cent. By contrast, food prices in Mali *fall* by around 0.25 per cent on impact (the possible reasons for the price fall were discussed earlier). By month 12, prices in all countries have begun to converge on their common long-run asymptote, a price increase of around 0.1 per cent, although there is still some substantial variation between the lowest and highest food price level. In the case of p^r_{it}, the largest effects on impact (in Côte d'Ivoire, Senegal and Togo) are only around 0.1 per cent, and in the other four countries they are insignificantly different from zero. By month 12, there has been rather more convergence on the asymptote than in the case of p^f_{it}.

In Table 9.3 these effects are quantified in more detail. Over the first four months after a hypothetical 1 per cent increase in m_t, average monthly food price inflation rates are highest in Côte d'Ivoire, Senegal and Togo. In these countries, the average inflation rate is about 0.03–0.04 per cent per month. This means that for a relatively large change in m_t (say, 16 per cent, the largest change observed in-sample), the average *monthly* inflation rate would be around 0.25–0.33 per cent. At the other extreme, a 1 per cent increase in m_t delivers an average rate of food price *deflation* in Mali of over 0.02 per cent per month in the first four months. Price effects in the other four countries lie in between these two extremes. If our perspective changes to the twelve-month horizon these stylized differences are still present, but the magnitude of the cross-country variation is much smaller. Average monthly inflation in Mali is now positive, as Malian prices are pulled up to the UEMOA average, and average inflation rates among the other countries are much less dispersed.

Table 9.3 shows that the variation in the response of non-food price to a 1 per cent increase in m_t is smaller. Over the first four months, average monthly inflation rates vary between about 0.02 per cent (Burkina Faso) and about 0.03 per cent (Côte d'Ivoire, Niger and Senegal). If we consider a twelve-month horizon, these differences have all but disappeared.

The profiles for a change in the interest rate, depicted in Figures 9.4–9.5, look very different from those for a change in the currency stock. First of all, the effects converge on zero: a change in r_t has no long-run impact on prices. Second, there are only a few cases in which the effects are statistically significant: relatively small changes in food and non-food prices in Burkina Faso and Senegal, and larger food price changes in Mali and Togo. (In interpreting the figures, remember that a change in r_t as large as 1 percentage point is quite an unusual event.) Some profiles indicate deflation in response to a fall in r_t, but none of these is significantly different from zero. By far the largest price response on impact is in Togo, where a percentage point fall in r_t generates an increase in food prices of over 3 per cent. There is a similar effect in Mali, but with a magnitude about half that in Togo. Otherwise, the estimated price responses are all less than 1 per cent, which is very small considering that the average change in the interest rate is only about 0.4 percentage points. Figures 9.2–9.5 show that in all countries the price response profiles decay quite quickly to zero. Table 9.3 reinforces this impression. Over a four-month horizon Togo stands out as the one country with a substantial monthly inflation rate (0.79 per cent) in response to the interest rate change. The effects in all other countries are very small, even at the four-month horizon. Over longer horizons the average monthly inflation rate in Togo is very much closer to the UEMOA average.

What do these figures have to say about the cross-country distribution of the costs of an increase in the stock of currency or a decrease in the interest rate? On average, the rate of growth of the currency stock is quite small, but from time to time there are substantial monetary expansions and contractions. So it makes sense to focus on the volatility of food prices that arises in response to a monetary expansion or contraction. A simple measure of volatility is the standard deviation of inflation in the different countries implicit in the price response profiles – that is, the extent of variation in inflation as prices adjust to their new mean level. Suppose that the BCEAO decides to generate an increase (decrease) in the stock of CFA currency by 10 per cent, implying a general price increase (decrease) of about 1 per cent in the long run. Such a change in m_t is larger than the average we have observed in recent years, but smaller than the largest observed change. This policy change might be motivated by a desire to boost (reduce) aggregate demand in response to a negative (positive) macroeconomic shock or – less likely – by an increase (decrease) in borrowing by one or other of the member state governments. Table 9.3 implies that the cross-country asymmetries in aggregate price responses will largely be due to asymmetries in the response of food prices. At all time horizons, the largest standard deviation in monthly inflation is in Mali (about 1.5 per cent at the four-month horizon, for a 10 per cent change in m_t). But the standard deviations of prices in Côte d'Ivoire and Senegal (0.8 per cent and 1.2 per cent at the four-month horizon, respectively) are also relatively high. Given that recent average inflation rates in the UEMOA have been of Western European magnitude – that is, less than 0.5 per cent per month – these effects are substantial. By contrast, the figures for the other four countries are much smaller, because food prices there respond much more smoothly to the change in m_t. So consumers in Côte d'Ivoire, Mali and Senegal will bear the burden of sudden (and, if the change in m_t is a shock, unpredicted) price movements.

If we consider an interest rate change, the picture is very different. Suppose that the BCEAO reduces (increases) r_t by 1 percentage point. Table 9.3 indicates that, over a four-month horizon, the standard deviation of food price inflation in Togo will be about 1.7 per cent. The standard deviation of food price inflation in Mali is about half as large as this, and in Burkina

Faso and Senegal about one-third as large; the corresponding figures for the other countries are very much smaller. So consumers in Togo and (to a lesser extent) Mali will bear the burden of sudden (and, if the change in r_t is a shock, unpredicted) interest rate movements.

The response profiles for hypothetical income groups

We have seen that the burden of a change in m_t, in terms of inflation volatility, falls on consumers in Côte d'Ivoire, Mali and Senegal; and that the burden of a change in r_t falls on consumers in Mail and Togo. Which consumers: the rich or the poor? Since food prices are more sensitive to changes in monetary policy instruments than non-food prices, it is likely to be the poor. Figures 9.6–9.12 and Table 9.4 provide evidence on the magnitude of this effect.

Figures 9.6–9.12 shows the response profiles of the aggregate consumer price index for three hypothetical households in a particular country, following either a 1 per cent increase in m_t or a percentage point decrease in r_t.

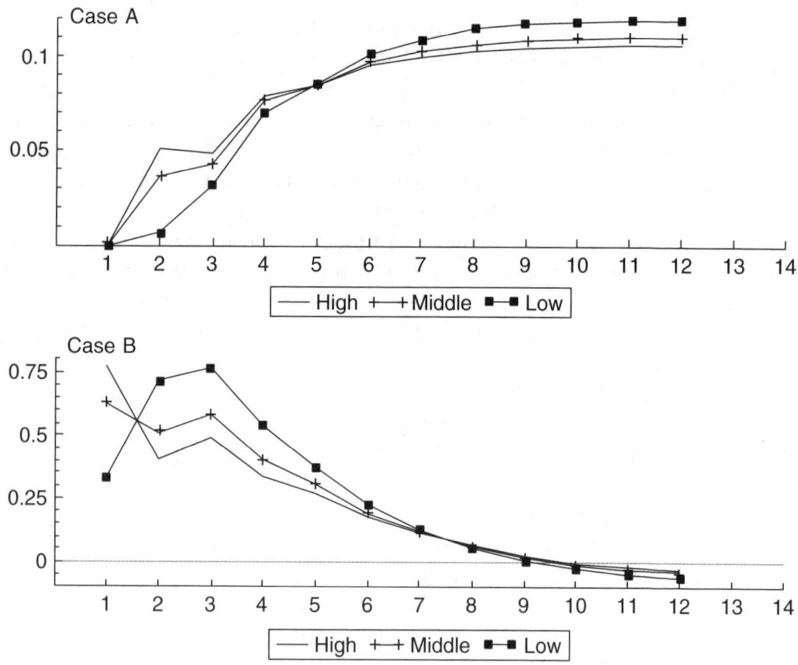

Figure 9.6 Response of hypothetical price indices for high-, middle- and low-income groups to a 1 per cent increase in m (case A) and a 1 per cent decrease in r (case B), Burkina Faso

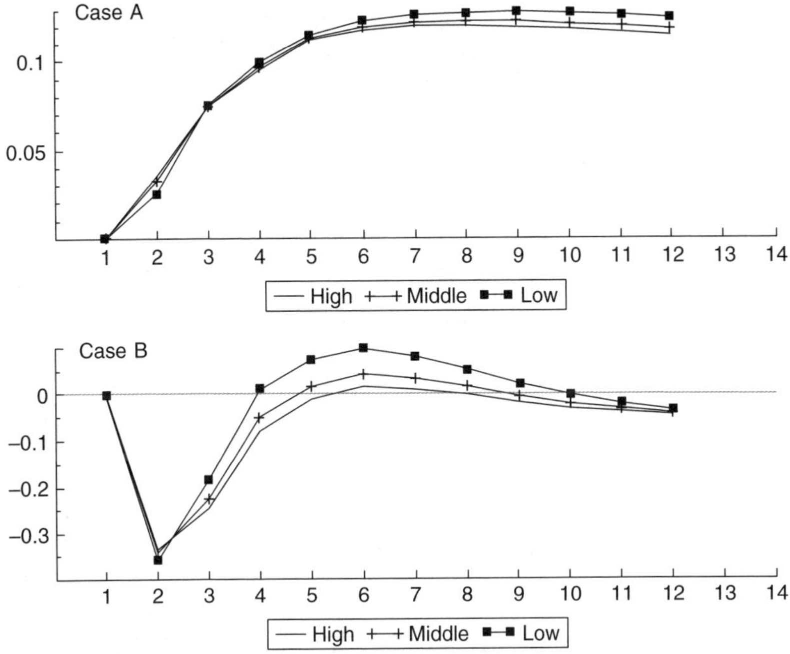

Figure 9.7 Response of hypothetical price indices for high-, middle- and low-income groups to a 1 per cent increase in *m* (case A) and a 1 per cent decrease in *r* (case B), Benin

The 'middle-income household' index is the Ivorian HICP. The 'low-income household' index is constructed with a weight on food prices twice that in the Ivorian HICP. The 'high-income household' index is constructed with a weight on food prices half that in the Ivorian HICP.[13] Of course, consumption patterns between high- and low-income households differ in ways other than the share of food in total expenditure, and we do not have enough degrees of freedom to fit a more disaggregated model of consumer prices. Nevertheless, the share of food in total consumption is likely to be the major difference between rich and poor households. Note that the scaling of the vertical axis varies from one chart to another.

Figures 9.6–9.12 show that in three countries – Benin, Burkina Faso and Togo – the three response profiles for a change in m_t are virtually identical. In these countries, food and non-food prices respond in a similar way to the initial change in m_t. In Senegal the same is true from the second month onwards, but inflation is much higher for the low-income group in the first month after the new currency creation. In Côte d'Ivoire, the initial upward jump in the price index for low-income households is also much

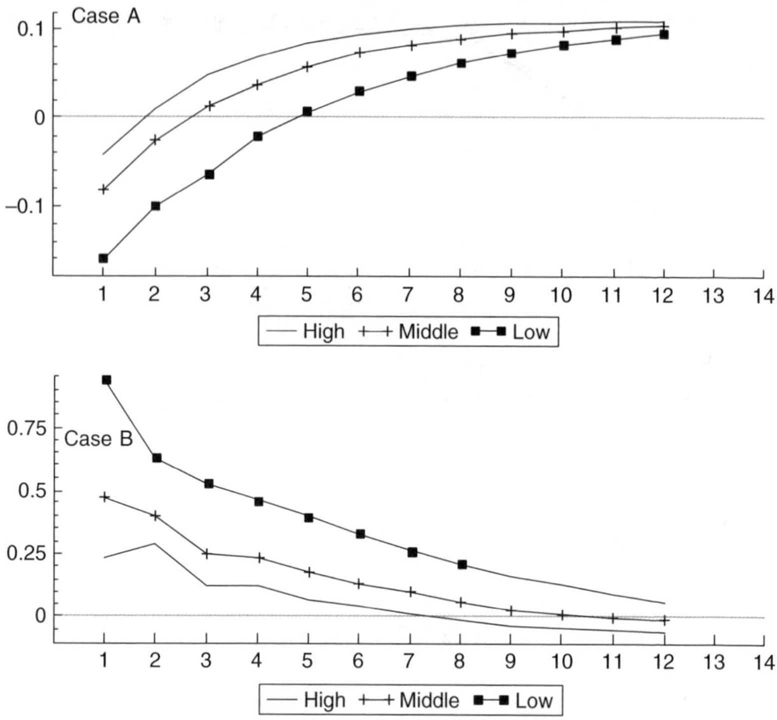

Figure 9.8 Response of hypothetical price indices for high-, middle- and low-income groups to a 1 per cent increase in *m* (case A) and a 1 per cent decrease in *r* (case B), Mali

larger than for high-income households, and moreover the gap between the price indices persists for some time. (Price convergence is relatively slow in Côte d'Ivoire.) In Mali, there is virtually no initial jump in the high-income price index, because the increase in non-food prices is offset by Mali's idiosyncratic decrease in food prices. But for low-income households, who spend a larger fraction of their income on food, there is a substantial *drop* in food prices after the increase in m_t, followed by a steady increase as food prices converge on non-food prices. So the price index for low-income households is much more volatile. In Niger, prices are somewhat *higher* for the high-income group in the twelve months following the increase in m_t, although the initial price increase is relatively small, and for all income groups the transition to the steady state is relatively smooth. This implies a relatively low inflation variance for all income groups.

Table 9.4 indicates the implications of these responses for the average inflation rate and the standard deviation of inflation in the twelve months

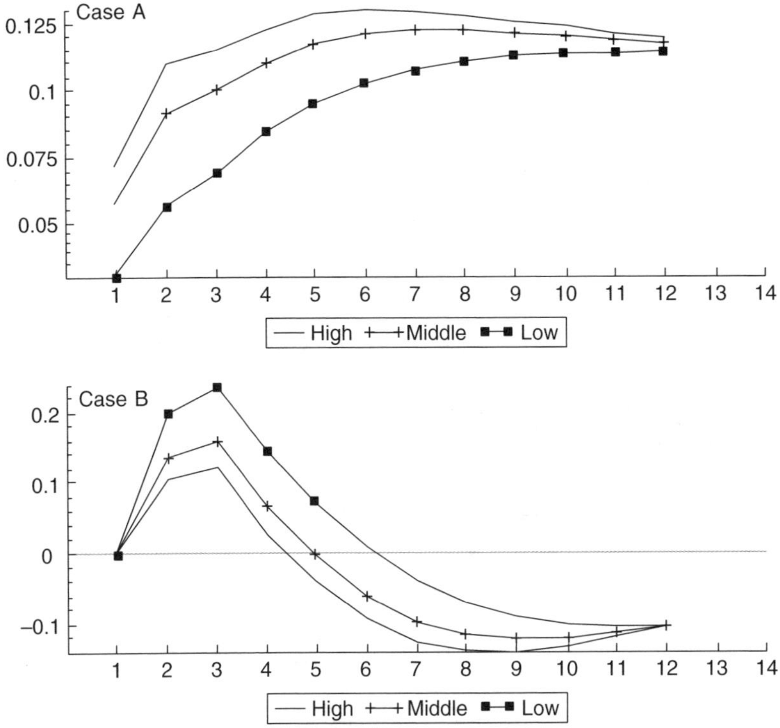

Figure 9.9 Response of hypothetical price indices for high-, middle- and low-income groups to a 1 per cent increase in *m* (case A) and a 1 per cent decrease in *r* (case B), Niger

following a 1 per cent change in m_t. Table 9.4 implies that groups experiencing the most inflation volatility are low-income households in Mali and Senegal. A 1 per cent change in the currency stock leads to a standard deviation of inflation of 0.1 per cent over the next four months for the poor in Mali, and of 0.09 per cent for the poor in Senegal. Other groups experiencing relatively high inflation volatility are middle-income households in Mali and Senegal and low-income households in Côte d'Ivoire (all with a four-month standard deviation of over 0.06 per cent). There is also substantial volatility for high-income households in Mali and Senegal, and for middle- and high-income households in Côte d'Ivoire.

The response profiles for changes in the interest rate are rather different. Only in Togo, and to a lesser extent Burkina Faso, Mali and Senegal, are there any quantitatively substantial effects. (The interest rate response profiles in Benin, Côte d'Ivoire and Niger, which are sometimes below the

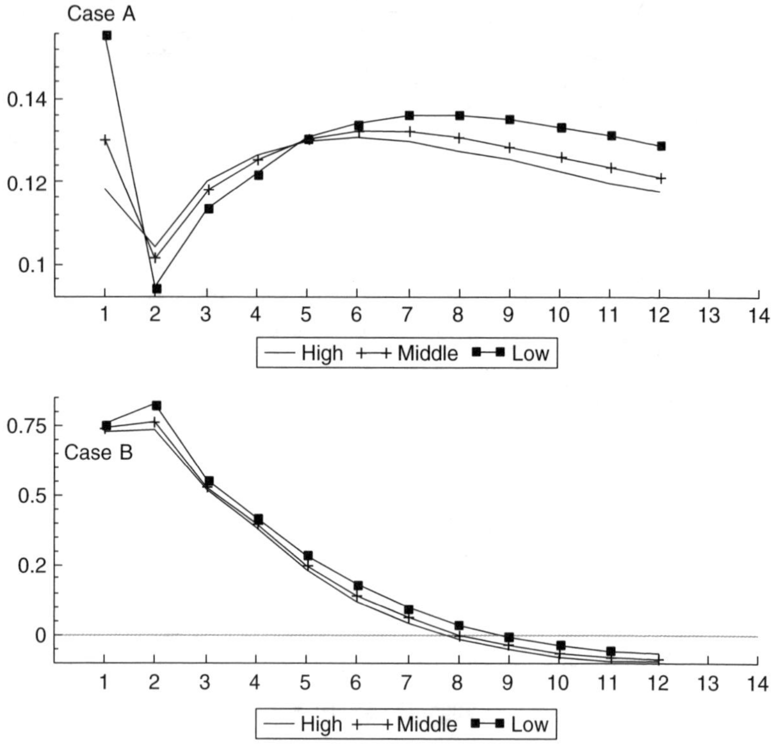

Figure 9.10 Response of hypothetical price indices for high-, middle- and low-income groups to a 1 per cent increase in *m* (case A) and a 1 per cent decrease in *r* (case B), Senegal

zero line, are not significantly different from zero.) In all cases the rise in prices following a fall in the interest rate is larger for low-income households, although in Burkina Faso and Senegal this difference is negligibly small. Table 9.4 implies that a 1 per cent change in r_t will lead to a standard deviation of inflation in the following four months equal to 1.1 per cent for low-income households in Togo. The corresponding standard deviations for low-income households in Mali, and for middle-income households in Togo, are about half this. In Burkina Faso and Senegal, all income groups experience a magnitude of inflation volatility that is marginally smaller again.

So, in general, monthly movements in either one of the monetary policy instruments can be expected to generate more price volatility for the poor than for the rich. But the volatility effects are concentrated in a limited number of countries: Côte d'Ivoire, Mail and Senegal for changes in m_t; Mali, Senegal and Togo for changes in r_t.

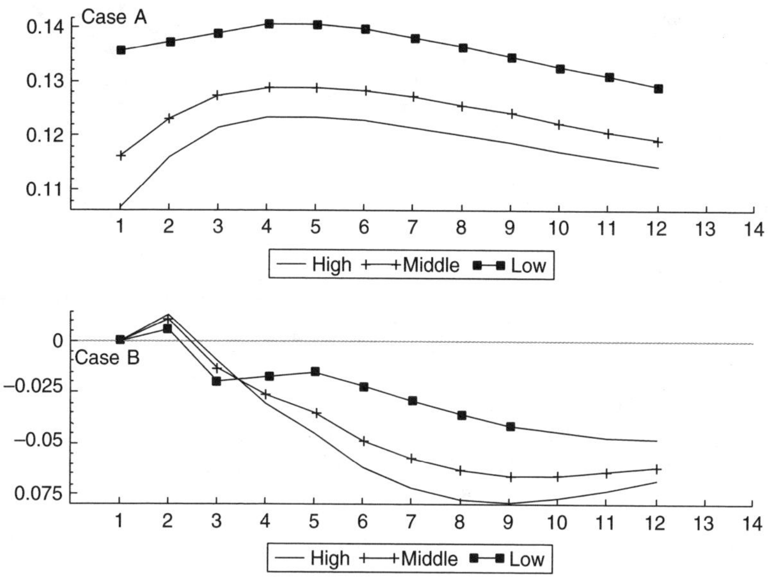

Figure 9.11 Response of hypothetical price indices for high-, middle- and low-income groups to a 1 per cent increase in *m* (case A) and a 1 per cent decrease in *r* (case B), Côte d'Ivoire

A note on orders of magnitude

How important are the magnitudes indicated above? If one just considers a single unanticipated change in a monetary policy instrument, then the conclusion will be that there is a small – but not entirely negligible – impact on welfare. For example, a 10 per cent contraction of the stock of currency causes the aggregate price index for our hypothetical low-income Malian household to rise by about 1.4 per cent in the first month, a figure that has declined to 0.2 per cent by the fourth month. If all of this price increase is met by a reduction in food consumption (because household income and other expenditure commitments, such as rent, are fixed in the short term), and if each household member eats one meal per day, then the consumption forgone is equal to about one-and-a-half meals per person.

However, if one considers the persistent volatility in inflation that is likely to result from frequent changes in monetary policy instruments (and remember that the standard deviation of deseasonalized monthly Δm_t is over 4 per cent), the figures calculated above are substantial relative to the inflation targets used by central banks in OECD countries. For example, the Bank of England aims to keep aggregate *annualized* inflation within 1 percentage point either side of a target rate. We have seen that a 10 per cent change in m_t

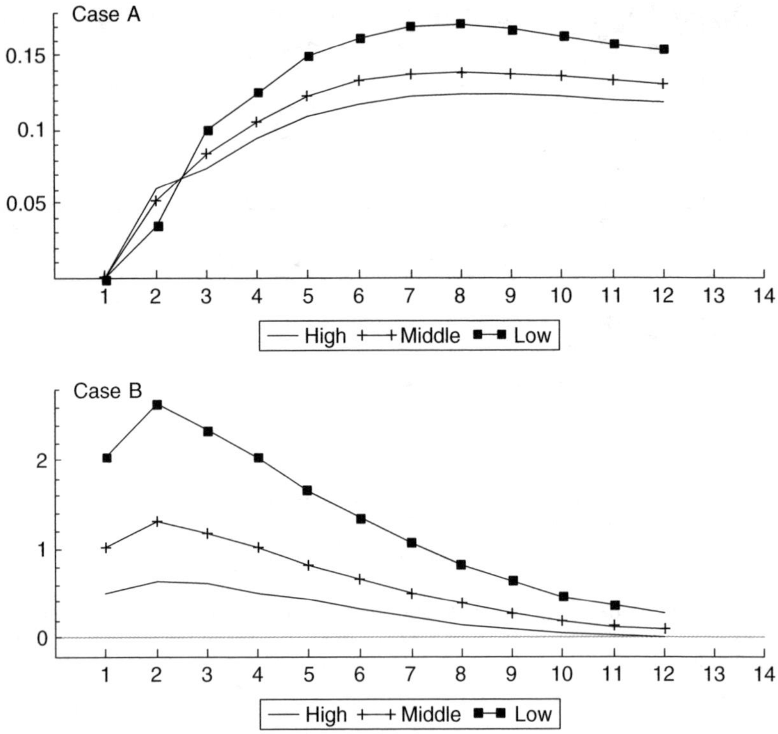

Figure 9.12 Response of hypothetical price indices for high-, middle- and low-income groups to a 1 per cent increase in *m* (case A) and a 1 per cent decrease in *r* (case B), Togo

results in an immediate *monthly* change in food prices in Mali of 2.5 per cent (Figure 9.2), and a corresponding change in aggregate prices for low-income households of 1.4 per cent (Figure 9.8).

Summary and conclusion

We have fitted a model of urban food and non-food prices to monthly time-series data for different countries in the UEMOA, in order to examine the asymmetries of price response that arise after a change in a monetary policy instrument. Although the countries share a common currency and a single central bank (the BCEAO), and although prices across the monetary union are cointegrated, there are some significant short-run asymmetries, both across countries and across commodities. We have explored the consequences of these asymmetries for different income groups in different member states.

Table 9.4 Simulated average values of *monthly* consumer price inflation for three hypothetical income groups in response to a 1 per cent increase in *m*/a percentage point decrease in *r*, for four and twelve months after the change

	high/*m*	**mid/*m***	**low/*m***	**high/*r***	**mid/*r***	**low/*r***
Twelve-month figures						
Benin	0.00961	0.00987	0.01039	−0.00354	−0.00333	−0.00289
	(0.01488)	(0.01507	(0.01593	(0.11847	(0.12428	(0.13743
Burkina Faso	0.00883	0.00922	0.00999	−0.00282	−0.00356	−0.00504
	(0.01600)	(0.01257)	(0.01198)	(0.26623)	(0.20728)	(0.18572)
Côte d'Ivoire	0.00952	0.00994	0.01078	−0.00566	−0.00510	−0.00399
	(0.03079)	(0.03362)	(0.03938)	(0.01138)	(0.00925)	(0.00784)
Mali	0.00901	0.00866	0.00796	−0.00468	−0.00140	0.00515
	(0.02244)	(0.03253)	(0.05623)	(0.09111)	(0.15174)	(0.30117)
Niger	0.00992	0.00978	0.00951	−0.00867	−0.00869	−0.00871
	(0.02240)	(0.01806)	(0.01010)	(0.05031)	(0.05756)	(0.07466)
Senegal	0.00978	0.01010	0.01073	−0.00783	−0.00715	−0.00580
	(0.03469)	(0.03933)	(0.04961)	(0.24115)	(0.24537)	(0.25458)
Togo	0.00987	0.01084	0.01278	−0.00015	0.00742	0.02255
	(0.01752)	(0.01707)	(0.02124)	(0.17173)	(0.34192)	(0.68327)
Four-month figures						
Benin	0.02383	0.02415	0.02479	−0.01979	−0.01211	0.00325
	(0.01778)	(0.01832)	(0.02073)	(0.22122)	(0.23315)	(0.25843)
Burkina Faso	0.01977	0.01905	0.01762	0.08341	0.10042	0.13443
	(0.02585)	(0.01845)	(0.01788)	(0.49323)	(0.36440)	(0.28252)
Côte d'Ivoire	0.03082	0.03228	0.03521	−0.00759	−0.00651	−0.00435
	(0.05067)	(0.05609)	(0.06701)	(0.01729)	(0.01506)	(0.01416)
Mali	0.01697	0.00941	−0.00569	0.02969	0.05790	0.11430
	(0.04051)	(0.06150)	(0.10521)	(0.16603)	(0.27737)	(0.55522)
Niger	0.03057	0.02745	0.02119	0.00682	0.01659	0.03613
	(0.03109)	(0.02343)	(0.00843)	(0.08064)	(0.09356)	(0.12096)
Senegal	0.03161	0.03122	0.03045	0.09563	0.09881	0.10517
	(0.05873)	(0.06901)	(0.09062)	(0.43106)	(0.43911)	(0.45660)
Togo	0.02375	0.02614	0.03092	0.12783	0.25476	0.50854
	(0.02574)	(0.02161)	(0.02662)	(0.27122)	(0.54783)	(1.10280)

Notes: See Table 9.3.

Households in a sub-set of the countries – especially poor households – bear the brunt of the price volatility that occurs in the wake of a change in the value of one of the instruments.

This does not mean that the BCEAO should abandon monetary policy. The policy instruments at its disposal are a potentially valuable set of tools to combat the price uncertainty that arises from exogenous shocks and increases the vulnerability of the poor. However, policy-makers do need to be aware of the distributional asymmetries that arise as a consequence of monetary policy interventions. There may be a need for targeted measures (for example, food subsidies), to reduce the price volatility that faces certain income groups in certain countries following a large monetary adjustment.

We should stress that the results here relate to urban prices. High-frequency time-series data for rural areas are not available. The heterogeneity we observe between cities and between income groups suggests that there might well be some heterogeneity between urban and rural areas. This is an important topic for future research.

Notes

I am grateful to Chris Adam and seminar participants at UNU-WIDER for comments on a previous version of this chapter, but all remaining errors are my own.

1. Azam (Chapter 7 in this volume) deals with the consequences of the devaluation episode for poverty in the UEMOA.
2. Although there is no evidence for PPP in levels between France and the UEMOA (Nuven 1994).
3. That is, Cotonou, Ougadougou, Abidjan, Bamako, Niamey, Dakar and Lomé.
4. Implicitly, the ε terms incorporate supply and demand shocks. The degree to which supply shocks are correlated across countries is reflected in the covariance matrix for the εs. (The εs might also reflect private sector demand shocks, but the identification of supply and demand shocks is not directly relevant to the main thrust of this chapter.) I do assume that the supply shocks are orthogonal to Δm_{t-1} and Δr_{t-1}.
5. See Appleyard (1999) for a description of migration patterns in the area.
6. The results that follow are consistent with Rother (1999), who finds no stable narrow money demand function.
7. This is still true if we exclude the interest rate from the regression.
8. The corresponding t-ratio is 1.801, so there is a marginally significant (but very small) correlation between the two variables.
9. Thus we are not directly concerned with impact of monetary policy *shocks*. Our aim is not to identify the consequences of unpredictable changes in monetary policy variables, but rather to inform policy by estimating the consequences of a planned policy change. We do make the assumption that the impact of unpredictable changes in m and r is the same as the impact of predictable changes; when looking at data at a monthly frequency, this seems to us to be a reasonable assumption.
10. All results reported in this and the following section were produced using Pc-Give 9.0 and Pc-Fiml 9.0.
11. Data on the cross-border movement of notes are limited. The BCEAO makes periodic attempts to track the *billets déplacés*, figures for which are sometimes reported in the *Rapport Annuel de la Zone Franc*, published by the Banque de France. These indicate that a substantial fraction of the currency issued travels from one country to another.
12. In the notation of Doornik and Hendry (2001), these are $V[\mathbf{e}]$ forecast error statistics that allow for parameter uncertainty.
13. The Ivorian HICP weight on food items is 0.3221.

References

Appleyard, R. (1999) *Emigration Dynamics in Developing Countries, 1: Sub-Saharan Africa*, Abingdon: Bookpoint.

Cardoso, E. (1992) 'Inflation and Poverty', Working Paper 4006, Washington, DC: NBER.

Cobham, D. (2001) 'Capital Account Liberalization and Poverty', Working Paper 70, Queen Elizabeth House, University of Oxford.

Doornik, J. and D. Hendry (2001) *Empirical Econometric Modelling Using PcGive*, 3rd edn, London: Timberlake Consultants Press.

Easterly, W. and S. Fischer (2000) 'Inflation and the Poor', World Bank (Country Economics Department) Working Paper 2335, Washington, DC: World Bank.

Fielding, D. (1999) 'How Does a Central Bank React to Changes in Government Borrowing?', *Journal of Development Economics*, 59, 531–52.

Fielding, D. (2004) 'How Does Monetary Policy Affect the Poor? Evidence from the West African Economic and Monetary Union', WIDER Research Paper 2004/2, Helsinki: UNU-WIDER, http://www.wider.unu.edu/publications/rps/rp2004–002.pdf.

Ganuza, E. and L. Taylor (1998) 'Macroeconomic Policy, Poverty, and Equality in Latin America and the Caribbean', Working Paper 6, New York: CEPA, New School for Social Research.

Im, K., M. Pesaran and Y. Shin (2003) 'Testing for Unit Roots in Heterogeneous Panels', *Journal of Econometrics*, 115, 53–74.

Nuven, D. (1994) 'Linkages in the Price Level and Inflation Rate Between CFA Franc Zone Countries and France', Working Paper WPS/94/93-EA, Washington, DC: IMF.

Pesaran, M., Y. Shin and R. Smith (2001) 'Bounds Testing Approaches to the Analysis of Levels Relationships', *Journal of Applied Econometrics*, 16, 289–326.

Romer, C. and D. Romer (1998) 'Monetary Policy and the Well-Being of the Poor', NBER Working Paper 6793, Washington, DC: NBER.

Rother, P. (1999) 'Money Demand in the West African Economic and Monetary Union–The Problems of Aggregation', *Journal of African Economies*, 8, 422–47.

Shortland, A. and D. Stasavage (2003) 'Country-Level Monetary Policy in the CFA Zone', Helsinki: UNU-WIDER, mimeo.

Sugimoto, K. (2001) 'One Money or Two Monies? Monetary Policy in the CFA Franc Zone, 1968–93', *Journal of African Economies*, 10, 64–91.

Index